WINNING

Market Leadership

WINNING

Market Leadership

STRATEGIC MARKET PLANNING FOR TECHNOLOGY-DRIVEN BUSINESSES

Adrian Ryans • *Roger More* • *Donald Barclay* • *Terry Deutscher*

John Wiley & Sons Canada, Ltd

Toronto • New York • Chichester • Weinheim • Brisbane • Singapore

John Wiley & Sons Canada, Ltd
22 Worcester Road
Etobicoke, Ontario
M9W 1L1

Canadian Cataloguing in Publication Data

Main entry under title:
Winning market leadership : strategic market planning for
  technology-driven businesses

Includes index.
ISBN 0-471-64430-7

1. High technology – Marketing. 2. Strategic planning. I. Ryans,
Adrian B., 1945-.

HC79.H53W56 1999   620'.0068'8   C99-932962-6

Production Credits:
Cover design: Interrobang Graphic Design Inc.
Text design: JAQ, RGD
Printer: Tri-Graphic Printing Ltd.

Printed in Canada
10 9 8 7 6 5 4 3 2 1

CONTENTS

ॐ

PREFACE
&c.

This book grew out of our work over the past decade with a number of leading global companies in technology-intensive industries. We have frequently been asked by senior executives to work with teams of their managers to help them develop strategic market plans to capture or retain market leadership. We all believed that winning market strategies are developed and implemented by committed teams of managers who have an in-depth understanding of their customers, their competitors, the relevant technologies, and the capabilities of their own organization. However, these teams also need a high-level vision of how their markets are evolving and how they might be driven to evolve.

Our challenge was to provide them with a simple, but powerful, process together with useful tools and concepts, so that they could develop the deep understanding that would help them win market leadership. Over time we developed teaching materials and action learning tools that seemed to really help managers from a variety of technology-intensive industries. The process itself evolved as we used it with different companies.

In developing the process and tools, we did not try to incorporate every nuance of current academic thinking. Rather we focused on those tools and concepts that the managers we have worked with really found helpful. The result is, we believe, a book that describes a systematic and highly integrated process for evaluating market opportunities and for developing strategies to win market leadership in chosen opportunities. The book focuses on the key issues and tough choices faced by executives and managers in these very demanding technology-intensive markets.

Executives and managers who embrace our book and its underlying process discover benefits including:

- Faster but more comprehensive planning
- Iterative planning that creates living plans that reflect current market and competitive dynamics
- A natural, not forced, involvement of cross-functional teams in the planning process
- A drive to "Yes/No" decisions as opposed to "Maybes"
- A clear emphasis on generating cash flow and profitability

ACKNOWLEDGMENTS
ဢ

Clearly we owe a huge debt of gratitude to the executives and companies we have worked with over the last decade. They challenged us to help them develop market leadership in their chosen markets. Fluke Corporation, General Electric, IBM, ICI, National Semiconductor, Nortel Networks, and Varian Associates are among the companies we have worked with in developing and applying the process. Patrick Brockett, Executive Vice President of Analog Products at National Semiconductor, gave us considerable latitude in designing a major management development intervention for business teams at National. Steve Mercer and Ken Brown at General Electric involved us in a major organizational change initiative at General Electric and were very supportive of our efforts. The book benefited greatly from our learning on both of these projects.

Many executives over the years have contributed ideas and concepts that have been shamelessly borrowed and used. Richard Levy, President and CEO of Varian Medical Systems, was one major contributor.

Clearly the book has benefited tremendously from the intellectual contributions of such people as Michael Porter and Geoffrey Moore. But perhaps the biggest intellectual debt is owed to George Day, who has shaped our thinking on strategic market planning more than any other individual.

We would certainly be remiss if we did not recognize the debt we owe to well over a thousand executives and managers in North America, Europe, and Asia who have applied this process and the tools to their strategic opportunities. Their puzzled looks, questions, and comments have caused us to continually refine what we do. Drafts of the book have also been classroom tested in Executive MBA and MBA programs, and in public executive programs at the Richard Ivey School of Business, The University of Western Ontario.

Behind every book like this are many unsung heroes. Karen Milner and Elizabeth McCurdy, our editor and assistant editor at John Wiley & Sons Canada, made many useful suggestions and helped keep the book on track. Diana Lee, the unofficial head of the marketing area group at Ivey, did a tremendous job in coordinating the preparation of the manuscript, keeping the authors relatively organized, and ensuring that the final product was of high quality.

Introduction

When Steve Jobs returned to Apple Computer as interim CEO in the summer of 1997, he faced a massive strategic market planning challenge. Apple was in deep trouble. Many users no longer saw the Macintosh's user interface as significantly better than Microsoft's Windows 95 interface, so its leadership in this important area was no longer clear. Apple's prices were still higher than those of PCs. In the still-growing personal computer market, its global market share was declining rapidly, from 8.2% in the fourth quarter of 1994 to about 3% in July 1997. The company had lost $1.6 billion over the preceding two years.

Jobs faced some very tough choices. Should Apple put more emphasis on "cheap" Macs that would be more competitively priced? This would help drive up unit volumes and reduce variable costs. Should he be more aggressive in licensing the Mac operating system to other computer manufacturers? This could both make the Mac platform more attractive to software developers and help lower costs on components and subsystems. Or would it just cut into Apple's own sales? Which market segments should Apple focus on? Should it still try to be a major player in the education market? Should it really focus on those segments, such as media and entertainment, where Apple had historically had a very strong following? Should it put more emphasis on new, emerging markets, such as personal digital assistants (PDAs) like the Apple Newton or on Internet appliances? And what should it do to stop its dealers and value-added resellers from abandoning Apple? How might it encourage software developers to continue to develop software for the Macintosh platform? It was an almost overwhelming set of questions in which each one could not be treated in isolation. Jobs and his team had to make some very tough, difficult choices very quickly, if Apple was to be saved.

Steve Jobs moved quickly and decisively to address many of the key issues.[1] Apple killed the Newton product line and began refocusing the business around its core Macintosh and PowerBook product lines. He initiated a crash program to develop a dramatic new consumer product, the iMac, which was launched with a big splash in August 1998. Apple also began paying a lot of attention to the top 100 software developers to ensure that they continued to develop the complementary software that was essential if customers were going to continue to buy Macs. Whether these moves were enough to ensure Apple's survival is debatable, but at least Jobs was making the hard calls. Without them Apple would almost surely have withered away.

Our book is designed to help executives and managers in technology-intensive businesses, like Apple Computer, grapple with the extremely challenging planning issues they face in their businesses. We propose a process for managers and executives to deal with these types of issues in a systematic way, so that all the major factors influencing the difficult choices are considered. The process is focused on winning market leadership—that is, identifying and creating attractive, profitable market opportunities and developing the market plans that will lead your company to capture a dominant and profitable share of the market.

When we talk about technology-intensive businesses, we are referring to the company's products and services rather than its supporting infrastructure. Technology-intensive businesses are characterized by rapid advances in technology that allow the company and its competitors to offer new functionality or applications to help customers solve existing or latent problems. Computer hardware and software, telecommunications, advanced materials, pharmaceuticals,

---

[1] "Back to the Future at Apple," *Business Week*, May 25, 1998.

semiconductors, electronic equipment, specialty chemicals, instruments and controls, and the services businesses built around these types of products are all examples of technology-intensive businesses. In addition, many pure service businesses, such as financial services, exhibit many of the characteristics of technology-intensive businesses.

The book presents an integrated strategic market planning process and a set of tools and concepts that are designed to address the particular issues faced by technology-intensive businesses like yours as you develop strategic market plans. The process can be used as the basis for the periodic planning process in your company, or for the more ad hoc analysis of new business opportunities or threats that emerge at unpredictable times and that must be screened and acted upon before the next iteration of the formal planning process.

The process and tools described here will help executives and managers to ask the tough questions and make the tough choices that need to be dealt with if your company is to achieve market leadership.

The Environment in Which Technology-Intensive Businesses Operate

A number of characteristics of technology-intensive markets makes strategic market planning a particularly challenging activity for the companies competing in these markets. They are as follows:

- Complex and Dynamic Market Chains
- Network Effects
- Speed of Change is High
- Blurred Market Boundaries
- Markets and Competition are Global

Complex and Dynamic Market Chains

In many technology-intensive businesses there is less vertical integration than in more mature, less technology-intensive businesses. This often results in long market chains with several different organizations playing, or potentially playing, key roles in the task of converting the raw materials into the solutions that the end users require. The market chain describes the organizations involved in creating and delivering the products and services you help create for customers or end users. A simple market chain is shown in Figure 1-1. The company whose perspective we are taking is always shown as the focal point of the market chain (in Figure 1-1 it is the manufacturer). Companies in technology-intensive industries find it very difficult to develop and maintain the necessary competencies in all the roles in the market chain that contribute to success in a market. In addition, at the downstream end of the market chain, close to the ultimate customer, there are sometimes many niche market opportunities. It is often very difficult for one company acting alone to access all these opportunities effectively. As a result, many high-technology companies must rely on a complex network of partners, such as system integrators, value-added resellers, or other third parties to work with them to develop these niche opportunities.

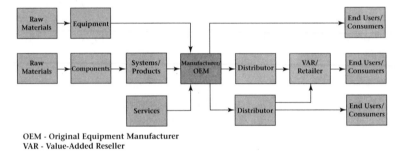

OEM - Original Equipment Manufacturer
VAR - Value-Added Reseller

FIGURE 1-1: Market Chain

Frequently, the market chains are not only long and complex, but also unstable. As companies in a market chain search for new opportunities to enhance their own profitability in a changing market, some of them see opportunities to move either up or down the market chain, absorbing some of the activities of their suppliers or customers. In 1999 Lucent Technologies, the world's largest manufacturer of telecommunications equipment, acquired International Network Services. International Network Services designed, installed, and maintained computer networks for many large U.S. corporations and telephone companies. In this role it had a significant impact on the amount of Lucent equipment that was installed in these computer networks. By buying International Network Services, Lucent hoped to gain greater control over these purchase decisions. Such moves can have a significant impact on the competitive dynamics within a market chain and within the broader market.

In any situation where market chains are long and relatively complex, relationships between the various players in the market chain can have a major impact on the success of the companies in the market chain. For this reason, successful competitors in technology-intensive industries often are companies that are very effective at developing both the internal and external relationships required for success. These relationships can take a variety of forms. Some are focused directly on sales, while others might be concerned with accessing critical information or technology, or influencing major stakeholders in the business arena. Some major successes in technology-intensive industries have occurred when a company has been able both to develop a new type of relationship for its industry and to successfully leverage that relationship.

Glaxo Wellcome was the first major pharmaceutical company to really exploit co-marketing relationships when it used this type of relationship in the 1980s to ensure the rapid global adoption of its anti-ulcer pharmaceutical, Zantac.[2] At the time Zantac was launched, Glaxo was a moderately successful pharmaceutical company based in the United Kingdom. Its strongest markets were in Europe and in the countries of the British Commonwealth (its sales in Nigeria were larger than its sales in the United States!). In order to gain rapid global market share with its new product against a very strongly entrenched competitor, SmithKline, it made alliances with a number of other pharmaceutical companies that were strong in certain geographical markets. These partners either marketed Zantac under their own brand names and paid a royalty to Glaxo or used their sales forces to sell Zantac in return for a share of the revenues. The approach was remarkably successful, and it helped make Zantac the largest-selling pharmaceutical in the world, with sales of almost $4 billion in 1994.

Network Effects

A significant number of technology-intensive industries also exhibit network effects. When the value of a product or service to the user depends on the number of other users, the product exhibits network effects.[3] Network effects are particularly pronounced in

---

[2] This example is based on INSEAD case study #592-045-1, *Zantac* (A) (Fontainebleau, France: INSEAD, 1992).

[3] Carl Shapiro and Hal R. Varian, *Information Rules: A Strategic Guide to the Network Economy* (Boston, Massachusetts: Harvard Business School Press, 1999).

communication technologies, such as e-mail, Internet access, and fax machines. Each of these products or services is more valuable to a user when the people the user wishes to communicate with also have the product. Network effects also exist for software products, since a community of, say, Macintosh users facilitates the exchange of files and encourages software developers to create additional programs for the Macintosh platform.

Frequently, products or services exhibiting network effects are slow to take off, but once a critical mass of users is established the growth can be explosive. The core technology for the Internet was available in the early 1970s, but it took about 20 years to reach the mainstream market, at which point the volume of traffic began to grow explosively.

The presence of network effects encourages companies to go to extraordinary lengths to establish market leadership and become the standard. It has now become common for companies to give away a basic version of their product to encourage adoption in order to become the standard. Netscape captured an early need in the Web browser market by using this strategy.

Speed of Change Is High

By their very nature most technology-intensive markets undergo rapid and continuous change. The turbulence of these markets requires that companies competing in such industries must be continually making decisions about their business definitions. That is, they must constantly be making choices about the customers they will serve, the functions and applications they will provide to these customers, the technologies and competencies they will use to provide the functions or applications, and their own value-added role within the larger market chain.

Some of the changes that occur in these markets involve significant discontinuities. These discontinuities, which may be brought about by changes in technology or markets, provide major opportunities for new firms to topple the current market leaders from their leadership positions. In many technology-intensive industries it is rare for a firm to maintain leadership across a major market discontinuity. For example, in the computer industry, IBM was unable to transfer its leadership position in mainframes to the emerging minicomputer market in the 1960s and 1970s. As a result, Digital Equipment Corporation and Hewlett-Packard emerged as the leaders in what became a very high growth segment of the market. When the next significant discontinuity in the computer industry, the personal computer, emerged in the early 1980s, Digital Equipment Corporation and Hewlett-Packard were both unable to gain a significant position in this new emerging industry. Leadership was assumed by new companies, such as Compaq, Dell, and Apple, and even a resurgent IBM.

The speed of change and the turbulence in technology-intensive markets place major stresses on the companies competing in these markets. New product development processes have to be responsive to deal with this turbulence. They must ensure a stream of timely new products that will earn a fast return on research and development investments in an environment where product life cycles are sometimes measured in weeks and months, not years.

> With rapid market change and a significant number of discontinuities, companies in technology-intensive industries cannot rest on their laurels. A company that has achieved market leadership must aggressively strive to maintain its leadership position. In many of these markets, sitting back and planning to be a "fast follower" is not a viable option.

By the time a market or market segment is clearly defined and measurable, it is too late. Other more aggressive companies will have staked out leadership positions in the most attractive segments of the market. In addition, they may have helped establish industry standards or shaped the market in ways that play to their competencies and strategies. Often third parties will emerge to provide support and complementary products for the market leader's products and services, buttressing its leadership position. Therefore, your company must either strive for market leadership or be satisfied with reacting to a market where the rules and standards are set by others. A purely reactionary strategy is unlikely to be a very profitable one.

Blurred Market Boundaries

A particular challenge in many technology-intensive industries is the blurred and changing nature of the market boundaries. Market boundaries are the hypothetical dividing line where one market, such as personal computers, ends and where a related market, such as engi-neering workstations, begins. As technology advances on a broad front in the areas around a particular market, new ways of providing a particular functionality or application to a customer group are con-tinually emerging. Sometimes these new technologies provide prod-ucts with dramatically improved price and performance for particular segments of the market and with the potential to displace the incum-bent suppliers.

In the mid-1980s, Aldus Corporation, in an alliance with Apple Computer and Adobe Systems, was very successful in creating the desktop publishing market with its software product PageMaker. Desktop publishing dramatically simplified the process and lowered the costs of developing newsletters, brochures, and other printed materials for individuals and organizations. But within a few years, the once-clear boundary around the desktop publishing market was gone as word processing packages, such as WordPerfect and Microsoft Word, added more and more desktop publishing features to their soft-ware packages. While this functionality did not meet the needs of the most sophisticated segments of the desktop publishing market, it did meet the needs of the casual user. Thus, Aldus found itself increas-ingly in competition with the large, well-financed, mainstream soft-ware producers.

Markets and Competition Are Global

Most of the major technology-intensive industries are either already global or rapidly becoming global. The globalization of these indus-tries is driven by a number of factors, including:

- converging customer needs,
- lower trade barriers,
- deregulation of markets (or lack of regulation), and
- the fundamental economics of many technology-intensive busi-nesses.

Most technology-intensive industries are, by their very nature, heavily research and development-oriented. Thus, large investments are required to develop a new generation of technology and its asso-ciated products. Once this investment has been made, large volumes must be sold to recoup the investment. Given the relatively short product life cycles in many technology-intensive businesses, the only way these volumes can be achieved is by aggressively selling the product in all the major markets in the world. A major new pharmaceutical product can require a cumulative investment of over $500 million.[4] In addition, it may take an ethical pharmaceutical company 10 to 12 years to develop the product and get the product through all the required clinical trials. With only a few years remaining before the patents expire or other competitors enter the market, the pharmaceutical company must achieve rapid worldwide distribution and market share if it is to recoup this enormous investment. In other technology-intensive businesses, such as notebook computers, the life cycle of the product may be measured in months, rather than years, making a strong global presence and global distribution an imperative.

The global nature of most technology-intensive industries sometimes results in the key players coming from different business cultures, each to a significant degree with its own objectives, competencies, and strategies. Taiwanese manufacturers in many segments of the electronics industry are well known for having very strong, low-cost manufacturing. They are often willing to accept low margins if doing so will allow them to achieve high volumes. This strategy has made them formidable competitors for North American or European manufacturers with different objectives, competencies, and business strategies. The mere fact that different global competitors in a technology-intensive industry have different business and marketing strategies can lead to more intense competition and require us to think about competition in new ways.

As companies competing in technology-intensive businesses try to penetrate the global market they must build and nurture relationships and strategic alliances with partners all over the world. Because of this, they must grapple with the difficult issues of building relationships with managers and executives from different cultures and business environments, which can be a challenging and time-consuming activity.

Not all technology-intensive industries have all the above characteristics: complex and dynamic market chains, network effects, high speed of change and frequent discontinuities, blurred market

---

[4] Such a figure is likely when one considers that a single successful product must cover the costs of all the other drug compounds that were developed but failed to make it through the preclinical testing and clinical trials or failed to get regulatory approval.

boundaries, and global markets and competition. But many of these characteristics are present in most technology-intensive industries.

Strategic Market Planning in a Technology-Intensive Business

Strategic market planning is the process by which a company selects and creates the business opportunities it will pursue, and develops the marketing plans that will propel it to market leadership in its targeted markets.

Who Should Be Involved in the Process?

It is the accepted wisdom in most businesses today that strategic market planning should not just be left to those individuals with "marketing" in their titles. This principle is particularly important in technology-intensive industries. Given the range of technologies that may be involved and the rapid changes occurring in the base technologies, market chains, and end users, it is almost impossible for an individual or a small group of individuals to keep abreast of developments in all these areas.

Many marketing managers find it difficult to fully appreciate complex technological issues, and technology managers can have difficulty appreciating the marketing issues. Furthermore, in most technology-intensive businesses it is not possible to divorce the technology decisions from the marketing decisions, or vice versa. This means at the very least that multi-functional and multi-level teams must be involved in the planning process and that the planning process actively encourage a continuing dialogue among all members of the team on these issues.

Planning Builds Mental Models

As Aries DeGeus, the former head of planning for Royal Dutch/Shell Group, has argued, the real purpose of planning is not to make plans, but to change the mental models that the decision makers carry in their heads.[5] Plans in fast-moving industries are often outdated, in at

---

[5] Arie P. DeGeus, "Planning as Learning," *Harvard Business Review* (March–April 1988), pp. 70–74.

least some details, the moment they are written. However, managers and individuals, even at low levels in the organization, have to make decisions that can affect the future of the company. They must make decisions about whether to pursue a new opportunity, such as a new contract, that was not contemplated during the planning process.

Being involved in the planning process increases the likelihood that each individual will have in her or his head a current "model" of where the business unit is trying to go. The individual can then quickly determine whether the unexpected opportunity will help move the company in the desired direction. If it will, the opportunity is seized; if not, it is quickly discarded without a lot of time being wasted. Given the turbulence in technology-intensive markets, it is not surprising that the actual realized strategy often differs significantly from the planned strategy as decision makers make adjustments over time in response to changes and opportunities in the environment (sometimes called the emergent strategy).[6] Thus, the planning process should facilitate the regular updating of the business unit's "mental model."

Planning Process Must Be Iterative and Continuous

All of this suggests that in many technology-intensive, fast-moving businesses with short product life cycles, total reliance on a ritualistic once-a-year planning process would be ludicrous. While the general direction of the strategy for the business should be revisited periodically, often on an annual basis, strategic evaluations or reevaluations of new emerging opportunities must be done on a more ad hoc basis—when they emerge and when they are needed. In fast-moving markets, waiting until the next periodic planning cycle may result in a strategic window being missed. Planning calendars have to be flexible, because a technology breakthrough or a major announcement by a competitor at a key trade show can significantly affect product and market dynamics and put existing plans into question.

---

[6] For a discussion of intended, emergent, and realized strategies, see Henry Mintzberg, *The Rise and Fall of Strategic Planning* (New York: The Free Press, 1994), pp. 24–29.

Planning Process Must Be Integrative

Planning processes in technology-intensive businesses must lead to an integrated set of choices to gain and sustain market leadership. The planning process should encourage such an integrated approach. Ideally, all members of the cross-functional team should work with the same process and the same language and set of tools, a procedure that improves communication within the teams.

> Keeping communication clear is a real challenge in an era when organizations frequently use a series of consultants over time, each with their own terminologies and "buzz words" and each leaving a legacy of terms and processes in the organizations.

Winning Market Leadership: An Integrated Approach

The strategic market planning process shown in Figure 1-2 is particularly well-suited to the environment and issues that technology-intensive businesses face. This planning process is focused on the issues faced by a strategic business unit (SBU). In a later chapter we will discuss how this process might interface with a typical strategic planning system in a large multi-business corporation.

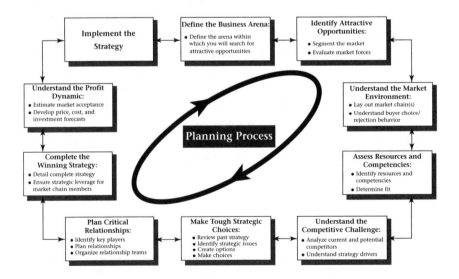

FIGURE 1-2: Winning Market Leadership—Steps in the Planning Process

In the next few pages we will briefly introduce the major steps in the process. The rest of the book will delve into each of these areas in depth with a chapter being devoted to each topic. We will deal with these topics in a logical order, beginning with choosing the arena where we will compete, but that is not to say that other sequences cannot be perfectly appropriate. In addition, the process is iterative—you may end up revisiting steps as your efforts in other areas raise new questions or generate new insights.

The process emphasizes the selection of the "right" set of market opportunities, which is a real challenge in many technology-intensive markets, where an organization may have dozens or hundreds of potential opportunities. The process also places heavy emphasis on market chains, which are often much more complex and more varied than they are for fast-moving consumer goods or for a mature business-to-business product or service. The complexity of the markets and the market chains, the blurred market boundaries, and the turbulent competitive environment mean that understanding the competitive environment is absolutely key in technology-intensive markets. And finally, winning in this complex environment means managing multiple shifting relationships. The process proposed here places particular emphasis on all these areas.

Choose the Arena

The first step in the process is to tentatively identify the broad business arena or arenas that are or will be targeted by the strategic business unit (SBU). An existing business unit will already be active in one or more arenas. A new business may be trying to decide whether there is a viable opportunity or opportunities for it. Each arena of opportunity should be tentatively defined along four major dimensions:

1. Potential customer segments that could be served
2. Potential applications or functionality that could be provided to these customers
3. Possible technologies or competencies that could be used to create these applications or functionality
4. Possible value-adding roles for the SBU in the market chain

The latter refers to your initial thinking on your organization's role in providing the customer value compared to the roles of the other players in the market chain, such as your suppliers, your distributors, or your system integrators. At this stage, all of the above decisions must be tentative ones and may very well be reconsidered and changed as you move through the strategic market planning process. Almost certainly you will pick only a limited set of the opportunities that are included in this initial arena.

The selection of the business arena is crucial in any strategic market planning process, since it places some tentative boundaries on the arena in which the organization will seek specific opportunities and profits, and puts some boundaries around the area that will be subjected to intense analysis.[7] Selecting the business arena is especially important for businesses operating in technology-intensive markets, where the business may theoretically take a new technology into dozens or even hundreds of product-market segments. As we all recognize, it is by no means a trivial task to understand just one or two of these opportunities in enough depth to be able to develop a strategy for achieving leadership in it.

Identify Potentially Attractive Opportunities

Once you have defined an arena to be the focus of the strategic market planning process, you need to begin gaining an in-depth understanding of its potential opportunities.

In some cases an opportunity will have presented itself to your company, perhaps as a result of a customer bringing a need to your attention or a technological breakthrough by your scientists or engineers. In other cases, the SBU may be actively searching for new opportunities, since the current opportunities it is pursuing will not allow it to meet its revenue or earnings targets.

Invariably, an important early step in identifying attractive opportunities is a thorough segmentation of the market to start developing a complete understanding of the applications or functionality the customers require, the technologies or competencies that the SBU might employ to deliver the application, and the value added they require from the market chain that will supply them.

---

7 George S. Day, *Strategic Market Planning: The Pursuit of Competitive Advantage* (St. Paul, Minnesota: West Publishing, 1984), pp. 16–17.

Having identified the segmentation, the management team must next try to develop an understanding of the likely profitability of serving particular market segments. If the market forces affecting a segment over the planning horizon are likely to be negative, so that none of the companies serving this market segment are likely to make money, you might eliminate this particular market segment from further consideration. By the mid-1990s, several market segments in the personal computer industry had become so unattractive that almost no company was making money in them. Thus, it was surprising when Sony, a leader in consumer electronics, announced its entry into the desktop market in late 1996. Even though the revenues in some of these segments might be high, these are not the market opportunities an SBU will typically wish to target, unless its management can see a way to change the business model or feels that for strategic reasons it has to have a presence in the segment. Sony clearly felt that the potential convergence of the home computer and home entertainment markets made it essential that it develop a strong presence in the home computer market. As the president of Sony Electronics said two years later, "The PC will be the hub of all the entertainment equipment for Sony."[8]

As you are conducting your analysis, be on the lookout for market segments where there might be the opportunity for you to drive the market by adopting a radically different strategy. These types of opportunities often arise as the result of major discontinuities occurring in a market, perhaps as the result of a technology breakthrough or deregulation or some other destabilizing force. Nortel Networks was able to become a major supplier of central office switching equipment to telephone companies in the United States during the late 1970s and 1980s by exploiting the breakup of AT&T and breakthroughs in digital switching technologies.

Once your team has developed one or more opportunities that look attractive, you can take the opportunities through the next three steps of the process either individually or as a group. Often small, cross-functional teams will do the analysis, drawing on other resources both inside and outside the business unit.

---

[8] David Kirkpatrick, "Is the PC Dead? Not Even Close," *Fortune*, December 21, 1998, pp. 211–214.

Understand the Market

To develop a deeper understanding of the opportunities that have passed the initial screen, a useful first step is to lay out the actual and potential market chain or chains that could supply the end users the SBU is targeting with its product or service. The market chains, extending from the major suppliers of raw materials for the product or service through the supply and distribution channels, may well be long and complex, but the visual representation is one that the team will return to many times as it does its analysis and develops its strategy.

While the main focus may be on the pieces of the market chain closest to the level in the chain where the SBU intends to focus, there are, as we shall see later in the book, some very good reasons to develop an understanding of the complete chain. This is particularly true for the "downstream" parts of the chain, between the SBU and the end users of the product or service.

The next step in understanding the market is to examine and understand buyer behavior in the potential target segments and the market chain or chains that serve (or could serve) them. If their needs are being met by other suppliers of the product or service the SBU hopes to provide, the team needs to discover what will cause the target customers to switch from that product to its product and the switching barriers that must be overcome.

In analyzing this choice/rejection behavior of all the players in the market chain, the SBU team needs to understand the decision making units that will be involved, the buying criteria of the members of the units, and the likely buying process they will go through. Again, the information the team will pull together in this process can be very helpful both in making the choices among opportunities and in developing implementable action plans to capitalize on the chosen opportunities. This analysis may expose some major barriers to the adoption of the proposed product or service that can't be overcome. Such findings may result in this opportunity being dropped from further consideration.

Assess Resources and Competencies

After looking at the external marketplace, it is necessary to consider the business unit's internal situation and assess the resources and competencies (or capabilities) that the business unit has to work with as it tries to seize the opportunities in the market arena.[9]

Resources are the tangible and intangible assets that the business unit and the company as a whole have developed and accumulated, such as its financial resources, technology platforms, intellectual property, manufacturing capacity, and brand equity. Competencies are complementary bundles of skills, knowledge, and collective learning that allow an organization to perform one or more important business processes effectively. Because of its strong process capability in new product development, 3M has been very successful in leveraging its technological competencies in substrates, coatings, and adhesives into hundreds of new products in a diverse set of markets.

Again, it may become apparent in the course of the assessment of an opportunity that the SBU and the company do not have the necessary resources or competencies, or the ability to acquire them. Again, this may eliminate the opportunity from further consideration.

Understand the Competitive Challenge

Although the competitive analysis is an important part of the analysis of the external environment, it is best done after the review of the business' resources and competencies. You are always in a better position to assess your competitors if you have carefully looked at your own resources and competencies first. In addition, any competitive analysis has two fundamental purposes: to determine your likelihood of winning a profitable position in a particular market and to develop the strategy and tactics that will allow you to achieve the winning position.

Clearly, an SBU's assessment of the first requires that it be able to assess the resources and competencies of its potential competitors not only in an absolute sense, but also relative to its own resources and competencies. For example, a semiconductor company may be considering a market opportunity where rapid development of prototypes will be a key factor in success. This may be an area in which it is one of the leaders—typically being able to deliver a prototype in two months. However, if the key competitor is a company that is

---

[9] Competencies and capabilities are used interchangeably in this book.

superlative at producing a prototype quickly and can typically deliver it in less than six weeks, the semiconductor company's two-month delivery becomes an area of relative weakness.

In order to conduct the competitive analysis, the team must first identify the actual, potential, and indirect competitors it will face. The indirect competitors are simply the companies that meet the same functional need of the customer by exploiting different technologies and competencies. If a company were looking at an opportunity in on-demand video for the home market using the cable TV infrastructure, indirect competition might come from telephone companies or direct-broadcast satellite companies, or even the local video store. If the team has done a good job of its market forces analysis earlier when it was assessing the attractiveness of the opportunity, this step should be straightforward, since all the likely competitors should have been identified as it went through that process.

The next step is to understand how each competitor or group of competitors competes, their current and likely future performance, and what the drivers are that underlie their business strategies. A good understanding of the business drivers and any changes in any of these driving forces can provide essential information for predicting their future moves. Sometimes changes in key executives, such as a new CEO, can signal a major shift in strategy, as when George Fisher moved from Motorola to become the new CEO of Eastman Kodak in 1993. Fisher sold all of Kodak's businesses that were unrelated to imaging and placed Kodak's embryonic digital imaging businesses in a business unit separate from its traditional silver-halide photography businesses. This increased focus on electronic imaging was an important development for both competitors and complementors in digital imaging.[10]

The final step in a competitive analysis is to pull together the implications of the competitive analysis for the opportunity being evaluated. These implications provide the answers to four major questions for each of the competitors, or strategic groups of competitors:

1. What is this competitor likely to do next?

2. What are this competitor's areas of weakness or vulnerability that you can potentially exploit?

---

[10] Linda Grant, "Can Fisher Focus Kodak?" *Fortune,* January 13, 1997, pp. 76–79.

3. How is this competitor likely to react if you do X, or Y, or Z?

4. What has your team learned from this competitive analysis that could be applied in your own organization to make you a stronger, more effective competitor?

Make Tough Strategic Choices

The essential step in any strategic market planning process is the identification of the strategic issues and making the tough choices associated with each issue. A strategic issue is one created by external or internal developments that:

- Has potential significant impact on the organization's future performance,

- Is controversial in that reasonable people can disagree on how to deal with it, and

- Has strategic consequences in that the resolution of the issue may mean implementing a change in strategy.[11]

Strategic issues involve tough choices which are controversial and where powerful arguments can be made for more than one alternative.

The strategic issues arise at two levels: at the level of the individual opportunity and at the level of the portfolio of opportunities the SBU is pursuing. At the level of the individual opportunity, two common strategic issues that arise are the selection of the best strategy for taking advantage of the opportunity and the decision as to whether this is an opportunity the SBU should pursue. The first issue addresses the question of winning. On the basis of the analysis the team has done, does it think it can develop a strategy that will allow it to achieve a leadership position?

The second addresses the question of what it will be worth to win. That is, is the market opportunity attractive enough and is the SBU's strategy powerful enough to generate a level of profitability that will meet its financial targets? Or if it won't be sufficiently profitable, are there other compelling reasons to proceed despite unacceptable financial results? For example, it might decide to proceed

11 William R. King, "Using Strategic Issues Analysis," *Long Range Planning* (August 1982), pp. 45–49.

with an opportunity that is not financially attractive if doing so positions the SBU to seize other opportunities that promise to be highly profitable. This was probably Sony's motivation for entering the PC business in 1996.

Winning profitable market leadership is about identifying and creating attractive market opportunities, where you can win.

FIGURE: 1-3 Winning Profitable Market Leadership

At the level of the portfolio of opportunities the business is pursuing, strategic issues often arise with regard to the fit with the other opportunities the SBU is pursuing or plans to pursue. Here the team is concerned about potential synergies within its portfolio of opportunities, such as leveraging a common technology or a market chain. An important issue is that the strategies for the various opportunities should be reasonably consistent, since the SBU is unlikely to be able to pull off two or more radically different strategies. For example, a strategy based on product leadership for one product line is unlikely to be workable with a strategy of cost leadership for a related line.

> Perhaps the most challenging aspect of any strategic thinking process is making the hard choices—saying yes to this opportunity and no to that one. But this is what any good strategic market planning process should get you to do: select the few truly attractive opportunities, concentrate your resources on these opportunities, and develop a leadership position in the selected areas.

This is exactly what Intel did in 1985 when it decided to exit the memory business and focus on microprocessors.[12] Too often, management puts off making the hard choices and dissipates its resources over too many opportunities, developing a leadership position in

---

[12] Andrew S. Grove, *Only the Paranoid Survive* (New York: Doubleday, 1996), pp. 85–89.

none of them. This is a sure way to "underwhelm" the competition![13] (see Figure 1-4 below).

FIGURE 1-4: How to Underwhelm the Competition

Sometimes an outcome of the strategic thinking process and the analysis that leads up to it is a decision to redefine the business arena. Perhaps you recognized that you don't have the competencies to win in most of the market opportunities within the original arena, but you now believe there are some promising opportunities outside the original arena, where your competencies will be applicable. In this case, you would redefine the business arena and work back around the process a second time to determine if some of these opportunities are truly attractive ones for you.

Plan Key Relationships

At this point, many of the key decisions will have been made: the various opportunities within the arena will have been evaluated and prioritized and the strategic objective for each of the selected opportunities will have been set. The initiative now usually returns to the team that did the analysis of the opportunity to finalize the strategy and build the implementation plan.

As a result of the earlier analysis, several of the major strategy decisions will also have been tentatively made. The target segments should now be clear. It should also be clear exactly what functionality and applications will be provided to the target segments, as well

---

[13] Based on a discussion with Richard M. Levy, President and CEO, Varian Medical Systems.

as the resources and competencies that will be employed to deliver this functionality. As a result of thinking through the market chain and market forces issues, both the value-added role the SBU will play and the market chain or chains it will use, should also now be clear.

The value-added role and the market chain help clarify the important relationships that the SBU needs to develop and manage if it is to be successful. In many technology-intensive industries, the management of these relationships is absolutely crucial. Some of these crucial relationships will be within the chain, such as those between an original equipment manufacturer (OEM) and its value-added resellers (VARs). Others will be with individuals or organizations outside the market chain—perhaps with a company that has a strong position in a technology of potential interest to you, or with a standards-setting organization that could affect the acceptance of your products, or with the developer of complementary products or services.

Complete the Winning Strategy

In order to complete the winning strategy, a number of additional issues need to be resolved. One crucial issue is the development of a clear positioning statement for the product or service, so that the target market will find it easy to buy. Other elements of the strategy that require attention are pricing and marketing communications. Both of these activities, if done skillfully, can help create the economic incentive for other companies in the market chain to work with you rather than with one of your competitors. You must create a strategy that will allow each of the key players in your market chain to achieve its business and personal objectives by working with you. Ideally, you want to give each member of the market chain a strong reason to adopt and aggressively push your product or service. The market chain members should find it more profitable to work with you than with any of your competitors. Otherwise, they will follow their economic self-interest and work with other partners.

Many technology-intensive businesses underestimate the importance of marketing communications, assuming that great products will "sell" themselves. Time and time again, we have seen companies with "inferior" products succeed, partly as a result of effective positioning and marketing communications. Many analysts feel that this has been one of the factors that has contributed to Microsoft's success in many software markets.

Understand the Profit Dynamic

In assessing the attractiveness of the various market opportunities being considered in the planning process and its ability to win in these opportunities, the SBU team is effectively assessing the potential profitability of the opportunities. Usually the financial analysis at those stages in the process is relatively crude, since a more refined analysis requires a detailed understanding of the complete marketing strategy and the associated costs. However, once the detailed strategy has been established, the team should understand the profit dynamic or financial model for each of the opportunities that have reached this stage in the planning process.

Understanding the profit dynamic requires an in-depth knowledge of the financial model underlying a market opportunity and each of the major cash flow drivers. With this knowledge, the managers and team members will have a clear understanding of the sensitivity of overall cash flow to changes in each of the drivers. As the team's understanding deepens, they may suggest modifications to the strategy that could enhance the present value of the cash flow stream associated with the opportunity.

Implement the Chosen Strategy

Implementation is the final key step in the strategic market planning process. No matter how good the strategy is, it will fail if it is not implemented effectively. Implementation is not something that begins when the strategy development process ends. Rather, the strategy development process should always have the implementation step in clear view and anticipate it. One important way to do this is by making sure that the individuals who will play the key roles in the implementation process are heavily involved in, and committed to, the strategy. If they are involved in the strategy development process, they will contribute to its development, understand the rationale for particular choices, and be able to make the dozens of minor adjustments in strategy that are needed as the theory behind the strategy hits the shifting reality of the marketplace.

As we discussed earlier, strategic market planning in technology-intensive industries requires the ideas and energy from all of the major functional units in the company. As the strategic market plan comes together, the supporting functional strategies in such areas as research and development, purchasing, manufacturing, and logistics must be finalized. Any barriers to implementation in these areas must be identified and overcome.

In technology-intensive businesses there is seldom a smooth transition from strategy development to implementation. The environment is too fast-moving for such a clear demarcation. Even as you begin the implementation process, the strategy will evolve, requiring adjustments to the implementation process. It is truly an iterative, evolving process that is difficult to timetable.

What Is Different About This Book?

Integrated Planning Process

This book presents an integrated strategic market planning process and a set of tools and concepts that are designed to address the particular issues faced by technology-intensive businesses in developing strategic market plans. The process focuses on the critical questions that must be addressed in developing winning market plans in technology-intensive markets. It is a process that can be used by all members of the cross-functional team responsible for the development of the strategic market plan.

Process Applies to New or Existing Business Opportunities

The process can be used in a variety of ways. As we discuss in Chapter 12, the process can dovetail very well with the strategic planning system used by a number of large, multi-business corporations. In such a planning process, the individual businesses may be looking at a number of potential opportunities that could be included in the plan they will be submitting to corporate management. The process described here will be very useful in identifying a coherent set of existing and new opportunities to be evaluated and in providing a systematic process for screening these opportunities to identify one or more subsets that should be presented to corporate management for approval.

Alternatively, the process can be used to screen opportunities that arise between iterations of the periodic (often annual) planning process. In the turbulent world of technology-intensive businesses, opportunities don't always appear at the appropriate time in the planning cycle. Opportunities appear as a result of an unexpected technological breakthrough by the company or a competitor, an unexpected move by a competitor, or the request of a customer. On some rare occasions, decisions can be delayed until the next iteration of the planning process. But usually, this is not possible and a quick decision is essential. In this case, a team should be quickly assembled and the opportunity run through the appropriate steps in the process. The critical questions raised by the process are generic and can be applied in either case.

Process Is Designed for Managers

The process is designed to help real managers make the tough decisions needed to gain market leadership in today's highly competitive technology-intensive markets.

CHAPTER TWO

Choose the Arena

Introduction

The first step you face in your strategic market planning process is to conceptualize the business arena for your strategic business unit (SBU). This arena should include both the market opportunities your business is currently pursuing and the markets where it will search for attractive opportunities that could be added in the future. Essentially, you are trying to put some boundaries around your current business and future opportunities to make the planning process a more manageable and effective one. This initial conceptualization of the business arena is only a starting point. One of the major outputs of a strategic market planning process is sometimes a reconceptualization of the business arena in which the SBU will compete. Thus, the process is often an iterative one.

In defining the business arena, it is important not to be too narrow. If you are, you may not spot emerging opportunities and threats in neighboring arenas. Microsoft was a fairly late entrant into Internet products and services, because it had apparently not included Internet opportunities within its business arena.[1] However, in 1994 some managers and executives began to become aware of the

---

[1] Kathy Rebello, "Inside Microsoft," *Business Week*, July 15, 1996, pp. 56–67.

opportunities and threats posed by the Internet for Microsoft. By late 1995 Microsoft was aggressively pursuing a number of Internet-related opportunities. On the other hand, if you define the business arena too broadly, it will become impossible to get the depth of understanding of all the opportunities in the arena that is needed for really effective decision making. So it becomes a difficult, but important, balancing act.

The business arena for a strategic business unit has four major dimensions:

1. The customers it is serving or could potentially serve
2. The functionality or applications it is providing or could provide for these customers
3. The technologies and competencies or capabilities it is using or could use to create the applications or functionality for its customers
4. Its value-adding role

The latter element, the value-adding role, refers to the portion of the value added that will be provided by the strategic business unit rather than by other members of the market chain. Generally, the customers we are talking about in the business arena are the end users for the product or service we are providing or to which we are contributing. These end users may or may not be direct customers.

The business definition of the SBU reflects the current set of choices a company has made about which specific market opportunities it will pursue within the broader business arena.

The choice of the specific market opportunities within the business arena is a crucial one for many technology-intensive businesses. Such organizations may have hundreds, if not thousands, of potential applications for the technologies they have developed. Thus one of the most important outputs of any strategic market planning process for these kinds of businesses is the selection of a focused set of opportunities within the business arena on which the SBU can concentrate (i.e., its current business definition).

Crucial First Step in the Planning Process

Later in this chapter we will discuss the importance of defining the business arena before beginning to plan. But first we should clarify the organizational unit in most companies where much of the strategic market planning is done, the strategic business unit (SBU).

Strategic Business Unit (SBU)

Most "start-ups" are initially focused on one or a couple of closely related market opportunities. But as the company grows and evolves, it may find itself with several businesses, some of which may have only tenuous links to each other. Starting with General Electric in the late 1960s, many companies have since found it useful to divide such a company into a number of SBUs that are each large enough to justify top management attention, yet small enough to serve as a useful basis for resource allocation.[2]

Ideally an SBU should look and act like a free-standing business. Generally, an SBU has an external market (as opposed to selling its products and services only to other units within the company) and has customers and competitors that are distinct from those of other SBUs within the same company. The SBU should also be strategically autonomous from the other SBUs. This allows an SBU to change its strategy without having a significant impact on the strategies or profitability of the other SBUs within the corporation. An SBU does not necessarily need to "own" all of its own resources. It might very well share research and development with other business units and use a shared sales force or marketing channel to reach its customers. However, it should have significant control over these resources and have some say in setting their objectives and priorities. Ideally, the profitability of an individual SBU can be measured, so that top management is able to make resource allocation decisions on an informed basis.

The business arena of the SBU describes the boundaries within which an SBU will search for specific, attractive market opportunities. By conceptualizing the business arena for the SBU clearly, the management team is able to narrow the area in which it must do its detailed market analysis.

---

[2] Frederick W. Gluck, "Strategic Planning in a New Key," *McKinsey Quarterly* (Winter 1986), pp. 18–41.

Existing Market Opportunities

For an established SBU, a good deal of the strategic market planning exercise will focus on existing market opportunities. One of the issues here is often whether the current business definition for these opportunities should be modified in some way by adding new market opportunities or deleting some of the existing opportunities. Some companies have been very successful at growing by means of a controlled expansion of their existing business definition.

Applied Materials is an excellent example of such a company. Throughout most of its history, it has focused on the same core group of customers, namely semiconductor manufacturers. It has provided these customers with leading-edge semiconductor manufacturing equipment. Over time, it expanded its business definition by moving into closely related market opportunities involving providing equipment for more of the steps in the semiconductor manufacturing process. In effect, it has gradually moved along the semiconductor manufacturing line providing its established customers with an expanding line of equipment. Since these opportunities often involved new technologies for Applied Materials, the company had to develop or acquire expertise in these technologies. By 1998 Applied Materials was serving 10 markets representing global revenues of $9 billion (see Figure 2-1). Applied Materials had total revenues of about $4 billion, and was the market leader in six of the 10 markets it served.

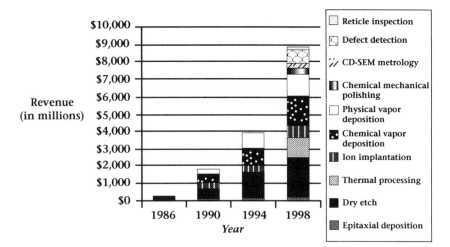

FIGURE 2-1: Applied Materials' Served Markets

New Market Opportunities

In some cases an SBU will be looking at new market opportunities that represent a significant departure from the current business in customers served, functionality/applications provided, technologies or competencies used, and/or value-adding role. In these situations the SBU management often has much less knowledge of these new market opportunities. This initial lack of detailed knowledge requires a highly iterative planning process. The team must often start by going through the process at a high level of abstraction and then with increasing depth as members begin to focus on those parts of the arena that seem to provide the really attractive opportunities for the SBU.

Thus for many companies a critical part of the strategic market planning process is identifying within the "big" cube that represents the SBU's broad business arena, the one or more "small" cubes that are the specific market opportunity or opportunities where the SBU has the potential to win profitable market leadership. See Figure 2-2. Over time, a really successful SBU may roll through several related opportunities to build on its previous successes and to build an almost unassailable position in its chosen arena. This is essentially what Applied Materials has done.

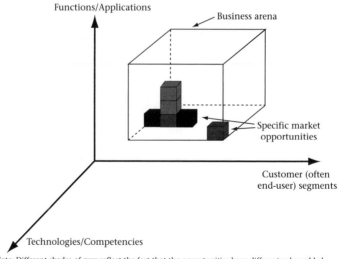

Note: Different shades of gray reflect the fact that the opportunities have different value-added roles for the company.

FIGURE 2-2: SBU Business Arena and Specific Market Opportunities Within It

Dendrite International is an example of a company that faced some challenging choices with regard to its business arena and growth directions in 1993.[3] The company was one of the world's largest suppliers of electronic territory management (ETM) software and services for pharmaceutical company sales forces. As the initial opportunities it had focused on reached saturation, it began to look for new opportunities. One of the first steps in this process was to specify the business arena in which it would search for new opportunities.

A simplified diagram of the business arena it selected is shown in Figure 2-3. Growth opportunities existed on all three of the dimensions shown in the figure, as well as on the fourth dimension, the value-adding role. It could adapt its core ETM software for other related industries, such as insurance or consumer packaged goods. Or it could expand its software for use in other related functional areas within the pharmaceutical industry or other related industries to help managers manage their operations more effectively. Or it could enhance its technology by adding new software modules that would provide new functionality for existing or new applications. In addition, it could make changes on the fourth dimension and adopt a broader value-adding role—perhaps by getting more involved in

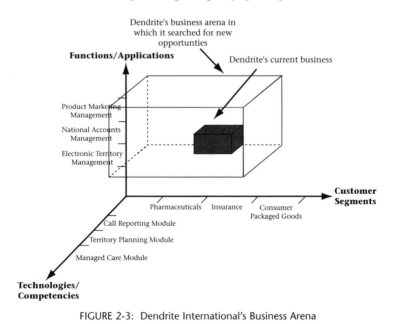

FIGURE 2-3: Dendrite International's Business Arena

[3] This is based on Harvard Business School case study #9-594-048 *Dendrite International* (Boston, Massachusetts: Publishing Division, Harvard Business School, 1993).

integrating its software with the databases of its customers. The combination of possible initiatives meant that Dendrite would potentially have to look at hundreds of market opportunities to determine the most attractive growth directions.

> One useful way of thinking about new market opportunities is to categorize them into product opportunities, service opportunities, or integrated product-service opportunities. Most product situations have service opportunities that go with them, and similarly, most service situations have product opportunities.

GE Aircraft Engine provides a useful example to illustrate this categorization. As shown in Figure 2-4, GE Aircraft Engine can be viewed as facing six different types of market opportunities. Each of these product/service situations is quite different in the way in which it produces profit and cash flow, and the time horizons involved. It is critical for GE to determine which type or types of opportunities are the most attractive at a particular time.

The top row of cells represents GE competing in the industry without getting involved with competitive products in any way. Cell 1 recognizes a GE product-centric opportunity where GE sells a particular engine to airlines and derives its profits and cash flow from product and spare parts sales. Cell 3 includes such opportunities as the servicing of GE engines. Cell 2 represents a more complex type of opportunity where GE markets an integrated engine product-service bundle to an airline. Here, GE might provide a fully serviced engine to an airline for a 20 year period, where the airline pays GE so many dollars per hour flown ("power by the hour"). The bottom row of cells represents an analogous set of opportunities based on competitors' products, rather than GE's. Cell 4 represents opportunities involving GE marketing a competitor's engine, perhaps for a segment where GE does not have an appropriate product of its own. Similarly, Cell 6 captures situations where GE might service a competitor's engine for an airline and Cell 5 sells an integrated product-service package based on a competitor's engine. Conceptualizing market opportunities using this matrix as a model might help you to identify some attractive new opportunities.

	Product	Integrated Product-Service	Service
GE Offering	**Cell 1** Markets GE product	**Cell 2** Markets integrated GE product and service	**Cell 3** Markets GE service
Competitive Offering	**Cell 4** Markets competitive product	**Cell 5** Markets integrated product-service based on competitive product	**Cell 6** Markets service based on competitive product

FIGURE 2-4: Conceptualizing New Market Opportunities at GE Aircraft Engine

Define the Arena

Customers Served

One of the crucial elements of the business definition is the choice of those customer segments the SBU will target. A complication is that many technology-intensive companies have a long market chain of direct and indirect customers. Most of these companies are not dealing directly just with the end users. There are some strong reasons for actively viewing all members of the market chain as your customers. Despite that, it is often useful to focus on the group of customers at one level in the market chain as the organizations or individuals whose needs you and most of the other members of the market chain are trying to serve. This is usually the "end user." Even though Intel was largely focused on designing and manufacturing microprocessors and selling them to PC manufacturers in the late 1990s, Andy Grove, the CEO of Intel, was attempting to drive Intel and the PC industry by focusing Intel's resources on "delivering information and interactive experiences to PC users."[4] Intel was clearly focused on meeting end-user needs in the PC market.

Another approach would, of course, be to focus on just the next level in the market chain (our immediate customers) and view those

---

[4] Andrew S. Grove, "A Revolution in Progress," Keynote Speech COMDEX/Fall 1996, Las Vegas, Nevada, November 18, 1996.

organizations or individuals as the customer, rather than trying to identify an appropriate end user as the focus in the strategic market planning process. There are some real dangers in just responding to the next downstream member in the market chain, and this approach no longer works in many technology-intensive markets. If the company is totally focused on the needs of the next player in the market chain, it may be unable to respond in a timely manner to the needs of this player.

In some cases, semiconductor manufacturers serving personal computer makers find that their product development cycles are longer than those of the personal computer manufacturers. For example, a personal computer manufacturer may want a semiconductor company to deliver a new semiconductor component in three months so that it can introduce a new personal computer into its market. The product development cycle for the semiconductor manufacturer may well be six months or more for a particular type of component. Therefore, unless the semiconductor manufacturer is anticipating this need of the personal computer manufacturer and is part way through its product development cycle, it will not be able to respond in a timely manner. By developing a good understanding of emerging needs throughout the market chain, a company should be in a better position to anticipate the needs of its immediate customers.

In addition, by having this good understanding of needs throughout the market chain, a company can build a competitive advantage over its direct competitors, who may take a more myopic view of the customer. Sometimes, a non-traditional view of the appropriate "end user" can give a company some useful insights. For example, one company competing in the diagnostic imaging market had traditionally focused on hospitals and clinics and the staff of these institutions as the appropriate end users for its equipment. In one strategic market planning cycle, they decided to move one step farther down the market chain and view patients as the appropriate end user. This led them to develop some product enhancements that made their equipment provide a more pleasant diagnostic experience for the patients. They believed that patients who were more satisfied would eventually result in a financial payback for the hospitals and clinics that used their equipment.

Applications/Functionality Provided

The second element of the business definition is the applications or functionality that an organization provides to its customers. Applications/functionality provided refers to the needs of the target customers you are trying to satisfy. For example, a manufacturer of diagnostic imaging equipment must decide which of its customers' particular diagnostic imaging needs it will attempt to meet. For example, it might focus only on the skeletal structure of patients. Or the company might decide it will try to provide a broader range of images, including those of soft tissue and nervous system activity.

Increasingly, as suggested in the GE Aircraft Engine example above, many manufacturers of products have been looking for services that they could bundle with their product or have been providing services that obviate the need for the customer to even own or use the product. For example, most major manufacturers of diagnostic imaging equipment provide financing and after-sales service and support for the equipment they sell. One can certainly envisage situations in which a diagnostic imaging company might own the equipment, rent space in a hospital, employ the radiologists and technicians, and sell diagnostic imaging services to the hospital and individual patients. Some hospitals might welcome this opportunity to outsource a complex, expensive, high-technology activity to a specialist supplier that had the potential to provide state-of-the-art imaging.

Technologies/Competencies Used

In many situations in technology-intensive industries, alternative technologies can be used to deliver particular applications or functionality to targeted customers. Again, if we use the diagnostic imaging example, several diagnostic imaging technologies are available. These include conventional X-rays, computed tomography (CT), magnetic resonance, ultrasound, magnetic source imaging (MSI), and positron emission tomography (PET) imaging. In some cases a company can meet the diagnostic imaging needs of doctors for a particular application with more than one technology. In this case, the company has to decide which of the technologies to pursue or whether it should pursue all the available technologies that might have the potential to be useful in that particular application.

Clearly, while the pursuit of several technologies may provide a better or more complete set of diagnostic images for the physician, it may be very expensive for the supplier in time to market and in research and development investment.

In addition to technologies, companies also need certain competencies or capabilities if they are to deliver particular functionality and applications to their customers. For example, if a company's strategy is to provide leadership products and services, it will need to have the competency to manage the innovation process better than its competitors. On the other hand, a company that is focused on delivering adequate functionality at very attractive prices will need real competencies in driving costs out of the various processes involved in the design, production, marketing, and delivery of its products and services.

Value-Adding Role

An important decision that faces many technology-based businesses is how much of the total value-added the company should provide itself rather than relying on other partners in the market chain or outside of the market chain. For example, many hardware manufacturers rely on system integrators or value-added resellers to customize the hardware or complementary software to meet the needs of individual customers. Most organizations are unlikely to want, or are not able, to do everything for the customers in all the market segments they are trying to serve. In these cases, it is important to pick those areas where the company has the greatest leverage in creating customer value and competitive advantage.

Strategic Drivers and Strategic Paths

Driving Force

As discussed earlier, an SBU's business arena has four major dimensions: customers served, functions/applications provided, technology/competencies used, and value-adding roles. For many SBUs, one or two of these dimensions of the business arena tend to be the strategic drivers and have a major impact on how the SBU's business evolves over time. Often for technology-based businesses, the strategic driver will be either the technology or technologies where it has a strong position or a particular set of customers. Applied Materials, discussed above, was driven by the customers it chose to serve; it focused on providing more and better integrated functionality in the equipment it supplied to its semiconductor manufacturing customers over time.

Sometimes a strong focus on one of the dimensions of the business definition, the strategic driver, may cause a company to re-examine the other dimensions of its business arena. Perhaps recognizing that a particular technology allows the company to pursue a whole range of new opportunities with new customers causes a major change in the conceptualization of the business arena.

Strategic Path

The advantage of choosing a strategic driver is that it simplifies and reduces the complexity of evaluating the opportunities within the business arena. For example, if you decide to focus on only one or a limited set of the possible technologies in the business arena, you have essentially limited your search to one slice of the business arena (see Figure 2-5). Furthermore, since it is likely that the choice of a particular subset of technologies limits the applications or functionality that you can provide, the range of customers you could serve and the value-adding role you could play will probably be limited.

In the mid-1980s, when machine vision was beginning to be used in a range of industrial applications, there were four major technologies underlying the applications. These were mathematical morphology, statistical pattern recognition, artificial intelligence, and signal processing. Different customer applications, such as surface inspection or 3-dimensional robot guidance, required one or a particular combination of these technologies. For example, if a company did not have a competence in mathematical morphology, it would be very difficult for it to provide state-of-the-art vision systems for surface inspection.

> The fundamental choice about which technology or combination of technologies a business will pursue has a huge impact on the functionality and applications it could provide to its customers, and hence which customer segments it could serve and what value-adding roles it could play.

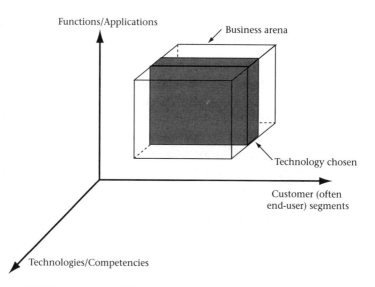

FIGURE 2-5: Impact of Choosing a Technology Strategic Driver on the Business Arena Area That Will Be Searched for Market Opportunities

By making such a sequential set of choices, we are defining a strategic path or set of paths for the SBU (see Figure 2-6). The danger of simplifying the task of evaluating market opportunities in this way is that you may miss some exceptionally attractive opportunities that are not on your strategic path. Periodically, you should at least quickly scan all the opportunities in your business arena to ensure that this is not happening to you. A potential danger of picking a technology as the strategic driver is that you may become so focused on that technology that you don't recognize the technology is maturing and you should be making a transition to other emerging technologies with a higher potential of providing the functionality and applications your customers will want in the future.

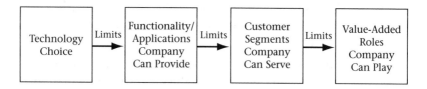

FIGURE 2-6: How a Strategic Path Limits Market Opportunities That Will Be Considered

Next Step: Identifying the Potentially Attractive Opportunities in the Business Arena

At this point, the SBU will have defined the "big" cube in its market—the arena in which, at least temporarily, it has decided to compete (recall Figure 2-2). The challenge facing the management team now is to do the analysis and strategic thinking that will allow the SBU to select one or more "small" cubes within the arena (i.e., the specific combinations of customer segments, functionality/applications, technologies/competencies, and value-adding roles). This cube or these cubes will be the specific market opportunity or opportunities where management believes the SBU has the potential to win profitable market leadership.

The process to make these choices is by necessity a highly iterative one and involves several steps:

- First, it will be necessary to segment the business arena—that is, identify the small cubes that represent the possible market opportunities, and identify which of those market segments has the potential to be an attractive market that will generate good profits for the companies competing in them. As part of this selection process, the SBU will be particularly seeking those opportunities where it has the potential to drive the market and to obtain market leadership.

- Second, as the opportunities are identified, the management team will need to deepen its understanding of the potential market chains that can be used to access each of the opportunities. And, for each of the relevant market chains, the team will need to develop an understanding of buyer behavior and the choice/rejection process operating at all levels in each of these chains.

- Third, as the management team's understanding of the key success factors for each of the market chains develops, they will need to assess the fit of each of the opportunities with the SBU's core competencies.

- Fourth, the team will need to understand the competitive environment they will face in each of the opportunities and, in particular, the specific competitors they are likely to encounter as they try to win market leadership.

- Fifth, the team will need to pull all the above information together in order to make the tough choices.

This process can be a really challenging one for the management team. As the information is pulled together for each market opportunity, it will become clear that some of the opportunities are not viable ones for the SBU. But often, even at the end of the process, there will be a range of opportunities available—far too many to be successfully pursued. Then there is a need for some strategic thinking and hard choices. The team will have a sense of the attractiveness of each opportunity and of the SBU's potential to win in these opportunities. This knowledge now has to be used to make choices about the best strategy for winning in each opportunity. The opportunities then need to be prioritized and the portfolio of opportunities that the SBU will pursue must be selected.

Key Questions for Executives and Managers

- Have you made clear and hard choices on all four dimensions of the business arena—customer segments you could serve, applications or functionality you could provide to these customers, technologies you could use, and the value-adding role you could play?

- Have you defined the business arena for your SBU appropriately–should it be broadened, narrowed, or changed? Is it broad enough so that you won't miss emerging opportunities and threats outside your arena? Is it narrow enough that your management team can develop the depth of knowledge about the market opportunities within the arena to be able to pick the best opportunities for you and to be able to develop strategies that will propel you to market leadership?

- Does it make sense for you to identify a strategic driver and to use that driver to help identify a limited number of strategic paths through the business arena? Or, if you have a strategic driver, is it making you myopic and leading you to miss some exceptional market opportunities?

CHAPTER THREE

Identify Attractive Opportunities

Introduction

Defining the business arena is a key first step in the strategic market planning process for a strategic business unit. But it is only the first step. Even a fairly narrow definition of the business arena can contain hundreds of specific market opportunities. The challenge for your management team becomes selecting and prioritizing a set of the most attractive opportunities that should be pursued in the next three to five years (or whatever is a reasonable planning horizon for your business).

In this chapter we explore some tools and concepts you will find useful for identifying potential opportunities and assessing their attractiveness. We also spend some time looking at those market driving opportunities which have the potential to allow a company to gain a leadership position in an emerging market.

Identifying Potential Market Opportunities

Market segmentation is a valuable tool to help the management team begin the process of selecting the most attractive market opportunities. By breaking a market into segments and making some tentative decisions on segments the company could target, the management team starts to make the selection process a more manageable one.

In defining the business arena, you made some tentative choices on each of the four dimensions: customers, functions/applications, technologies/competencies, and value-added roles. Now you need to get more action oriented and often more specific. For example, as in the Dendrite example in Chapter 2, you may have made choices on the customer dimension by identifying a couple of potential end-user industries. But now you need to find ways to break these end-user industries into smaller segments that can form the base of a market opportunity. You will need to break apart the other three dimensions of the business arena in a similar way.

In segmenting a market, you are trying to aggregate customers into homogeneous groups so that one or more of those groups can become the targets in your marketing plan. In essence, you are trying to find sensible ways to build those small "cubes" in the business arena from individual customers. Each of the resulting "cubes" is a homogeneous group of customers with certain functionality/applications needs that can be satisfied by a certain combination of technologies/competencies and supporting products and services provided by the market chain.

Usually, the primary market segmentation is done at the end-user level, since that is where most market opportunities originate. This segmentation is particularly important in markets where development cycles at the upstream end of the market chain are long. The upstream players must be anticipating emerging customer needs so they can respond quickly as the downstream players in the chain begin to respond to changing end-user needs. Once you have identified a potential opportunity at the end-user level, you need to determine actual and potential market chains that could be used to access the end-user opportunity. See Figure 3-1 on the opposite page.

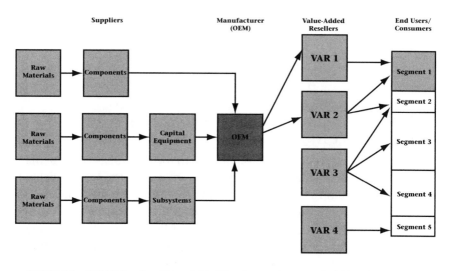

FIGURE 3-1: OEM Using Two Value-Added Resellers to Access an End-User Opportunity

Sometimes the segmentation at the end-user level leads to no interesting new insights into market opportunities. In these cases, it might be useful to move back up the chain one level at a time to see if you can identify attractive opportunities at higher levels in the chain, even when there are none at the end-user level. A good example of such a process occurred in the telecommunications market in the 1990s. The move toward deregulation of the telecommunications industry in North America and Europe created some interesting new market opportunities for telecommunications central office switch manufacturers, as new companies began providing telephone service. The deregulation did not create significant changes in the needs of the end user as far as what they wanted from a telecommunication supplier, but it did allow a number of new suppliers of telephone services to compete to fill the end-user needs for telecommunication services.

One such group of customers, or segment, was cable TV companies, who now had the opportunity to offer telephone service to their customers in several countries. Coming from very different backgrounds and cultures than the traditional telephone companies, they had somewhat different needs with regard to equipment specifications and they often wanted the equipment suppliers to play a much bigger role in financing and providing before and after sales service and support. This involvement required the equipment suppliers to modify their strategies in order to meet the needs of the new players. The suppliers that responded successfully to the needs of this emerging segment made some significant inroads into the market segment, as the Finnish manufacturer Nokia did in the United Kingdom.

Benefits of Thinking About Market Segments Early in the Process

One of the major advantages of starting to focus on market segments early in the planning process is that the management team quickly begins to develop a mental picture of the specific customers and their needs, decision criteria, and decision processes. An early, more focused picture of the potential opportunities develops, which may lead to some of the unsuitable opportunities being eliminated before much time and energy have been invested in looking at them. If the management team tries to look at too many segments in depth, the task will rapidly become overwhelming.

Segmenting a Market

There are an infinite number of ways of segmenting a particular market. A good segmentation scheme will result in segments that meet three major criteria:

1. Segments should have a distinctive response profile. The customers in a segment should have a distinctive set of needs or must respond in a distinctive way to the product or product class. If the segment is not distinct, competitors targeting a broader segment, which includes your targeted segment, may achieve economies of scale and hence gain an advantage over your company. If none of the segments are distinct from the others, you need to try other segmentation variables.

2. Segment members are identifiable. For marketing programs to be efficient, it is important that segment members be identifiable so that salespersons can be sent to knock on their doors, advertisements can be placed in appropriate media, or direct marketing lists can be selected for use.

3. A segment should be large enough to represent a viable target. If it isn't, the company may be unable to make a reasonable return on its investment in the segment.

Possible Segmentation Bases

In considering possible segmentation bases, it is useful to divide them into two groups—those that are to do with identification and those that are to do with the response profile. We will consider each in turn.

Identification Bases

In business-to-business markets, a wide range of bases have been used to help segment markets, including organizational "demographics" and a customer's approach to doing business.

Organizational "demographic" variables, such as size of company, growth rate of company, geographical location, North American Industry Classification System (NAICS) codes, and end-user industry, have all been successfully used as bases for segmenting markets. Perhaps one of the most widely used bases in many technology-based industries is the end-user industry, or vertical market.

One of the classic applications of this segmentation base was in the mainframe computer industry, where companies started using the end-user industry as a segmentation base in the late 1950s and early 1960s. At that time, companies like IBM began to recognize that business success required more than the basic computer hardware. Customers often needed specialized peripheral equipment, specialized applications software, and specialized sales representatives who understood the particular challenges of their business as they related to computers. Each of these customer requirements was expensive to meet, so early in the evolution of the mainframe computer business, some of the vendors began developing particular capabilities in certain industries, such as NCR in retailing and Burroughs in financial services.

> Today, specialization by end-user industry has become even more extreme, and some sizable companies live and die in very narrow vertical markets.

Triad, a California-based supplier of integrated hardware/software "solutions," specializes in a couple of very narrow niche markets, such as auto-parts wholesalers.

But Triad, like many similar companies, has found that the better it gets at understanding the customers in its niche markets, the more effectively it can develop specialized solutions to meet their needs and to build barriers that keep out its competitors.

Another base that has become increasingly relevant in recent years is the potential customer's approach to doing business. As companies re-engineer and downsize, they will often, within the same industry segment, adopt very different strategies with respect to how they run their businesses. Some companies continue to be quite self-sufficient and integrated, whereas others may outsource a lot of their non-core business activities. Clearly these two strategies represent very different business opportunities for suppliers—some customers want to buy computer equipment, whereas others want to buy an integrated product-service, such as an information technology service to do their payrolls or manage their database infrastructure. The sale of services and integrated product-services has become one of fastest-growing and largest businesses in IBM.

Consumer markets have analogous types of segmentation bases. Demographic factors, such as income, education, size of household, and family life cycle stage, can all be useful segmentation variables for technology-based consumer products and services. The initial penetration of home computers and Internet access was much greater in higher income and higher education households. For many products and services, psychographics are an increasingly important base for segmentation. Psychographics measures an individual's attitudes, interests, and lifestyle, all of which can have a major influence on her or his purchasing behavior. Whether or not an individual purchases a cellular telephone may depend as much on the individual's attitudes and lifestyle as it does on income level or education.

Response Profile Bases

Customers can vary tremendously in their needs and buying behavior. Any one of these differences can be the basis for segmenting a market. Two broad types of differences exist: those that are related to *why* a customer might buy a particular product or service and those that are to do with *how* a customer goes about buying a product or service. Most of our discussions will be focused on the first area, but the second area can be important. For example, a company may decide to concentrate only on those companies or organizations which buy products and services in a particular way. Some companies have decided to focus on government agencies, which in certain countries go through a complex and unusual buying process. By developing an in-depth understanding of the process and the individuals involved in the process, they can develop a strong competitive advantage over competitors who have failed to develop this in-depth knowledge. When we turn to why a customer might buy a particular product or service, we find many potential segmentation bases, including product benefits sought, price, marketing communications, distribution, and buying behavior. We will look at typical examples in some of these areas, but this is where the creativity of the segmenter can pay big dividends!

When people buy a product or service, different segments of the market may be seeking different benefits from the product or placing different priorities on the different benefits the product can provide. In the early 1970s, Jim Treybig, a young marketing manager at Hewlett-Packard's computer division in California, noticed that some potential customers for Hewlett-Packard's minicomputers seemed to be obsessed with one aspect of a computer's performance, its reliability. Given that a customer, such as an airline, could lose $25,000 every minute its reservation system was down, this was not surprising. When Treybig discussed this issue with some of the engineers at Hewlett-Packard, they suggested a technical solution to the reliability problem.

By connecting multiple processors together with some innovative software, they believed they could keep a computer system up and running, even if one of the processors failed. When venture capitalists indicated a willingness to invest in a company selling such a product, Jim Treybig left Hewlett-Packard and founded a new company, Tandem Computers. Tandem ultimately became the world leader in fault-tolerant computer systems with over 80% of all automated banking machines (ABMs) in the world running on Tandem servers by 1996. Revenues were about $2 billion in 1996, and in August 1997 Tandem was acquired by Compaq Computer Corporation. This is an excellent example of a company identifying an important customer need that customers did not perceive other computer companies as meeting, and developing an innovative solution to meet that need.

Pricing is another area that some companies have used as one of their segmentation bases. Two price-based segments of customers have been identified in several industries. One segment is very oriented to initial purchase price and puts much less emphasis on the postpurchase costs of ownership, such as costs of installation, operation, spare parts, and service. Another, often more sophisticated, segment of customers focuses on total life-cycle ownership costs. These latter customers are willing to pay a premium for a product if the supplier can demonstrate to them that the initial premium is more than offset by lower operating costs or other post-purchase costs. In some industries, such as certain parts of the electrical distribution industry, some manufacturers offer two lines of products: one line targeted at those customers who are oriented to low purchase price and another more expensive line (but with lower post-purchase costs) targeted at those customers who are most concerned about life-cycle costs.

A very successful example of a company segmenting a market on the basis of a particular dimension of customer behavior was ABB, a global manufacturer of energy, industrial and transportation systems. In the 1980s, ABB was trying to increase its electrical equipment market share in the United States.[1] After a great deal of sophisticated market research, it was able to segment its customers on the basis of their loyalty to their suppliers of this type of equipment. ABB divided its customers into four loyalty segments:

1. **ABB's loyal customers.** These were customers who saw ABB as much superior to other suppliers. They tended to buy from ABB unless ABB was unable to meet a particular set of specifications or could not deliver a product in a timely manner.

2. **Competitive.** These were customers who perceived ABB as slightly superior, but saw at least one of ABB's competitors as being nearly as good.

3. **Switchable.** These were customers who preferred one of ABB's competitors, but ABB was seen as being almost as good.

4. **Competitor loyal.** These were the customers who were loyal to one of ABB's competitors and ABB was simply not in the running for these customers' business.

---

[1] This example is based on Dennis H. Gensch, "Targeting the Switchable Industrial Customer," *Marketing Science* (Winter 1984), pp. 41–55 and Dennis H. Gensch, Nicola Aversa, and Stephen P. Moore, "A Choice-Modeling Market Information System That Enabled ABB Electric to Expand Its Market Share," *Interfaces* (January–February 1990), pp. 6–25.

After analyzing this situation in some depth, ABB decided that in certain regions of the United States it would reduce the sales and other marketing communications effort allocated to the first and last segments and focus the freed-up resources on the competitive and switchable segments of the market. ABB management felt that these were the segments where increased marketing effort would pay off in increased sales. And it did. In the two regions of the United States where the new strategy was implemented, awarded contracts rose by 15% in the following year compared to a decline of 10% in the region that continued to do business in the traditional way.

The number of ways to segment a market is limited only by the creativity of the segmenter. In many situations we may try several segmentation bases before we end up with a useful segmentation scheme. In the ABB example above, the customer loyalty segmentation was combined with another segmentation based on the benefits different segments of customers were seeking from their supplier of electrical distribution equipment. These 12 benefit segments involved a combination of type of customer (utilities, rural electrification cooperatives, municipal, and industrial), geographical location of customer, and size of customer. The benefits the 12 segments were looking for helped drive both new product development efforts and the marketing communications messages that were delivered to specific customers through personal selling and direct mail.

Segmentation Process

As discussed above, for a segmentation scheme to be useful and able to be acted on, managers ultimately need some descriptors of the segment that can be used to identify segment members for targeting purposes, as well as an understanding of the process by which they make choices and the buying criteria they use in making their choices.

Sometimes the process might start with the customer buying process or the customer response profile. In essence that is how Jim Treybig at Tandem started. He noticed that there were some customers who put a heavy emphasis on the reliability of their computer system and he thought that this concern could represent a business opportunity. However, for this segment to be a useful and profitable opportunity these customers needed to be clustered in some way. If they were clustered in certain end-user industries, such as banking, or in certain applications, such as on-line transaction processing, this would result in efficiencies in developing a complete solution and in marketing the solution to the target customers.

In other cases, the manager of the segmentation process begins with identifying descriptors rather than the response profile. For example, a new additive for high performance ceramics materials might start with an a priori segmentation based on an identifier such as company size, creating segments comprising small, medium, and large ceramic manufacturers. The manager might then do market research to determine if these three segments have different needs, buying processes, etc., which could have implications for marketing strategy. Perhaps in the small customer segment, decision making is at the most senior level in the organization and the decision makers at this level are more responsive to a business case for the new product than a technology case. In addition, small customers might need more technical support and would be less sensitive to price. These differences between the segments have direct and obvious implications for strategy.

But whether you start with the identifiers of the buying unit or the response profile of the buying unit, you ultimately will need both in order to develop practicable marketing plans (see Figure 3-2).

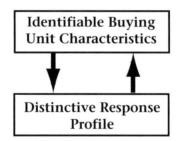

FIGURE 3-2: Process of Market Segmentation

Targeting Issues

Once the management team has identified a number of market segments, both existing and new, that are to be considered during the planning cycle, the members face some real challenges in selecting those market segments that represent the most attractive opportunities for the SBU. The selection process is not simple. Numerous factors must be taken into account. We will consider a few here before we move into a discussion of market segment attractiveness.

Balance

Most organizations must strive for balance in selecting market opportunities to pursue. One important balance issue for a business is finding a portfolio of opportunities or segments that will generate
current sales and profits, future sales and profits, and "invisible
assets."[2] Many businesses become so totally focused on short-term
financial results that almost all management's attention is focused
on the segments that are producing today's sales and profits. But for
many businesses, if sales and profits are to continue to grow, they
need to be actively developing those opportunities that will generate
sales and profit growth. In addition, some market segments and
market opportunities don't directly generate much in the way of
sales and profits today or even in the foreseeable future, but are key
opportunities for the future of the business. For example, one segment might be a small group of particularly demanding customers
that generate very little revenue and may even be unprofitable. But
these customers might be the very ones with the most demanding
applications that push the R&D organization to develop the next
generation of technology.

Some of the medical centers associated with major teaching uni-
versities play this role in medical devices and equipment. In fact,
manufacturers often give these medical centers free equipment and
research grants. This results in their being "unprofitable" accounts.
However, these medical centers are where the next generation of doctors is trained and where the breakthrough scientific papers are written. Success with this segment of customers is a good example of "an
invisible asset"; although these accounts don't produce profits today,
they can often be leveraged into a leadership position in the more
mainstream hospitals where the bulk of the revenues and profits are
generated.

Leveraging Success

In more general terms, as we think about market opportunities, we
should always be thinking broadly about the linkages between segments. Sometimes success in one key segment of the market can be
leveraged into success in other related segments. These opportunities

---

2 Hiroyuki Itami, *Mobilizing Invisible Assets* (Cambridge, Massachusetts: Harvard University Press, 1987).

might be new applications for existing customers or existing applications in a new segment of customers. Documentum, a California-based software company that developed and marketed enterprise document management systems, had its earliest major success in providing document management solutions for regulatory filings by pharmaceutical companies. By 1996 it had established itself as a leader in this market segment, and it was able to move into other applications of document management systems in pharmaceutical companies, such as in manufacturing. It could also leverage its success with regulatory filings in the pharmaceutical industry into other industries faced with challenging document management issues concerning regulatory filings.

Market Segment Attractiveness

When we talk about the attractiveness of a market segment, we are trying to estimate the total profit that a particular market will generate for all companies competing in that market segment over a reasonable planning horizon. In too many organizations, market size and market growth rate are used as surrogates for market attractiveness. This error can lead to companies participating in very big market segments where there are few barriers to entry and many competitors, with the result that very little of the revenues in the market "drop down" to anybody's bottom line. Thus, you have to get beyond revenues and market growth rates in order to determine a market's ability to generate profits for the players both today and over the planning horizon.

> It is important to spend time trying to estimate the attractiveness of a market segment, because this is often the major factor driving the profitability of a business. It is no use winning market leadership in a market or market segment that is chronically unprofitable.

We might be much better off being the number two player in a small, highly profitable market segment than being the market leader in a large market segment where nobody can make significant profits. In the personal computer software business in the late 1980s and early 1990s, some software companies found that paradoxically they made more money in the smaller, low-growth Macintosh market than in the much bigger, high-growth Windows market. This success occurred even though the total size of the Windows software market was more than five times as large as the Macintosh. However, the Macintosh market was often less competitive as a result of fewer players and significantly lower advertising and promotion costs.

Determining the Attractiveness of a Market Segment

Michael Porter's competitive forces model is a very useful starting point for helping to assess the attractiveness of a market or market segment.[3] Of course, all markets are embedded in market chains, which involve a series of activities that result in the conversion of some raw materials into a finished product or service that is provided to the end user. In some cases, most or all of these activities are carried out by one vertically integrated player. In other situations, the activities will be carried out by a chain of different companies. Each of the activities in the market chain helps create a package of benefits for which the end user is willing to pay a certain amount of money. A powerful customer may, of course, be able to bargain and obtain a much lower price than the value of the benefits it receives.

Market attractiveness analysis focuses on estimating the profitability of the opportunity in total and how much of the potential profit in the market chain will accrue to the players at a given level in the chain. For example, in the personal computer business, we could look at the market attractiveness of making microprocessors for personal computers, making the personal computers, or retailing the personal computers to businesses and individuals. The attractiveness of these different opportunities will obviously be related to each other and will vary depending on the particular market forces operating at that level in the market chain.

Porter has argued that the profit potential of an industry or market depends on the collective strength of the market forces created by direct competitors, customers, suppliers, potential entrants, and substitute products or services. If the collective strength of these forces

---

[3] See Michael E. Porter, "How Competitive Forces Shape Strategy," *Harvard Business Review* (March–April 1979), pp. 137-145. Much of the discussion of competitive forces in this chapter is based on this article and George S. Day, *Market Driven Strategy: Processes for Creating Value* (New York: Free Press, 1990).

is strong, this will have a negative impact on the profit potential of the market segment. Even a relatively strong player in that segment is unlikely to generate high profits. In many technology-intensive businesses, complementors are a sixth market force that can have a major impact on market attractiveness.[4] A complementor is a company that provides complementary products or services for your product or service. These complementary products or services make customers value your product or service more than they would if they had your product alone. For example, great games make a Nintendo or Sega video game machine more valuable to a customer, so there is a big incentive for Nintendo and Sega to encourage software developers to develop exciting games for their platforms.

Some of the factors determining whether these six market forces will have a negative impact on market attractiveness are shown in Figure 3-3. Many of these factors are drawn directly from Porter's analysis. Some of the major factors are discussed below.

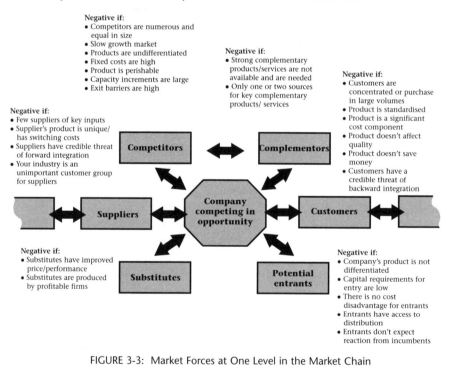

FIGURE 3-3: Market Forces at One Level in the Market Chain

[4] See Andrew S. Grove, *Only the Paranoid Survive* (New York: Currency, 1996), p. 29, and Alan M. Brandedburger and Barry J. Nalebuff, *Co-opetition* (New York: Currency, 1996).

Direct and Indirect Suppliers

When suppliers to an industry have considerable bargaining power, they can price their inputs to the industry at a level which captures much of the value the market chain is creating for the ultimate end user.

Suppliers tend to be powerful and have a negative impact on market attractiveness when one or all of the following conditions exist:

- Their product is unique and has high switching costs. A classic example of this was the very powerful position Intel was able to create for itself in the PC industry in the 1980s and 1990s with its microprocessor. It developed a leadership position in the X86 architecture and managed to stay ahead of its direct competitors. Its direct and indirect customers faced massive switching costs if they tried to move to another type of microprocessor. Therefore Intel and Microsoft (which had a similar position in PC operating systems and application software) were able to capture most of the profitability in the PC market chain, even though they accounted for a relatively small part of the revenues generated by the players in the chain.

- The suppliers pose a credible threat of forward integration. Again, this was one of the sources of Intel's power, since it had a real potential to forward integrate into the manufacture of PCs. It manufactured not only the microprocessor, but also the motherboard (the key assembled component of the PC). In addition, for a small set of customers it produced complete private label PCs.

- There are relatively few competing suppliers and they are more concentrated than the customers they serve.

Direct and Indirect Customers

When industry customers have considerable bargaining power, they can drive prices down to a level that leaves little profit for their suppliers, making a market opportunity less attractive.

Customers tend to be powerful when:

- They are few and purchase in large quantities. Customers have particular leverage when the product they are purchasing involves high fixed costs, since producers have a strong incentive to keep their capacity utilization high even at the expense of lower prices. This is a continuing situation in many segments of the chemical industry when the industry is in over-capacity situation due to either an economic downturn, or the addition of significant new capacity by one or more of the players.

- There is little product differentiation or there are low switching costs. In these cases, the customers can readily switch from one supplier to another and may use this threat to extract lower prices.

- The customers have a credible capability to backward integrate if they feel they are not getting satisfactory terms from their suppliers. In recent years this has become a powerful tool for customers in some segments of the electronics industry; many companies now can design their own integrated circuits and can contract with a foundry to produce the parts. This development put heavy pressure on some semiconductor companies.

Customers tend to have a bigger incentive to use their power when:

- they themselves are under severe profit pressure,

- the product or service has little capability to differentiate the customer's product from other competing products, or

- the product or service represents a significant proportion of the customer's total costs.

Even one very powerful player or group of players in the market chain can strip much of the potential profitability out of the market chain, creating major pressure on the other players in the chain to capture for themselves as much as possible of the remaining profit. This pressure reverberates throughout the market chain and related chains. For example, as Intel and Microsoft stripped much of the profitability out of the PC market chain, they placed tremendous pressure on even the largest PC manufacturers, such as Compaq. Compaq reacted to this by trying to extract the most favorable terms from its other suppliers, in turn threatening their profits.

Complementors

A factor that influences the attractiveness of many technology-intensive markets is complementary products and services. Often the adoption of new technology and the growth of the market are affected by the degree to which complementary products and services are available from complementors for customers. If few complementors are available, customers may be unwilling to adopt. For example, customers are unlikely to adopt the latest, most powerful Intel microprocessor until there is software and hardware available that will take advantage of the power. This is one of the reasons Intel spends so much time and money encouraging complementors to develop new applications, such as voice recognition and voice processing, which require a lot of processing power. Intel is one of the biggest venture capitalists in Silicon Valley with many of its investments being in suppliers of complementary products and services.

If complementary products and services are required by any of your customers down the market chain and they are not available, the market opportunity is unlikely to develop into a large and profitable one for you and your competitors. In addition, if there is only one source for a key complementary product, the company with this product will have great bargaining power and may be able to capture a lot of the profitability in the market opportunity. If one or both of these conditions are present, then complementors become a negative market force.

Direct Competitors

The intensity of rivalry among the company and its direct competitors can vary dramatically from market to market, and even from market segment to market segment within the same broad market. Rivalry tends to be more intense when the following conditions occur:

- There are many competitors of roughly equal size. When there is a clearly dominant player in the market, competition tends to be muted, as it was for many years in the mainframe computer industry, when IBM was clearly the dominant player.
- The industry has a high fixed cost structure or the product or service is perishable. This results in the competitors trying to

capture volume, often by engaging in price-cutting activities. The airline industry is a classic example.

- The industry is mature and experiencing slow growth. In this environment, a company must capture additional market share to increase its sales volume. This move invites retaliation from the competitors who are being affected. In a fast-growing market, companies can gain share without any other player losing sales or customers.

- The product or service is undifferentiated or lacks switching costs. In industries where companies have been successful in establishing strong proprietary standards and hence high switching costs, the competitive rivalry becomes less intense.

- The competitors have different objectives and strategies. One of the major effects of globalization in many industries is that in a given geographic market the direct competitors now include foreign competitors, who have different objectives and play the game in different ways. Some Asian companies have upset stable competitive markets in North America and Europe by placing more emphasis on gaining market share than on current profitability. Where strategies vary among the competitors, any environmental event, such as a recession or a technology breakthrough, tends to benefit some of the players more than others. Often the only thing the disadvantaged players can do in the short run to defend their market shares is to reduce prices, a move that will eventually lead to an overall erosion of profitability in the industry.

- Exit barriers are high. Any time one or more companies are reluctant to leave an industry even when their earnings are poor, it tends to reduce the average profitability in the industry. Sometimes this is the result of companies being unwilling to write off the assets and negatively affect earnings; sometimes management is unwilling to close down a business for political or loyalty reasons.

Potential Entrants

The degree of threat posed by new entrants depends on the barriers to entry and the perceived ability of the incumbents to respond effectively to new entrants. If the barriers to entry are low, an industry's customers may use the threat of new entrants to get lower prices or better terms from its suppliers. In cases where the suppliers have failed to respond adequately, customers have encouraged suppliers from other countries or neighboring industries to enter the market. Barriers to entry tend to be high when the following conditions occur:

- Incumbents have substantial economies of scale in research and development, production, marketing, and after-sales service and support. New entrants with strategies similar to the incumbents will need to invest heavily to achieve similar economies of scale or they will be forced to operate at a cost disadvantage. Xerox was extremely successful in the 1960s in building some massive barriers to entry through its patents on the xerography process; its huge research and development investments; its heavy investment in a vertically integrated manufacturing capability and worldwide direct sales and service; and its investment in an extensive leasing program for photocopiers. Smart new entrants will, of course, search for innovative ways to compete in the industry where the existing scale economies have little value. Japanese photocopier companies, such as Canon and Ricoh (marketed in North America initially under the Savin name), were successful in competing with Xerox by generating a totally different business system to develop, manufacture, market, and service small photocopiers. Ricoh and Savin's system used a simple and more reliable technology that allowed it to focus on outright sales to customers through office supply dealers. These same dealers were able to service the less complex Ricoh technology.
- New entrants face cost disadvantages unrelated to size or scale. Sometimes incumbents have cost advantages due to lower-cost raw materials, lower labor costs, or access to proprietary technology.
- The incumbents have been able to achieve strong product differentiation or high switching costs.

- New entrants have difficulty gaining access to distribution channels. In many high-technology businesses, one of the most important barriers to entry is not making the product, but accessing an effective channel of distribution. There is only so much space on the shelves of distributors and retailers, and there are only so many effective value-added resellers (VARs) that can access a particular market segment. Often channel members see few benefits from adding more product lines to their range—any additional margin may be more than offset by higher inventory and training and sales costs. Some entrants to a market have been forced to develop their own channel of distribution. The difficulty of accessing traditional computer retailer channels was one of the factors that led Dell to create an extremely effective and profitable direct marketing operation.

The barriers to entry will also be affected by the perceived ability and willingness of one or more of the incumbents to react strongly to a new entrant. If one or more of the incumbents has access to resources and has a demonstrated willingness to use price or other weapons, new entrants will be discouraged.

Substitute Products or Services

Many high-technology industries seem particularly vulnerable to the impact of substitute products and services. It seems that almost every time a nice, profitable market segment gets established, substitutes start appearing around the edge of the market and start eroding the market's profitability. Facsimile machines had developed into a large and growing business by the early 1990s. Then substitutes began to affect demand significantly. Fax-modem cards for personal computers, e-mail systems tied into the Internet, and Lotus Notes and other document sharing software all began to grow rapidly, eroding the potential market for fax machines.

Substitutes are a particular threat when they are marketed by companies that have the resources to invest in market development and where the substitute's price performance is improving more rapidly than the product's they are threatening. Clearly some of the substitutes for fax machines have big advantages on some of these dimensions.

Assessing Overall Market Attractiveness

In order to assess the attractiveness of a market or market segment, you must carefully evaluate each of the six market forces. The overall attractiveness is seldom based simply on the average of the six forces. Even if only one of the market forces is very negative, the market is likely to be unattractive and the profitability of the players competing in the market or market segment will be low. For example, electronic communications in all its forms, videoconferencing, electronic mail, conference calls, etc., is a powerful substitute for other forms of communications, such as air travel and courier services. Furthermore, as a substitute it will continue to benefit for the foreseeable future from rapidly improving price performance as a result of rapid technological advances, which both improve performance and lower costs, and greater competitive opportunities as government regulation of the industry declines and traditional market boundaries are blurred. In addition, many strong and well-funded companies, such as AT&T and British Telecom, are committed to developing the market as rapidly as possible. Therefore electronic communication is a substitute that is likely to make many segments of other communication markets increasingly unattractive over time.

The electronic communications example also points out that external forces, such as technological change and the government and regulatory environment, can have an important moderating effect on the strength of the market forces. Government intervention and regulation can have a major impact on the strength of certain market forces and thus the attractiveness of a market. In most countries, governments initially restricted the number of cellular telephone network suppliers to one or two, creating artificial monopolies or duopolies. In the pharmaceutical industry, the lengthy and expensive approval process for new pharmaceuticals, which can involve the expenditure of over $500 million and 10 to 12 years, restricts entry to only the best-funded companies.

In assessing the attractiveness of a market or market segment, you must take a dynamic perspective and try to project the changes in the market forces over the planning horizon and the likely impact of these changes on the attractiveness of the market or market segment.

The attractiveness of a market can change very rapidly. Personal computer manufacturers' average net income as a percentage of sales dropped from about 6% in 1988 to about -1% in 1991 as a result of some massive changes in the strength of the market forces in the industry and because of the recession.[5]

Using the Market Forces Model

A good understanding of the market forces and market attractiveness can have a powerful influence on strategy. Sometimes a company can significantly improve its profit prospects by focusing on those segments of the market where the market forces are relatively weak resulting in a more attractive market. For most of the 1990s, the margins in the PC market were highest in the server segment, intermediate in the notebook/laptop segment, and lowest in the desktop segment. Companies that developed strong positions in the server and notebook segments of the market tended to enjoy higher levels of profitability.

In some cases, companies have an opportunity to shape the market forces so that their market becomes more attractive for them. Intel did a masterful job of this in the microprocessor market in the 1990s. It undertook a number of steps to ensure that its customers, the personal computer manufacturers such as IBM, Compaq, Dell, Packard-Bell, and Toshiba, did not become a strong competitive force. It moved new technology into the market as rapidly as possible, so that other microprocessor manufacturers at the time, such as AMD, Cyrix, and NextGen, were not able to catch up to Intel's technology. Intel became essentially a monopoly supplier to the PC manufacturers. It also promoted its technology directly to the PC consumer with its Intel Inside campaign and advertised the merits of it latest microprocessor to these consumers. This move made it difficult for the PC manufacturers to offer outdated technology.

Incorporating the latest microprocessor technology into a PC presented an increasingly difficult engineering challenge, so Intel provided reference designs to PC manufacturers and motherboard suppliers and eventually complete motherboards, so that even

---

[5] "Deconstructing the Computer Industry," *Business Week*, November 23, 1992, pp. 90–100.

companies with very little engineering talent could enter the PC market and produce the latest designs.

As discussed earlier, Intel has encouraged complementors, sometimes by investing in them, to develop complementary products and services. Through these and other actions, Intel contributed to the PC industry becoming highly competitive with numerous players, several of whom had similar market shares and none of whom had power approaching Intel's. With their margins squeezed as a result of the intense rivalry within the industry, none of them was able to differentiate itself significantly from its competitors to assume strong leadership and pose a threat to Intel.

Sometimes it makes sense for a company to look at the market forces operating at other important levels in the market chain, either at the level of a key supplier or a key customer. This examination can help the management team better understand the situation facing this key member. The process may suggest actions the company can take to help its customers deal more effectively with the market forces affecting them. It might help the company to understand whether a supplier will continue to be the best supplier of the critical product or service.

Understanding Choices Among Market Chain Opportunities

In high-technology businesses more than one market chain may be operating in a particular market or market segment. Figure 3-4 shows a situation where a system manufacturer has three potential market chains it can use to reach its target market of consumers or end users. In some cases, companies have to make tough choices about which of these market chains they will participate in. Sometimes this is because it is difficult to compete in two or more market chains at the same time. For example, market chain members may be unwilling to work with a supplier who is also supplying a competing market chain, or the two market chains may require such different strategies that it is difficult to execute both strategies successfully within the same organization. In other cases, particularly for smaller companies, they simply do not have the resources to develop and exploit two or three different market chains simultaneously, particularly if they need to develop and maintain complex relationships.

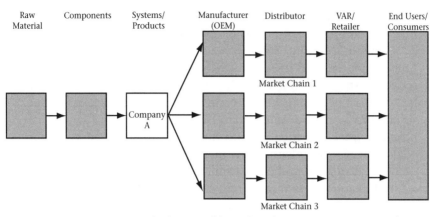

FIGURE 3-4: Company With Three Possible Market Chains to Access Target Market

In some cases a company cannot identify any market chain that will allow it to access an opportunity at the end-user level, and an otherwise attractive opportunity will need to be abandoned.

In situations where more than one market chain is available to access the market opportunity, your management team will need to determine which of the market chains is likely to be the most successful over the planning horizon and which will provide the company with the overall most attractive market opportunity. In some cases, the company will find that it faces much weaker market forces in one of the chains than the others, suggesting the opportunity for higher profits.

Even after the management team has chosen to compete in one market chain, it may also have to make some tough choices about which subset of players in that chain it will work with. The company may not have the resources or it may not make good strategic sense to try to work with all the players.

Market-Driving Opportunities

A particularly attractive type of market opportunity is a market-driving opportunity. Market-driving opportunities are created by discontinuities in a market that create the potential for a company to displace the current leaders or develop a totally new market. Sometimes a company can drive the market itself. In cases where the company is not as well positioned, it can partner with one or more other companies that are better positioned to drive the market.

Cirrus Logic identified such an opportunity in the mid-1990s. At that time, up to 30% of an analog cellular network was idle, even in the busiest times. Cirrus Logic recognized that a technology, Cellular Digital Packet Data (CDPD), could be used to turn that idle capacity into low-cost wireless data links for mobile computing applications. As a manufacturer of semiconductors, Cirrus Logic was not well positioned to drive this market opportunity itself. But, by working with partners such as McCaw Cellular and other carriers and IBM, who had access to potential users and mobile computing hardware, and by developing the base stations and subscriber units itself, Cirrus Logic was able to put together a complete solution for the potential end user. By early 1995, Cirrus Logic had shipped over 2,500 base stations to carriers and thousands of subscriber units to early adopters, who began using the technology in the United States. Unfortunately, the market did not grow as rapidly as Cirrus Logic and its partners had hoped, because no complementary data applications for CDPD gained widespread market acceptance.

In order to exploit market-driving opportunities to develop a leadership position, a company must identify the opportunity early and move rapidly and forcefully to exploit it. It must act rather than react.

Exploiting Environmental Change

Change in the business environment covers a continuum from evolutionary change to discontinuities (or breakpoints) involving sudden radical shifts in the rules of the business game. The turbulence in most technology-intensive markets means that there are an unusually large number of market-driving opportunities. This is not true in many other markets, such as consumer packaged goods or many of the more mature business-to-business markets. In the case of hard disks for computers, for example, perhaps 50% of the improvement in performance has come from evolutionary changes and the other 50% from more radical changes that have often been associated with a change in the size of the platter (or disk) on which the data is stored.

Big changes in competitive position are often associated with a company or companies exploiting a major discontinuity or breakpoint in their industry. Digital Equipment Corporation became a major influence in the global computer industry by developing and exploiting minicomputers. Similarly, Compaq was successful in exploiting the emergence of personal computers to become the global leader in what by the mid-1990s was the largest segment of the computer market.

Sources of Discontinuities or Breakpoints

Important breakpoints can occur as the result of a variety of factors, including technological, economic, social, and political changes. Aldus Corporation was successful in creating the desktop publishing market by exploiting three technological advances: Apple Computer was eager to find applications for its laser printers; Adobe had developed its Postscript language that allowed sophisticated printing; Aldus itself had developed PageMaker software that gave the end user an unprecedented ability to create sophisticated documents with minimal training and investment in hardware and software. By effectively pulling together these technologies, Aldus was able to create an attractive market opportunity for itself.

Major discontinuities are often a function of a complex interplay of a variety of environmental forces. ROLM, Northern Telecom, and Mitel became major players in the private branch exchange (PBX) market in the 1970s by exploiting a number of environmental changes in the telephone equipment market. Advances in hardware and software permitted much greater flexibility in cabling and the features that could be offered on the telephone system. A rapid increase in business long-distance calling made it critical for companies to take advantage of software that would allow them to monitor and control toll charges. With organizational structures becoming more fluid and changing more often, some companies required technology that would make it easier and cheaper to move telephones and change people's telephone numbers as the organization changed.

The power and perceived inflexibility of AT&T and its Bell operating companies had led to an anti-Bell feeling in some organizations, making them more willing to switch to other suppliers for their telecommunications equipment and services. And a regulatory decision in the late 1960s, known as the "Carterfone decision," allowed users to connect equipment not owned by the telephone company to the public switched network. The combination of all these developments created a major opportunity for new players to enter and gain leadership positions in the PBX market.

A company must be very sensitive to underlying forces as they gather momentum if it is to take full advantage of a discontinuity. Ironically, sometimes the companies that do the best job of meeting their existing customers' needs fail to identify a major discontinuity affecting their industry. For example, a new technology may at first meet the needs only of customers outside the mainstream market. This is what happened when 3 1/2" disk drives for computers first appeared on the market.[6] Their initial performance lagged that of the older 5 1/4" technology, in which Seagate was the market leader. Seagate's mainstream customers wanted the higher performance of the 5 1/4" drives, and this need led Seagate to initially ignore the new technology. However, some desktop personal computer manufacturers were willing to use the new, lower-performance drives because they allowed a smaller "footprint" on the desktop.

Manufacturers of portable computers were also early adopters. Once disk drive manufacturers, such as Conner, were able to gain entry to the market, they improved the performance of the new drives by more than 50% per year, and soon the new technology met the performance needs of mainstream customers. By the time Seagate recognized the threat posed by the new technology, Conner was well positioned to take over leadership in the industry. As we can see from this example, too intensive a focus on current customers (or current technologies or applications) can sometimes blind you to emerging threats and opportunities in your business arena.

As this example suggests, any company in a technology-intensive industry should be constantly on the lookout for market-driving opportunities in its business arena. They often represent attractive opportunities, but sometimes they also represent opportunities for your competitors to displace you in an attractive market. The earlier they are spotted, the more time you will have to develop an appropriate strategy.

---

[6] Joseph L. Bower and Clayton M. Christensen, "Disruptive Technologies: Catching the Wave," *Harvard Business Review* (January–February 1995), pp. 43–53.

Next Step: Developing a Deeper Understanding of the Market Opportunities

As you prepare to move on to the next steps in the process, you will have identified through your market segmentation of your business arena a number of market opportunities and potential market chains that you might use to access each of the market opportunities. By analyzing the market forces influencing each of these opportunities, you will have determined which opportunities might be attractive ones for your company with the potential to generate significant profits.

But this is only one step in the process. The next step is to drill down one more level and to start developing a detailed understanding of each of the remaining opportunities, looking at the market chains accessing the opportunity and the buyer behavior within each of the opportunities.

Key Questions for Executives and Managers

- Are you segmenting your business arena insightfully? How might an aggressive new entrant into this market segment it?

- Do you know the key success factors by market segment? Can they be changed in your favor?

- Have you done an effective job of identifying and assessing the major environmental and market forces influencing the market opportunities in your business arena? How they will evolve over the planning horizon? What are the implications of this for the attractiveness of the market opportunities?

- Have you also assessed the market forces affecting key levels in your market chain? What are the implications of this analysis for you?

- Are you making the tough choices about which market chain or chains you should participate in?

- Are there any discontinuities occurring in your market that could represent attractive market-driving opportunities for you or for a competitor?

ༀ

Understand the Market

Introduction

In Chapter 3, we looked at some tools and concepts useful for identifying potentially attractive opportunities in your business arena. While you may have started with a number of opportunities, it is quite likely that you will have eliminated a number of them as you developed a deeper understanding of the market forces influencing the opportunities both today and over the planning horizon. Your next managerial challenge is to develop a deeper understanding of the market for each of the remaining opportunities. In this chapter, we will begin to "lower the microscope" on a specific market opportunity (see Figure 4-1).

An important tool for developing this understanding in technology-intensive businesses is the technology adoption life cycle. Understanding this technology adoption life cycle, and where your products and services are positioned relative to this adoption life cycle, can give you some important insights into buyer behavior. These insights can have powerful implications for developing winning marketing strategies. Closely related to this, we will try to help you better understand buyer choice/rejection behavior. It is important to recognize that before buyers can choose your product or service, they must invariably reject some current behavior, since they probably already have found some way of meeting their underlying need.

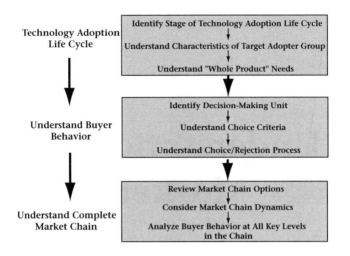

FIGURE 4-1: Process for Analyzing Technology Adoption, Buyer Behavior, and Market Chains

Having gained a better understanding of buyer behavior at key levels in a market chain, you need to broaden your analysis to look at the total market chain in which your customers are embedded. You have to recognize that winning leadership in a particular market requires that all the members of the market chain must adopt your product or service. If adoption does not occur quickly at any level of the market chain, your chances of gaining leadership and earning high profits will be seriously jeopardized.

Adoption of New Products

An important concept in understanding the market for technology-intensive products or services is the technology adoption life cycle. The technology adoption cycle is equally useful for new and existing opportunities. In both cases you will be introducing new products and services and, in the latter case, probably also reviewing the strategies for existing products. In order to do this successfully, you need to understand the current state of development for the market and where it is likely to move next. By understanding buyer behavior of both organizations and individuals at each of the key stages in the technology adoption life cycle and how that buyer behavior is likely to evolve over time, a company can substantially increase the probability of developing winning new products and successfully introducing them into the market.

Types of Innovations

While most technology-intensive companies strive to develop innovative products and services, the degree of innovation represented by each product or service can vary quite significantly. Some new products represent "continuous" innovations. These new products or services feature minor improvements or updates of existing products or services. A new, very light, and quite compact cellular telephone, Motorola's StarTAC, was viewed by many as a significant advance in the mid-1990s.

Similarly, each new generation of Intel's microprocessors in the 1980s and 1990s represented a significant advance in the functionality that was incorporated in the integrated circuit. However, the adoption of these products by customers did not require massive changes in behavior or the development of radically new infrastructures to use or support the product. Thus both of these products can be viewed as being toward the "continuous" end of the innovativeness continuum (see Figure 4-2).

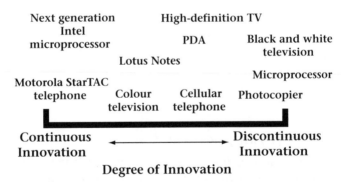

FIGURE 4-2: Innovativeness Continuum with Selected Examples

Now let's consider more radical new technologies, such as the personal computer, personal digital assistants (PDAs), black and white television, and photocopiers. These "discontinuous" innovations require some very significant changes in people's behavior and, perhaps, the modification of other complementary products and services if the customer is to adopt them. For example, widespread adoption of the personal computer required the development of "killer" software applications, new marketing channels, educational services, and a variety of peripheral and complementary equipment. Clearly, from a marketing perspective, these kinds of products and services represent a massive challenge. Other innovations, such as color TV or high-definition television, probably fall somewhere in between continuous innovations and discontinuous innovations (again see Figure 4-2).

When a new technology is developed, and you have the first products or services utilizing that technology, you have some latitude in how that innovation is positioned in the marketplace. For example, when Personal Communications Service (PCS) wireless telephone technology was introduced to the market, the equipment manufacturers and service providers could have positioned the technology either as an extension of traditional analog cellular technology or as an innovative wireless technology that offered significant benefits beyond traditional cellular technology.

In some cases, positioning a product as a logical extension reduces the perceived barriers to adoption and speeds up the adoption process. In other cases, you will want to differentiate the new technology from existing technology to appeal to a segment that has not adopted the old technology, because it was not seen as useful or user friendly, or because it had failed in the market.

An in-depth understanding of the technology adoption cycle is most valuable if you are introducing a discontinuous innovation. However, it can also provide useful insights for any product or service that has discontinuous elements in it.

Technology Adoption Life Cycle

Individuals and organizations vary greatly in their willingness to adopt new products or new technologies. Based on early research on the diffusion of innovations in such areas as agriculture and education, Everett Rogers identified five categories of adopters based on the relative time at which they adopted an innovation (see Figure 4-3).[1] Geoffrey Moore has taken this early work by Rogers and extended it; he has given these adopter categories names more attuned to

---

[1] Everett M. Rogers, *Diffusion of Innovations* (New York: Free Press, 1962).

technology-intensive markets.[2] The size of each of these adopter categories as a percentage of all adopters is shown in Figure 4-3, but these numbers should be considered as only approximate.

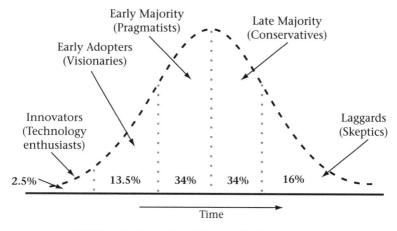

FIGURE 4-3: Technology Adoption Life Cycle Segments

Adopter Categories

The earliest adopters are the innovators or technology enthusiasts. For these people, certain areas of technology are a central focus of their lives. They are usually very knowledgeable about the technology and appreciate elegant technical solutions. They like to try out or test new technology. And, very importantly, they don't need a complete "solution." If the solution isn't quite there yet, they will jerryrig whatever hardware or software is needed to make the technology function. These innovators or technology enthusiasts are the kinds of people who bought personal computers in kit form in the mid-1970s. They wrote some of their own software and shared this software with other similar technology enthusiasts. Innovators want lots of information on the technology so they can understand how the technology works.   In many cases, they will read leading scientific journals in the field and attend technical conferences.

While these technology enthusiasts represent only a tiny fraction of the total market potential for an innovative product or service, they are critical in legitimizing the product and convincing other potential users that the technology does in fact work. They are, in

2 Geoffrey A. Moore, *Crossing the Chasm* (New York: HarperCollins, 1991) and Geoffrey A. Moore, *Inside the Tornado* (New York: HarperCollins, 1995).

essence, the gatekeepers to the next adopter group, the early adopters.

The early adopters, or visionaries, are the next group to adopt a new product. While these people have some familiarity with the underlying technology, they are not sophisticated technologists. Rather, they can see the potential benefits, both personal and organizational, that will accrue to them if they aggressively use the technology to achieve competitive advantage. These visionaries can imagine high-leverage applications of the technology and are willing to take substantial risks to gain the potential rewards. If they can see lots of leverage from applying the technology, they are also willing to invest their resources to create a complete solution.

Early adopters, or visionaries, are crucial for any high-technology innovation, since these are the people who can demonstrate the business value of the technology. American Airlines worked with IBM in the 1960s to develop a computerized reservation system (called SABRE), because visionaries at American Airlines saw that such a system could create significant competitive advantage for the airline.

The third adopter category, the early majority or pragmatists, also has an appreciation for the business benefits that the new technology can provide. However, they are more risk averse than the visionaries and are looking for proven solutions that can give them a competitive advantage. These pragmatists like to work with the supplier who appears to be the market leader in their vertical market segment. There are a number of reasons for this. The market leader's product may not be the best option on the market, but usually it will be a reliable product.

In addition, a number of third parties often enter the marketplace to provide either competitive or complementary products and services that work with or enhance the market leader's product and related services. These include value-added resellers, who work with the market leader's products to create the complete solution for the buyer, or third-party service organizations that provide maintenance and repair services for the market leader's products in competition with the market leader.

Even if the market leader is not being totally responsive to the needs of its customers, these other suppliers emerge to provide the required level of support and service. Pragmatists want complete solutions, either those provided by the supplier or by the supplier and those firms providing the complementary products and services. The pragmatic nature of this adopter group also means that they want to see successful applications of the technology in their own market segment before they adopt. Again, this helps them reduce the perceived risk of adopting the new technology.

The late majority, or the conservatives, adopt new technology only under duress. They are driven to adopt the new technology in order to reduce costs and to remain competitive in their markets. They are less comfortable with technology and are quite sensitive to price. They need a complete solution and they prefer a simple, standardized, pre-assembled solution that just works. Because of the price sensitivity of this adopter group, it is important to have a low-cost product and access to a low-cost market chain that effectively reaches these customers.

The fifth, and final, adopter category is the laggards or skeptics. These individuals are very skeptical of new products and services and the business cases that vendors use to sell them. They are very late to adopt new technology and they prefer not to adopt it at all. In business-to-business markets, a skeptic located in an influential position in a company can delay, or stop, the adoption of a new technology. The challenge in these situations is to find some way to work around the skeptic or to neutralize the skeptic, so that other, more innovative individuals within the organization can support the adoption of the new technology.

While understanding the differences in buyer behavior among the different adopter groups is most crucial in the case of discontinuous innovations, it can be valuable even for products and services that are toward the continuous innovation end of the continuum. Although in some ways this discussion exaggerates the differences between the groups, the reality is that most managers treat the different adopter groups far too homogeneously. Figure 4-4 summarizes the key characteristics of each of the five adopter groups and their needs. It also describes the role of each group in the adoption of a new technology.

Driving the Adoption Process

Understanding the adoption process has some clear implications for you as you try to speed the adoption of an innovative new product or service. When you are introducing an innovative new product or

	Innovators (Technology Enthusiasts)	Early Adopters (Visionaries)	Early Majority (Pragmatists)	Late Majority (Conservatives)	Laggards (Skeptics)
Focus	• Technology	• Breakthrough that will create competitive advantage	• Proven solutions that can give lower costs and/or competitive advantage	• Remain competitive	• Avoid change
Key characteristics	• Very knowledgeable about technology • Appreciate elegant technical solutions • Like to test new technology • Don't need complete "solutions"	• Can imagine high leverage applications • Willing to take risks • Willing to invest resources to create a complete solution • Not price sensitive	• Comfortable with technology • Pragmatic rather than risk takers • Like to work with market leaders • Have a "wait and see attitude" • Don't like surprises	• Less comfortable with technology • Resistant to change • More price sensitive • Risk averse	• Very skeptical of technology and business cases • Very risk averse
Needs	• Early access to emerging technologies • Access to all information on technology	• Lots of support • Want to move quickly	• Complete, proven solution • Want credible reference accounts in their own industry	• Prefer simple solutions that are easy to install and operate • Want to buy the established standard	• Technology may need to be "hidden" from them • Need to be convinced that all other solutions are weaker
Role in adoption process	• Confirm viability of technology	• Help commercialize the technology • Give visibility to technology	• Are entry point into huge, mainstream market	• Represent significant portion of the total market • Can be quite profitable	• Obstructs change • You should usually try to avoid or neutralize them

FIGURE 4-4: Key Characteristics, Needs, and Role of Adopter Groups

service, you will be able to use your knowledge of the characteristics of the different adopter categories to swiftly reach a sustainable position as market leader. Ideally, you would work with technology enthusiasts to demonstrate the viability of the technology and to jointly educate the early adopters or visionaries. Once the innovative product has attracted the attention of a few visionaries, you need to work with them to develop a complete solution to their needs, so your company can develop a pool of satisfied customers. Some of these visionaries may serve as useful references for pragmatists in their own (often vertical) market segments.

Your company then must try to leverage this success in one segment to other related segments (Moore has termed this the "bowling alley" strategy). For example, a company's initial success with one specific application in one industry might be leveraged in two ways. First, managers in your company might try to identify other vertical markets with almost identical applications and move to penetrate them. Second, they might look for new, different, but related applications in the vertical market in which your company is already established. With this approach, one success (the first bowling pin) can lead to multiple successes (the next row of pins) and so on until your company has succeeded in knocking down all the bowling pins in the market.

Once the company has begun to successfully implement the bowling pin strategy and penetrate the early majority or pragmatists, revenues grow very rapidly (Moore has termed this the "tornado"). If the company is able to establish itself as the market leader, its technology will become viewed as the accepted technology for addressing a wide range of similar problems. With the large volumes and experience gained as market leader, the company should then strive to prepackage and commoditize the product in order to make it inexpensive enough to attract the conservatives. During this period, a company will introduce a number of specialized variants of the product targeted at particular niche opportunities within this mainstream market to maximize the penetration of the technology.

Hewlett-Packard has been particularly successful in this, with both its inkjet and laser printers. For example, in 1997 it developed a high-quality, low-cost inkjet printer that was targeted at the home digital photography market and another printer that was targeted at very young children.[3]

---

[3]"HP Pictures the Future," *Business Week*, July 7, 1997, pp. 100–109.

The key in all of this is to keep the momentum going and to smoothly roll from one adopter category to the next. Moore has forcefully pointed out that things don't always work quite this smoothly. With innovations that are toward the discontinuous end of the innovativeness spectrum, the products may get a warm reception from the innovators and the early adopters, but then sales may stall as the product or service has difficulty gaining acceptance with the early majority or pragmatists. Moore has called the gap that often emerges between the early adopters or visionaries and the early majority or pragmatists, the "chasm" (see Figure 4-5). In recent years a number of products and services have had difficulty "crossing the chasm."

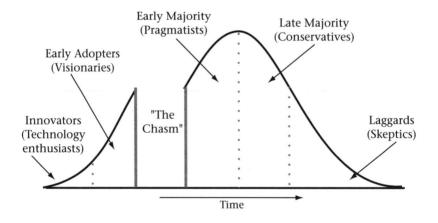

FIGURE 4-5: The Chasm in the Technology Adoption Life Cycle

Digital photography "stalled" for over a decade before crossing the chasm in the mid-1990s. Some of the factors that held it back were the lack of powerful personal computers and software that could manipulate digital images, networks that couldn't handle the large volumes of data required for digital images, and the absence of inexpensive input and output devices that generated acceptable quality images and printed output. Personal digital assistants also seemed to stall for several years before moving across the chasm in the mid- to late-1990s.

Chasms are much less likely to occur for innovations toward the continuous end of the innovativeness continuum.

A number of indicators warn of an emerging chasm. After an initial burst of sales to innovators and early adopters, revenues flatten out and selling cycles and selling costs rise. The next wave of potential customers, the pragmatists or early majority, show some interest in the product or service, but do not buy. A typical response of the selling company is to talk to these customers and try to determine their objections. Often, the objections are associated with some deficiency in the whole product. That is, the product or service does not provide a complete solution to the customer's need. The company may then interview a cross-section of customers and develop a "wish list" of the things they feel will have to be done if they are to adopt the product. Sometimes these customers are spread out over several different market segments. In some cases, approaching a wide range is intentional as the company does not want to put all its eggs in one basket by focusing on one market segment. With the wish lists in hand, the various functional groups go to work trying to deal with each of the issues. After months of effort, they usually have made significant progress in dealing with the issues and they return to the customers. Invariably, they have dealt with some of the issues for each customer group, but have not dealt with all the issues for any one customer group.

So, again, adoption is not likely to happen. The customers tell them that they are doing good work, and they should keep at it and come back when they have finished the complete list. Meanwhile, valuable time is passing and competitors may very well be overtaking the innovating company.

Frequently, a better way to proceed is by totally focusing your efforts on one particular market segment, usually a vertical market segment. By really focusing in this way, you are more likely to develop a complete solution that meets the needs of that particular segment. If it provides real competitive advantage for the customers in that segment, the adoption of your technology by one or two customers may lead to a rapid adoption by all of the other major players in the segment if they are to remain competitive.

A classic example of a company successfully adopting this strategy to cross the chasm was Documentum. Documentum was founded in 1990 to supply enterprise document management software, which can sort and compile critical information located in many niches within a company. By 1992, sales were $500,000 a year and were not growing.

In late 1993, the company's managers decided to focus. They carefully examined some 75 different application scenarios for Documentum's product and decided to focus on the pharmaceutical industry with the first application being the automation of all the document processes involved in producing a new drug submission for regulatory approval. In this application, Documentum software promised massive savings in time that could result in large incremental revenues and profits for the adopting companies. Within six months of Documentum entering this market segment, it had signed up 15 to 20 major pharmaceutical companies and by the end of 1995 it had added another 15 to 20 companies.

Today, almost every major pharmaceutical company in the world uses Documentum software. Once Documentum had achieved leadership position in the new drug submission application, it began to leverage that success into other applications within the pharmaceutical industry and into related applications in other industries (the next bowling pins). With continued success, Documentum might at some point hope to become the standard solution for a wide range of enterprise document management applications. In 1998, the company had revenues of almost $125 million and was quite profitable.

A vital element in Documentum's success was to create a compelling case for customers to buy the product by creating a complete solution for their needs. This included not only the generic software product, but also everything else the customer needed.

Achieving Market Leadership

In the early stages of the adoption of a new technology, it is difficult to determine who will become the ultimate market leader. While pioneers have an initial advantage, they sometimes have trouble getting across the chasm, or their early efforts are swamped by a fast follower with deeper pockets and a good strategy. But once a new technology has moved beyond the first two adoption categories and into the mainstream market (pragmatists and conservatives), it becomes difficult for a new entrant to displace the market leader, unless the market leader makes some major mistakes. It doesn't mean that a new entrant can't capture a part of the market, but it is unlikely to become the leader, or even one of the top two or three companies, unless it is able to bring unusual resources and capabilities to the market.

Entrants into the mainstream market (or losers in the battle for market leadership) end up competing in two major ways. Sometimes niches emerge in the market that have specialized needs not met effectively by the market leader. Specialist producers may be able to become the dominant player in these niches through great products and/or very close working relationships with customers. The other way of competing is on the basis of low cost. Some segments of end users, and certainly some members of the market chain, want low-priced alternatives to the market leader's product. Retailers and value-added resellers want a low-priced option on their "shelves" to help build traffic and to have a low cost offering for the price-sensitive customer.

Whole Product or Complete Solution

The importance of understanding what the whole product or complete solution is for the target market cannot be overemphasized. Take a new pharmaceutical product, for example. A naive observer might see the "product" as the pharmaceutical compound. However, the whole product includes not only the pharmaceutical, but such other things as educational materials and seminars for physicians, 24-hour-per-day support for the physician, clinical data on the pharmaceutical's effectiveness, value data demonstrating the economic value of the pharmaceutical, references to opinion leaders using the product, reimbursement information, pharmacological data, and guidelines for the doctor in how to prescribe the pharmaceutical (see Figure 4-6).

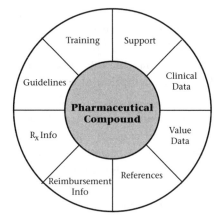

FIGURE 4-6: Whole Product for a Pharmaceutical

As the earlier discussion suggested, as a product or technology moves from one adopter category to another, the nature of the whole product changes. With the innovator, the core product is a big part of the whole product. By the time the product has reached the late majority or conservatives adopter group, the success of the product will depend much more heavily on the non-core elements of the product rather than the core product itself. Thus the core product is increasingly taken for granted and becomes a less important determinant of choice as the product moves into the later stages of the adoption cycle.

Understanding Buyer Choice/Rejection Behavior

In this chapter we have argued that ensuring the successful adoption of technology-intensive products and services requires a thorough understanding of the technology adoption life cycle. We have also demonstrated that some aspects of customer buying behavior change as a product or service moves from one adopter category to the next. In this part of the chapter we will focus on some of the more generic aspects of buyer choice/rejection behavior. However, we should recognize that some of the specifics will be dependent on the adopter category your customers are in.

The first step is gaining an understanding of buyer behavior at the critical level in your market chain. This buyer will be either the end user of the product or service or the organization that will be the key driver of adoption for your product or service. For a component or sub-system manufacturer, this buyer may be the original equipment manufacturer (OEM). But always there is tremendous value in understanding buyer behavior at all the other decision points in your market chain, since you may be able to do things to your whole product that will influence adoption at each level in the chain.

Having an in-depth understanding of organizational, and often individual, buying behavior is absolutely essential in high-technology businesses. As a seller, you need to understand the process by which organizations and individuals establish the need for a particular product or service and then go about identifying, evaluating, and making choices among alternative suppliers.

Some of the crucial elements in gaining this understanding of the process are identifying the members of the decision-making unit and their relative power and influence, the criteria these individuals will use in the choice process, and the nature of the decision process itself. In some cases you will be able to identify generalizations that apply to all the organizations in a market segment. However, in almost every case the fine tuning of the tactics will require buyer behavior analysis by the individual sales representative or manager on an account-by-account basis. At this stage in the planning process, you should be looking for useful generalizations that can be used to develop an understanding of the market and to make broad strategic decisions.

You may also have to think about the buyer's decision-making process for upstream members of the market chain, i.e., those that supply the products and services you use to develop the products and services you market to your customers. Perhaps you have to convince a subsystem or component supplier to build certain functionality into its product or to accelerate the development of the product if you are to win in the market. Therefore, you need to be concerned about all members of your market chain, both upstream and downstream.

Decision-Making Unit

The decision-making unit, or buying network, is a group of individuals that have some influence on whether to buy a particular product or service and, if the decision is made to buy the product or service, the particular brand of that product or service. It is important to recognize that in many decisions involving technology-intensive products or services, individuals external to the customer organization may very well become involved in the process. For example, it is not uncommon for consultants to be brought into a company to help that company make choices about a major non-routine product or service it should purchase.

It is also important to recognize that the key individuals in the decision-making unit may very well evolve over time. Sometimes, the individuals who are essential in getting an organization to make a decision to buy a new product or service may be much less influential in choosing the particular brand of that product or service. A CEO or the head of a business unit or function might be convinced that the extensive use of videoconferencing in the company will significantly reduce cost, increase productivity, and improve organizational responsiveness. She might persuade the rest of the top management team that this is a good idea and gain their support.

The decision about what sort of videoconferencing network to set up and which equipment to buy might then be delegated to a task force of middle managers from different areas of the organization and the company's information technology group.

It is also essential to understand the power and influence of each individual in the decision-making unit. This task can be challenging, particularly in industries that are in transition. For example, companies selling medical equipment to hospitals have in recent years seen the power and influence of doctors decline and the power and influence of administrators increase, as pressures to contain the cost of health care increasingly control the health care system. This shift in power and influence has resulted in companies having to respond more to the decision-making criteria of administrators rather than of the doctors.

In general, the better the selling organization understands its customers and the composition of the decision-making units, the roles and influence of the different individuals in those units, and the relationships between these individuals, the better it should be able to design products, services, and marketing strategies that will influence decision-making units to decide in its favor.

Choice Criteria

A second important element is the choice criteria that individuals in the decision-making units bring to bear as they attempt to make a decision. These criteria are related to both organizational and personal objectives. In a complex purchase decision, the individuals may bring very different criteria to the process, resulting in conflict. For example, in the mid-1980s, General Motors invested heavily in some highly automated systems to try to improve both product quality and cost position relative to its Japanese competitors.

The individuals involved in making the decision about buying this equipment had very different criteria. Some people in the head office manufacturing engineering group wanted to adopt leading-edge technology because it promised the biggest cost savings and biggest improvements in quality. However, the manufacturing engineers in the assembly plants where the equipment would be used were much more concerned about the reliability of the equipment and their ability to meet production quotas if the equipment was installed. They did not want to be at the "bleeding edge" of technology. The industrial relations group were concerned about potential job losses and the impact of these job losses on their relationships with the United Auto Workers union. Individuals from the sales organization were interested in equipment that would improve quality and reduce warranty claims. The finance staff was looking for data that would help them develop a business case to show a good return on General Motors' investment in the automation equipment.

Clearly, from the perspective of the sellers of this automation equipment, it was a challenging task to respond to this wide range of needs. To complicate matters even further, many of these automation systems incorporated equipment from several different vendors. These vendors each wanted to work with other vendors who had the capability to quickly put together a system that really worked. The faster a system was installed and running to General Motors' satisfaction, the sooner they got paid! For this reason, some vendors encouraged General Motors to include their preferred partners on the team whose responsibility was to supply and install the complete system. As any decision process proceeds, different decision makers, each with his or her own set of choice criteria, will increase or decrease in importance.

With regard to choice criteria, you can differentiate yourself from a customer's existing choice—what he or she is currently using—and a customer's other potential choices on one or a combination of two basic types of buying criteria: product criteria and process criteria. Product criteria refer to the fit of the product attributes to the customer's need. Does the product or service have the functionality, quality, reliability, speed the customer is seeking? Process criteria refer to the degree to which your product or service fits the customer's needs from a purchasing, usage, and disposal perspective. Some organizations call this the customer interface strategy. For example, some customers want to deal with a company with knowledgeable, consultative salespersons, who are available when and where the customer wants them and who will help the customer make the appropriate choices. Other, perhaps more sophisticated, customers may be much more comfortable downloading information from an Internet site, configuring the product or system they want to buy on the Internet, and placing the order over the Internet. They might also appreciate 24-hour-a-day availability of skilled telemarketers, if they have questions.

> In coming to an understanding of customers' decision criteria, it is important to develop useful insights on both these aspects of choice. Too often companies pay attention only to the product-based criteria and miss important, and sometimes more sustainable, opportunities to both better meet customer needs and differentiate their product and service offerings from those of the competition.

Later in the strategic market planning process, this information on choice criteria by market segment can be absolutely critical as you design your product and service offerings and as you decide how best to position them relative to customer needs and competitive offerings in the market. What you are searching for are those one or two compelling reasons that will get customers to reject the product or service they are currently using and to enthusiastically adopt your new product or service. These reasons could be based on product or process.

The Choice/Rejection Process

The third element in understanding buyer choice/rejection behavior is the "how" question—how the customer goes about making decisions in the choice/rejection process.

When a company develops a new product or service, it faces a number of issues. Most of the potential customers for the new product or service are already using something else that, to a greater or lesser degree, meets their needs. Thus, in order for them to adopt the new product or service, these customers need to switch from their existing choices. That is, they must reject their existing solution. Even if you are successful in getting customers to reject their existing solutions, you may not be successful in getting them to adopt your new product or service. Customers might find it easier to reject your new product or service and choose the product or service of an alternative supplier. We can imagine the customer going through a process similar to that shown in Figure 4-7.

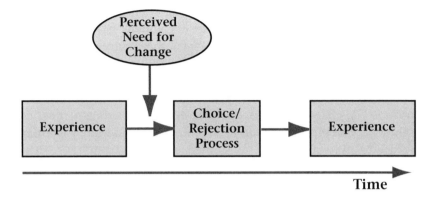

FIGURE 4-7:   Choice/Rejection Process Over Time

Consider a relatively simple example. As mentioned earlier in this chapter, one product that had some difficulty in crossing the chasm was the personal digital assistant (PDA). If we look at this product from a choice/rejection perspective, we may begin to understand why it has taken so long to become a mass market product. One of the major functions of a PDA is to keep track of an individual's calendar, important addresses and telephone numbers, "to do" lists, business expenses, and the variety of other things a person needs to keep track of and use on a daily basis. Historically, most people with this sort of need used an annual planning diary or a pencil-and-paper-based personal organizer. For many people, probably the bulk of the market, this solution was acceptable.

The challenge for manufacturers of PDAs was to get past the technology enthusiasts and the visionaries and to help the mainstream pragmatic customer see the potential value of a PDA and the need for change. In order to do this effectively, PDA manufacturers needed an excellent understanding of the skills and knowledge of these potential customers and how these people use their paper and pencil tools and the frustrations, or potential frustrations, they might have with such tools.

One of the major frustrations for individuals who use an annual planning diary is the annual "changeover." At some point close to the end of the calendar year, people have to transfer a great deal of information from the old planning diary to the new one. This might involve several hours of copying information from one book to another. This is less of an issue to users of the bulkier personal organizers, since these tools take advantage of a rolling calendar with new pages being added as needed. The growing use of computer-based scheduling software within companies resulted in another source of frustration because many people had to keep their diary or organizer schedule identical to that on the computer-based system.

In the late 1980s and early 1990s, most of these individuals did not see early PDAs, such as Apple's Newton, providing a superior solution. Many people found it difficult and inconvenient to enter data into PDAs and the PDAs seemed to be very complex. They offered a great variety of functionality, but to many users this variety was achieved at the cost of great complexity. In addition, it was inconvenient to transfer data between the PDA and a computer, to make a hard copy of the data on the PDA, or to back up the PDA data. In addition, many of the PDAs were large and relatively heavy.

The most successful PDA in the 1990s was the PalmPilot, which finally began to propel PDAs into the mainstream market. This product dealt with many of the concerns of the pragmatist buyer. It was compact, fitting in a pocket or purse, and had limited functionality, but that functionality included the main applications most users wanted. It used a relatively easy to learn handwriting recognition technology and was easy to synchronize with a personal computer. It was also inexpensive relative to the Newton and some of the other fully featured PDAs on the market.

For many potential users, the combination of functions and price provided a compelling reason for them to switch from a pencil-and-paper-based system to an electronic system. Once these customers had gone through the choice/rejection process, the challenge for 3Com, which had acquired the PalmPilot in 1997, was to create barriers that would reduce the chances of these PalmPilot users rejecting the PalmPilot solution and moving on to another PDA or back to paper and pencil. 3Com tried to do this by continually improving the basic product, adding line extensions to meet the needs of particular market segments, adding optional new functions that would allow the user to use the PalmPilot for a greater variety of tasks (such as e-mail and expense tracking), encouraging third-parties to develop other applications that could be downloaded to the PalmPilot, and stimulating a whole infrastructure to allow the community of PalmPilot users to learn from each other. In 1998 3Com started sending e-mails to registered owners to keep them informed about new developments, new software, and new complementary products.

With this example, we can see in a microcosm some of the difficulties that suppliers of innovative products and services have as they try to achieve market penetration. If customers are reasonably satisfied with the current solution to their need, it may be quite difficult to get them to adopt a new solution. The difficulty is likely to be a function of the degree of satisfaction the users have with the current solution. There are also major switching barriers, such as the costs of converting to the new system. These barriers include the need for training, the cost of the new solution, and the lack of a supporting infrastructure to help the user get the full benefit from the new solution.

Also, significant risks are often associated with new solutions. For example, there is the constant threat of obsolescence, the possibility that the product or service the user has adopted will not meet standards that emerge in the new market, and the possibility that the supplier of the new product or service might decide to exit the business, leaving the customer without spare parts and support. The longer the customer has been using the existing solution, the more difficult it may be to get it to switch. For example, companies that used Macintosh computers in the mid-1980s were reluctant to switch to Windows-based systems in the 1990s, even though it appeared that Apple was in serious trouble and that Windows-based applications software was by then leading in many areas. This reluctance to switch was because the customer had built a network and infrastructure around the Macintosh, and its employees were comfortable with Macintosh-type technology. Thus the switching barriers were very high, both personally and organizationally.

As we saw in the case of the PalmPilot, once the customer has adopted the new solution, it is important to spend time and effort ensuring that the customer does not reject the solution. In essence, you are trying to build massive switching barriers around the customer so it will be very difficult for the customer to change suppliers. You must ensure that customers use the product correctly, that the benefits of using your solution are visible to customers, and that they get good service and after-sales support. The more customers invest in making your solution work for them, and the more satisfied they are with the results, the less likely they are to switch to another supplier.

Some of the ancillary products and services a company provides to create the whole product the customer is seeking, and to build barriers to switching, can turn out to be attractive market opportunities themselves. Such things as customer training, customer support departments, and accessory products can turn out to be profitable activities. For example, Intuit has successfully built a number of complementary profitable businesses around its core personal finance, small business management and tax preparation software. These businesses include technical support billed by the minute, payroll services, and forms and supplies.

In summary, the three critical issues in the adoption of any new product are:

1. the rejection of the existing solution (OUT),

2. the adoption of the new solution (IN), and

3. the building of barriers to discourage future switching (BUILD BARRIERS).

The development of the whole product or a complete solution can help with each of these issues.

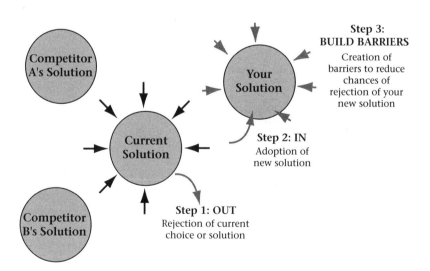

FIGURE 4-8: The Three Critical Issues in Any Choice/Rejection Process

Market Chains

As discussed in Chapter 1, a market chain (sometimes called a supply/demand chain) is simply the chain of organizations a company uses that play key roles converting raw materials into solutions that meet end-user requirements. The portion of the market chain between your company and the end users is made up of one or more market channels. If your new product is to be successful, all members of your market chain have to choose to work with you. The issue of buyer choice/rejection is critical, not only with respect to the end user or the key members of your market chain, such as OEMs, but also for all the intermediaries between you and the end user in your selected market channels.

In this book, we view market chains as live, profit-driven, value-creating networks of companies that compete with other value-creating systems in the market. Market chains have to be actively managed over time if you are to achieve leadership in your chosen target markets. The notion of active management is important. In fast-moving, technology-intensive markets it is a big mistake to wait for the emergence of a market chain that is aligned with your interests. Rather, you must cajole, negotiate with, and motivate other players, both up and down the market chain, to get them aligned with you and with the targeted end users in order to help you achieve your market leadership objectives. In some cases, this will require you to create new types of market chain members that heretofore did not exist. In several industries, including computers and robotics systems, manufacturers have had to build networks of value-added resellers or systems integrators in order for the manufacturers to be effectively able to serve their end-user customers.

Choices Among Market Chains

In many market opportunities companies are trying to serve several different market segments. Unfortunately it is seldom possible to reach all of the target segments effectively with one market channel. This means that the company has to employ several different market channels in order to reach all the different segments, and it may have to use two or more market channels to reach all the sub-segments within one target segment. This can lead to complex market chain structures with a high potential for channel conflict that can be a real challenge to manage. An example of such a complex structure is shown in Figure 4-9.

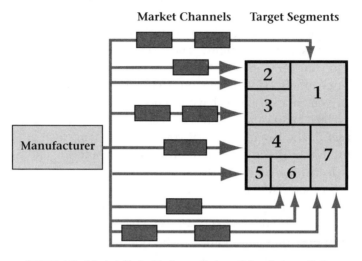

FIGURE 4-9: Market Chain Challenge Facing a Manufacturer Trying to Reach Multiple Target Segments

Here a full-line manufacturer is trying to reach all seven segments in the market. In some cases, there is one market channel that effectively accesses the segment, i.e., Segments 1, 3, 4, and 5. In the other cases, i.e., Segments 2, 6, and 7, some customers prefer to buy directly from the manufacturer, whereas others prefer to use a distributor. The total of all the market channels a company is using together with its network of suppliers is a company's market chain.

When there is more than one market channel that can be used to access a certain end-user market opportunity, you will have to choose which channel or channels to include in your market chain. Sometimes these potential market channels are very similar, with the issue being which company or companies you should try to work with at each level in the channel.

An example of such a set of market channels is the one being used by Motorola for the antilock braking system (ABS) market (see Figure 4-10). As can be seen from this figure, there are a large number of paths that Motorola or one of the other semiconductor manufacturers could use to reach the ultimate end user—the car buyer. While Motorola may have no control over the market channel choices beyond the ABS manufacturer, it can, in designing its circuits and the associated services, have an influence on choice all the way down the market channel to the driver of the car with ABS. Thus the semi-conductor companies need to have a good understanding of buyer choice/rejection throughout the potential market channels.

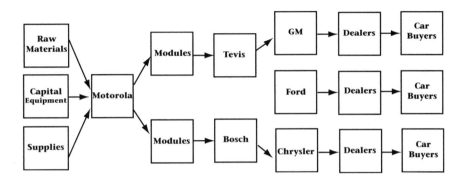

FIGURE 4-10: Two Potential Market Channels for a Manufacturer of Semiconductor Components to Access the Antilock Braking Systems Market

In other cases, the possible market channels will be quite different from each other. An example of this would be a personal computer company targeting the corporate market. It can choose to reach this market through one or a combination of different market channels, including value-added resellers, systems integrators, and direct marketing. In the latter case, which is the path Dell and Gateway 2000 have taken, they eliminate all downstream market chain members and deal directly with customers largely by personal selling, by telephone, or over the Internet.

In choosing the market channel or channels to use, a company should take account of a number of considerations. First, it should use channels that represent an attractive opportunity for it. Other things being equal, it should focus on the channel(s) most likely to be successful in gaining market share, growth, and profitability. These channels will be ones where there is an excellent fit between what the channels can deliver and the needs of the end user.

Second, if a company is aiming to capture leadership in the opportunity, it should focus on those channels where it can clearly emerge as the market leader relative to competing companies using the same chain. It will need to present powerful reasons for the market chain members to work closely with it and to aggressively market its products.

Some of the factors that can create this sort of enthusiasm among the market chain members and influence them to choose the company include the promise of a series of winning products and marketing programs that will help the individual market chain members differentiate themselves from their competitors. These products and programs should clearly create strategic leverage for the individual market chain members. By strategic leverage at any point in the market chain, we mean the ratio of the payoffs to the market chain members from working with a company to the investments that market chain member must make to support the activities of that company. For example, if a value-added reseller sees that a modest investment in training its staff and in inventory will lead to a dramatic increase in both market share and unit margins, it will likely be enthusiastic about working with a particular manufacturer. It will be particularly enthusiastic if these returns are clearly higher than it could obtain from working with one of the company's competitors.

Finally, since relationships play such an essential role in many market chains, all members of the market chain need to feel that they can build strong and professional relationships that will endure over a reasonable time.

Market Chain Dynamics

It is especially important to use a reasonable planning horizon in technology-intensive businesses, since change in market chains is inevitable in fast-moving industries as different players reassess their business definitions and adjust their strategies accordingly. Market chains in technology-intensive markets are living, dynamic organisms. The optimal market chain today may be totally obsolete in five years, as the underlying technology moves through its adoption life cycle. Professional managers recognize this, albeit reluctantly. They recognize that over time, each of the players in the market chain may have to choose partners in order to protect their individual market positions. For example, in many technology-intensive markets, the players considered most important in a manufacturer's market chain may initially be systems integrators but over time become the value-added resellers, then the retailers as the underlying technology moves through its life cycle. Often these players are totally different companies.

Conflict is frequently a major issue as the transition from one set of market chain partners to another is underway. Compaq experienced this conflict in 1998 and 1999 as it attempted to move more of its sales from indirect to direct channels.

Two fundamental types of strategic change underlie many of the dynamics we see in a market chain. At one extreme, we see companies changing the functionality or applications they offer their customers over time, but not changing the basic structure of their market chain. This move is frequently accompanied by adding or changing the technological or other capabilities the company uses. For example, a semiconductor manufacturer might provide more functionality on its integrated circuits (ICs), or integrate the functionality that had been on several ICs onto one IC, or simply enhance the performance of the product.

Sometimes this will reduce the value-adding role of the other players in the market chain. Some players will welcome it, since it may allow them to use these advances to create greater value for customers, or to engage in other value-creation activities that might promise greater returns. From the perspective of the semiconductor manufacturer, this strategy can be called horizontal upscaling (see Figure 4-11).

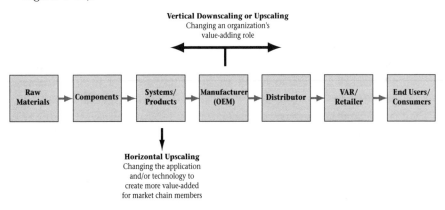

FIGURE 4-11: Downscaling and Upscaling

Vertical upscaling represents a fundamentally different strategy. Here one member of the market chain simply takes over all or part of the value-adding role of a neighboring member or members of the market chain and bypasses them entirely. For example, if Motorola decided to begin making ABS modules and shipping them directly to

Tevis and Bosch, it would have engaged in vertical upscaling and would have eliminated the module manufacturers from its market chain (see Figure 4-10). If, on the other hand, a semiconductor manufacturer, such as Motorola, decides to withdraw from, or outsource, certain activities, such as distributing its products, it is engaged in vertical downscaling (see Figure 4-11).

In reality we seldom see pure examples of vertical upscaling unless they are the result of acquisitions. Usually a company developing a horizontal upscaling strategy sees that it could quite easily bypass a neighboring player in the market chain, since that player is no longer creating much value-added. It moves ahead and effectively executes a mixed upscaling strategy. The emergence of custom and semi-custom integrated circuits together with advanced semiconductor design tools, design centers, and foundries in the 1980s led several companies in a number of industries to rethink their strategies and market chains. A number of companies that had previously bought all their semiconductor devices from merchant suppliers began to design some of their own semiconductors and have them manufactured by silicon foundries. In some cases, using custom integrated circuits allowed the manufacturers to build highly differentiated products and to reduce their costs. For the merchant semiconductor companies, it meant the loss of some attractive opportunities in certain markets.

Sometimes we see key players in the market chain actively encouraging other players in their chain to engage in upscaling to allow the key players to focus on those few areas of their business where they have strong core capabilities. All the North American automobile manufacturers were actively pursuing this strategy in the mid- and late 1990s, creating tremendous upscaling opportunities for some of their important suppliers.

Market Chains as a Series of Choice/Rejection Processes

One of the major challenges in any technology-intensive business is getting new products to the market in a timely manner. Often end-user sales develop much more slowly than anticipated. This can be the result of the marketing strategy not being responsive to the realities of buyer behavior at the particular stage in the adoption life cycle. It can also be due to some key players in the market chain not adopting and aggressively marketing the new product in a timely manner. These lags can cumulate in a market chain and can have a massive impact on sales and cash flow and the ultimate profitability of a market opportunity.

Managers don't usually pay enough attention to adoption along each of the market channels that make up the market chain. Each market channel can be viewed usefully as a series of choice/rejection processes, which must be actively managed by the company or companies trying to drive a particular market opportunity. Each of the companies in the market chain has its own choice/rejection process to go through.

Most companies will be existing businesses that carry a certain set of products and services and operate in certain ways. The new product or technology you are offering may require them to switch from one product to another and perhaps change the way they operate their business. They may face a number of barriers to switching. For example, they might have a high inventory of their existing product line, or their staff might not have the skills to sell and service the new product. Even if you are successful in showing them how to overcome the barriers, they will often have other suppliers or customers (if you are downstream from them) who might provide a similar opportunity. You will have to convince them you are the best option.

Once they have adopted, you or other players in the market chain will need to work with them and develop programs that solidify the new behavior. To do all of this effectively requires that you or other committed partners in the market chain understand the decision-making unit, the choice criteria, and the choice/rejection process at all levels in the market chain.

Next Step: Assessing Your Resources and Competencies

At this point you have developed a much deeper understanding of the markets for your opportunities. You know where they are in terms of the technology adoption life cycle and the characteristics of customers at that stage of the cycle. You also should have developed an in-depth understanding of buyer choice/rejection behavior and the market chains you intend to use to reach the targeted end users.

The next step is to assess your resources and competencies (or capabilities) and to determine the fit between them and the market opportunity.

Key Questions for Executives and Managers

- Where does your product or technology fit on the continuum from continuous to discontinuous innovations?

- At what stage in the technology adoption life cycle is the underlying technology for your product or service? If this product or service has not yet crossed the chasm, what will be your strategy for crossing it? Are you trying to attack this market too late in the technology adoption life cycle, when competition will be too firmly entrenched for you to gain a leadership position? If not, what are the key characteristics of the buyers at this stage and the next stage of the adoption life cycle? What are the implications of these characteristics for your marketing strategy?

- What are the elements of the whole product or complete solution for the customer segments you will be targeting over the planning horizon?

- Do you have a good understanding of buyer behavior of companies and individuals in your target segments? Specifically, do you understand:

  - who is in the decision-making units, the role and power of each player, and how the decision-making unit is likely to evolve over the decision process?
  - what buying criteria these individuals are going to use as they make their decisions?
  - what choice/rejection process they will go through? How are the individuals or organizations currently meeting the underlying need? Is there a compelling reason for them to reject their current behavior and move to a new product or service? Are you taking advantage of both product and process opportunities to differentiate your offering

---

from competing offerings? How might you build barriers to reduce the likelihood of adopters defecting from your solution?

- Have you clearly mapped all the alternative market channels that could be used to access your potential market opportunity? Have you carefully made the choice about which channel or channels to use, and do you have a clear map of the total market chain you will be using? Do you understand the buyer choice/rejection process at each key level in each channel? How will you create strategic leverage for each level in each of the channels in your market chain?

- Are you being realistic in estimating the speed of adoption by all members of the market chain? Do you see potential lags in adoption that could threaten your drive for market leadership and high profitability? What can you do to overcome these potential lags?

CHAPTER FIVE

Assess Resources and Competencies

Introduction

In previous chapters, we outlined an iterative process for identifying a market opportunity within a business arena and examining the market chains associated with it. Then we discussed customer choice/rejection behavior at the key stages within the chain as a foundation for understanding how you can create customer choice for your product or service.

In this chapter, the focus shifts to exploring the resources and competencies (or capabilities) you bring to the opportunity. How well does the opportunity fit with your existing competencies? Does it require resources and competencies that you don't possess? In areas that are lacking, can you obtain the necessary resources and competencies internally, by forming a strategic alliance to access them, or by outsourcing them to another firm? Answering these questions will put you in good shape for assessing the competitive challenges and determining whether it is realistic for you to expect that taking advantage of the opportunity will be profitable for you. These are the central topics of the next chapter.

The Process of Assessing Resource/Competency Fit

In simplest terms, this chapter is about gauging how well your competencies and resources can create sustainable competitive differentiation in the market opportunity. Your success will depend on how well your strategy fits the needs of the market you hope to enter compared to how well the competitors' strategies fit. Figure 5-1 portrays this process.

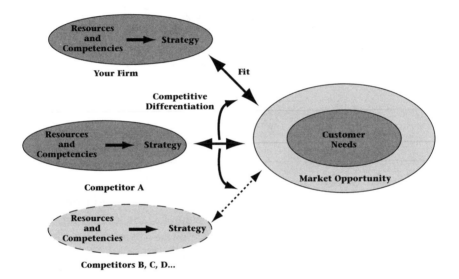

FIGURE 5-1: The Process of Assessing Resource/Competency Fit

Several concepts in Figure 5-1 need explanation. Again, market opportunity describes a specific strategic situation defined by four dimensions (customers, functions/applications, technologies/competencies, and value-adding roles). This could involve a situation in which you are reviewing your strategy for exploiting an existing opportunity or where you are developing a strategy for taking advantage of a new one. The opportunity will continue to be the focus for this chapter. At the core of a market opportunity are specific customer needs, which must be satisfied in a competitively differentiated way if the opportunity is to have potential.

Resources are assets that the strategic business unit can utilize for competing in a market opportunity. They can take one of three forms:

1. physical resources, such as plant and equipment;
2. cash and financial capacity;
3. intangible resources such as a patent, a brand name ("Intel Inside"), or a reputation.

Competencies are organizational capabilities, particularly people-based skills, knowledge, and collective learning, that are used to implement strategic activities. In the next section of this chapter, core competencies, which are unique sets of resources and capabilities, will be discussed. Particular attention must be paid to them, because they may well be the basis for winning market leadership. Furthermore, they have strategic implications that go beyond evaluation of the current opportunity.

Fit is derived from the match between a firm's strategy, which is necessarily based on its resources and core competencies, and the requirements for achieving success by meeting customer needs in the marketplace. In a subsequent section of the chapter, assessment of fit will be discussed using an example from the cancer treatment area.

Competitive differentiation is a concept that describes how well your resources and competencies, and your strategy which employs them, fit the opportunity relative to another competitor. Ultimately, the size of your firm's competitive differentiation determines how much of the business in a market opportunity you can win, and how much of the pool of potential profit from the opportunity you can win. Core competencies play a significant role in determining competitive differentiation.

Core Competencies

What Is a Core Competency?

A core competency is a unique and integrated set of resources and capabilities that allows a firm to perform some critical process better than any of its competitors, creating differentiated value for its customers.[1] The core competency can be applied to a number of opportunities over time to produce profit. There are three key elements to this definition.

A Unique and Integrated Set of Resources and Capabilities

A core competency is not a single strategic skill, but rather it is multidimensional. It is a unique combination of skills and resources, with particular emphasis on people's skills, knowledge, and collective learning. For example, consider the competencies required to reduce cycle time between order generation and fulfillment, or to incorporate customer ideas for improvement into a product. These skills typically don't all reside within a single function in the organization, but instead, they reside in a number of different functions. Embodied in a core competency is the ability to cut across traditional functional boundaries to link these capabilities to "act" in the situation. For example, Motorola's well-known focus on continuous quality improvement has required skills to be integrated across senior management functions (communication), human resources (training in their corporate university for quality), quality assurance (statistical process control), purchasing (supplier management), and manufacturing (teamwork).

The fact that core competencies are multifunctional undeniably makes them more difficult to acquire. It is very difficult, if not impossible, to buy core competencies, because they depend on the linkages between functions in an organization rather than residing in a particular technology, in a patent, or in the minds of one or two important individuals. In September 1995, EDS, a large professional services firm in the information technology field, paid more than $600 million to acquire the consulting company A.T. Kearney. EDS, which had a strong competency in the operations and implementation side of the information technology business, was hoping to acquire A.T. Kearney's core competency on the strategic side of information services and systems. The feeling at the time of the acquisition was that merging these two strong competencies would lead to new synergies across the amalgamated organization and produce new operations-oriented business with the former clients of A.T.

---

[1] This section borrows from Gary Hamel and C.K. Prahalad, *Competing for the Future* (Boston, Massachusetts: Harvard University Press, 1994).

Kearney and new strategic consulting with previous clients of EDS. However, these synergies proved to be very difficult to realize, primarily because the two groups had very different cultures.[2]

Of course, the plus side of the difficulty of acquiring core competencies is that competitors would have similar difficulties. They can't duplicate the differentiation that comes from a core competency by buying a brand-new piece of equipment, or even by hiring the people who designed it. Therefore, a core competency that is properly exploited and defended can be the basis of sustainable competitive differentiation in the marketplace.

Creating Customer Value

Core competencies aren't focused inward; instead, a core competency can readily be translated through strategy into a benefit for customers that will make them operate more successfully. Usually, if the customers in question are corporations themselves, more successful operations translate directly into more profitable operations. In other situations, particularly in consumer goods, while the core competency doesn't necessarily translate directly into increased profitability for end users, it does clearly produce differentiated value for them. For instance, a core competency in designing and producing the explosive igniter which fires a passenger-side airbag in an automobile (a difficult task because of the volume that the bag must hold) doesn't make the end customers for the automobiles more profitable, but it does have value for them. Likewise with the superior small engines that Honda builds for its motorcycles and other products. The fact that a home-owner's lawn mower starts more easily and runs more reliably doesn't necessarily have much of a direct impact on household profitability, but the added convenience has undeniable value for many consumers.

Competitive Differentiation

Core competencies aren't necessary preconditions for market entry, in the sense that all competitors must perform them at a high level in order to compete in an industry. If a given set of resources and

---

2 "What's Dragging Down A.T. Kearney?," *Business Week*, May 10, 1999.

competencies were possessed by most of the major firms competing in the industry, they couldn't be the basis for winning profitable business by beating the competition. The day that the chief competitors in an industry catch up in, for example, order fulfillment processes is the day that order fulfilling ceases to be a core competence for any of these firms. Core competencies are the foundation of strategies which create competitive advantage over most or all of the major companies in the industry.

Core competencies are distinctive from one firm to another. Merck and Glaxo were widely recognized as the two most successful pharmaceutical companies of the 1980s and early 1990s. However, the two firms developed distinctly different sets of capabilities in research, development, and marketing. Merck was renowned for its ability to identify opportunities very early in a broad range of therapeutic categories and then move multiple projects successfully through development. Glaxo, on the other hand, had a much narrower range of development projects, but it developed a significant core competency in bringing a few new products (Zantac was the major example) rapidly into global markets. Undeniably, both firms were very successful. However, they followed different paths to success and developed different core competencies in order to do so.

What Is a Constraining Incompetency?

A constraining incompetency, or a capability gap, is an inability to carry out strategic actions which are vital for success in an opportunity. These gaps can be the result of lack of resources or lack of skills. Constraining incompetencies have the power to cripple an organization's strategic response to an opportunity; they must be overcome or circumvented if you are going to capitalize on the market opportunity. Otherwise, you should drop the opportunity from consideration, because you can't win with it.

One leading business school concentrated for many years on residential management development programs that were two weeks or more in duration. The school successfully offered a problem-based, integrated experience to participants, staffed entirely by its own faculty. The faculty was made up of excellent classroom instructors, particularly skilled at leading case discussions. When the school attempted to develop, market, and conduct shorter courses of one to three days', duration, it discovered that it had several capability gaps.

First, it lacked the marketing competency to recruit large numbers of participants for these courses. This problem was compounded by the fact that not many of its faculty had names which were widely enough recognized in the target market to "pull" much new business.

Next, the school's residential facilities, which had been managed quite successfully for the two-to-five-week programs, were not well suited for integrating a number of short courses alongside the current programs. Scheduling the two types of programs was problematic, because the first-come, first-served tradition now meant that long courses were in danger of preemption by lower-margin short courses. Finally, the faculty did not enjoy the brief teaching slots because there was insufficient time to get to know the managers and their problems. Some of these deficiencies could have been overcome by hiring new instructors or using off-site facilities. However, the school was unable to make a profitable business out of the opportunity. Its capability gaps could not be overcome while maintaining profitability in the business.

Identifying Core Competencies

Widely shared agreement on what an organization's core competencies are is a necessary requirement for managing them. To utilize the notion of core competencies in evaluating market opportunities, you must first have a realistic idea of just what they are, and what skills and resources will be necessary to maintain them or to develop new ones.

Some rough guidelines are helpful for identifying core competencies. It is likely that a successful organization (or a strategic business unit in a large corporation) will have only a very few such competencies, say two to five, but not twenty-five or thirty. Core competencies are more than long lists of corporate strengths. Furthermore, although core competencies can lead to competitive advantage, the converse isn't necessarily true: not all competitive advantages are necessarily linked directly to core competencies. For example, readily available inexpensive labor or available production capacity might constitute a competitive advantage at a given time, but neither would qualify as a core competency. Neither one is necessarily sustainable, which is a key dimension of competitive advantage.

The common way of identifying core competencies is through brainstorming and subsequent discussion by senior managers, often as part of another process such as re-engineering or strategy development. Mapping essential corporate processes is one way of uncovering core competencies, because these processes will show activities crossing functional boundaries. Distinguishing between a resource or skill of an organization and a core competency is important, because investments to develop and preserve core competencies must be given a high strategic priority. They are the basis of a strategic business unit's competitive differentiation.

Identifying Your Organization's Core Competencies

Here are some questions that can help identify your organization's core competencies:

- Can the competency be related to a bundle of skills and resources rather than a single skill or resource? Usually, core competencies are the result of a considerable accumulation of practical experience, knowledge, and training. For instance, consider Wal-Mart's powerful supply chain management competency, anchored in its cross-docking system, which enables it to break down and reship orders from suppliers to its stores within 48 hours of receiving them. This requires links among many of its functions in order to manage hugely complex flows of information and materials. Retail store management, purchasing and supplier relations, inventory management, and warehousing all must be linked, not just by a data network and software, but also by shared goals and experience in working together. A major resource commitment is required to manage this process, including, in this case, Wal-Mart's investments in its own software development and satellite capacity for data transmission.

- Can the competency be linked directly to increased customer value? In most circumstances, at least one of a successful organization's core competencies connects with meeting customer needs and delivering the product or service to it. This means, as the previous chapter discussed in connection with the market chain, that the customer's business is well understood, so that the supplier can ensure that its products or services create value for the customer.

- Can the competency be easily matched by competition? If so, it is really not a core competency. Because core competencies don't reside in a single person, or a single function, and much of their power is based on experience at cross-functional cooperation, they can't easily be copied. To illustrate this point, let's return to the Wal-Mart example for a moment. By spending millions of dollars in resources, a firm could build a replica of the logistics system and information technology which underlies this core competency, and even buy its own satellite to transmit the necessary data, but it couldn't duplicate the experience base and values that the Wal-Mart organization has developed in working to reduce inventory without reducing customer service levels.

Managing Core Competencies

In the long-term success of the business, core competencies are the foundation of profitable market strategies. One example of an organization that has done an excellent job of nurturing a core competency is 3M Corporation. 3M is widely known for its success in managing the process of innovation. What underlies this core competency? The answer is multifaceted:

- An organizational culture that supports innovation. A new venture can draw on resources, such as technical or scientific expertise, anywhere in the organization. All individuals are allowed to spend up to 15% of their time on their own projects, if they feel they may ultimately benefit 3M.

- Organizational systems that measure achievements in innovation. All divisions have goals of realizing at least 25% of their revenue from products introduced in the last five years.

- Tolerance for well-intentioned failures.

- Insistence on market involvement by its research and development people. They are encouraged to meet with customers early in the development process, show them what is being produced, listen to their feedback, and, if possible, sell them something. This "make a little, sell a little" philosophy helps insure that no large investments are made on products that miss the market by not satisfying customer needs.

- Patient money. 3M's microreplication technology, which is now projected to produce $10 billion of sales in the early 2000s, has required 30 years of investment.

If you are to maintain profitable leadership in the areas where you choose to compete, it is imperative that you maintain leadership in the core competencies which underpin that leadership. In fact, there might even be some shifts in core competency requirements as a new product ages. The competencies required to introduce it (e.g., innovation, working with early adopters) might well be somewhat different than those required after it has "crossed the chasm" (e.g., large-scale production and efficient order fulfillment processes).

Should You "Make" or "Buy" Strategic Activities Associated with Core Competencies?

Key strategic activities associated with core competencies should not be outsourced, or you could be creating a chance for your competitors to cut your lead in critical areas.[3] At the same time, you might well outsource other strategic activities that compete with the core competencies for scarce resources in your company. That way, more of the critical resources are devoted to building leadership in the core competencies that the company has defined for its future. Honda is well known for its small motor design and manufacturing core competency. In order to preserve its lead in this "mission-critical" area, it does all small-engine research and development internally, designs and builds much of its own specialized tooling, and produces all critical parts for these motors in its own closely protected manufacturing facilities. If Honda permitted outside machine tool builders to manufacture its production equipment, some of the capabilities which underpin its core competency could "leak" through these suppliers to its competitors.

In practice, there can be a considerable benefit to a clear designation of an area that is to be protected and developed as a core competency. There can be considerable momentum associated with leadership in an area. It attracts the most challenging assignments from customers, typically at high margins, which affords your people

---

[3] This discussion is based on James Brian Quinn and Frederick G. Helmer, "Strategic Outsourcing," *Sloan Management Review* (Summer 1994), pp. 43–55.

the opportunity for further development as they stretch to deliver on state-of-the-art commitments. For example, Porsche takes on some of the most challenging engineering problems facing other automotive manufacturers so that it can insure state-of-the-art assignments for Porsche engineers, which will further develop its engineering core competency.

Furthermore, the chance to work with the leading people in an area, and the leading-edge customers, is attractive to the qualified high-potential people in the hiring pool. The highly skilled employee base then helps in attracting the most challenging development jobs, thereby building further on the core competency and making the firm even more attractive for the next round of hiring. Microsoft is currently benefiting a great deal from these factors. Throughout the '90s, the company has consistently attracted many of the best university graduates in computer science and engineering, because it is seen as the leading firm in the industry.

Customer Value and Profit Creation Model

By a combination of strategic investments and a process of continuous improvement, some companies have been able to create extremely powerful customer-value and profit-creation "engines." These engines or models link some or all of the organization's competencies and core competencies into a powerful profit-creation entity that is tightly focused on creating value for its target customers. This value is superior to that created by any of its competitors. The activities that these firms perform in the customer-value and profit-creation engine are consistent with each other and reinforce each other.

An ideal scenario for such a firm is if one or more of the new opportunities being assessed is a good fit with the existing customer-value and profit-creation model in the business. Applying the model in a related new situation is likely to lead to new learning, which may very well allow the firm to improve its performance in the opportunities it was originally pursuing. Honda represents a good example of such a company. From its early days in the motorcycle business, it developed core competencies in two major areas: the design and manufacturing of engines, and all aspects of the development and management of widespread networks of servicing dealers. It was able to manage a powerful customer-value and profit-creation model leveraging these two core competencies from its original motorcycle business into such varied businesses as automobiles, snowmobiles, lawnmowers, and portable generators. In doing this, it further refined its original competencies and thereby enhanced its competitive position in its original businesses.

Mapping Competencies and Customer Requirements

Figure 5-2 suggests that your competencies can be arrayed on a continuum by comparing them with leading competitors.

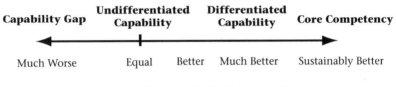

FIGURE 5-2: An Array of Competencies

Capability gaps, or constraining incompetencies, are areas where your performance is significantly worse than your best competitor's, and core competencies reflect areas where you perform much better than the best competition. The most serious of these capability gaps can be major constraints on your ability to respond to an opportunity. They are areas where a competitor has a core competency in an area where you are seriously deficient.

Figure 5-3 extends this map by adding in considerations about the opportunity which might go beyond customer requirements. What are the requirements for success? Which are absolutely critical? Which are merely "nice to have" with regard to strategic importance?

Eight zones are delineated in the chart. Clearly, if any of the requirements for success in the market opportunity are in the upper left area, you are at a significant competitive disadvantage, because you have a capability gap on a critical success factor. A manufacturing and order fulfillment process that is unable to meet customer requirements in an industry moving toward "pull system" manufacturing

Resources and Capabilities for the Requirement

	Capability Gap	**Undiffer- entiated**	**Positive Differentiation**	**Core Competency**
Critical	Losing Position	Standoff	Advantage	Winning Position
Minor	Minor Disadvantage	Zone of Indifference	Minor Advantage	Advantage

Importance of Opportunity Requirement (shown between the Critical and Minor rows on the left)

FIGURE 5-3: Mapping Capabilities vs. Requirements for Success

(where customers want high service from suppliers so they can cut their inventory investments) would be a deal-breaker. Competencies which fall into the "Losing Position" cell in the figure must be addressed if you are to have any chance at winning profitable business in the opportunity. If they can't easily be addressed internally in a timely fashion, or remedied through some sort of strategic alliance, the opportunity should be abandoned rather than incur losses in trying to exploit it from a weak competitive position.

On the other hand, if one or more of the opportunity's chief requirements match your firm's core competencies (i.e., they are located in the upper right corner in the diagram), you have the potential to develop strong differentiation in the market, and the chance to leverage these core competencies into significant positive cash flow.

The second column in Figure 5-3 contains capabilities in which you and the best competitor are not differentiated, and in the third column, you are ahead, but probably not in a sustainable manner, as your lead is not based on a core competency. Overall in the chart, the bottom row contains the less important requirements for success. The most important positions are in the upper row, in the left and right columns.

Assessing a Market Opportunity: Fit With Core Competencies

At this stage, you have defined the arena of opportunities that you are prepared to consider, identified a particular market opportunity for consideration, and developed an understanding of buyer choice/rejection behavior at important points in the market chain for the opportunity. Next, you need to assess how well this opportunity fits with your competencies, particularly with your core competencies.

The first step is to define the *key requirements for success* in exploiting the opportunity. Some of these will connect directly to needs of the end customer, and some will relate to other players in the market chain. Consider the situation of QLT Phototherapeutics (formerly known as QuadraLogic Technologies), a biotechnology company in Vancouver, Canada. In 1988, QLT was confident that it was on track for successfully developing the science behind photodynamic therapy, a fourth modality (in addition to radiation, chemotherapy, and surgery) for treatment of certain forms of cancer. Photodynamic therapy was based on the development of a light-sensitive biochemical compound with an attraction to rapidly growing body tissue. When introduced to the body, the chemical would collect at the site of a tumor. Then, if the tumor could be reached with a laser via fiber optics, the chemical could be activated, destroying the nearby tissue and the tumor.

The opportunity under consideration was a pharmaceutical biotechnology compound for treatment of certain kinds of cancer (characterized by localized tumors that could be reached by the fiber optic filament). The product would be initially targeted at markets in the United States and Canada. Key requirements for success in bringing this product to market were:

- research and development on the biotechnology product;
- development of the laser and fiber optic system for this application;
- expertise in obtaining regulatory approval from the FDA and its counterparts in Canada, and subsequently Europe and Japan (designing, executing, and presenting data from extensive clinical trials is critically important here);
- marketing expertise in building a strategy for introducing the product;
- a sales force which understands the decision-making process at cancer treatment facilities and is capable of influencing it;

- cash for completing the research, and surviving until the venture could generate positive cash flow, a period of at least five years, and possibly more.

Once the key requirements for success are understood, the questions presented in Figure 5-4 can be asked. Analysis proceeds with one key requirement at a time, beginning at the top left of the diagram. The first question addressed for each requirement is whether it is related to a core competency that your organization either currently possesses or is well on its way to developing. If the answer is "Yes," the follow-up question asks whether you can now satisfy the requirement. Another "Yes" response here, and this key success requirement is recorded as a significant match for the organization. A "No" on this latter question indicates the need to build the necessary competency, because deficiencies on core competencies must be remedied internally if at all possible. Otherwise, you risk relinquishing your core competency.

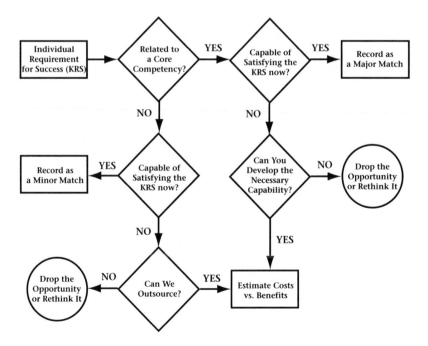

FIGURE 5-4: Assessing Corporate Fit with a Key Requirement for Success

On the other hand, if the key success requirement is not related to a core competency (so the answer to the first question in the upper left of Figure 5-4 is "No"), the next test is: "Can you satisfy the key success requirement now?" In other words, is this a requirement which, although it doesn't relate to a core competency, can still be met by the organization? For example, cash requirements or production capacity could play this role. If the answer is "Yes," this key success requirement is recorded as a match with organizational capabilities. If it's a "No," the next question is "Can we go outside our organization to meet the requirement—by outsourcing, or through a strategic alliance?"

The vital issue around outsourcing is whether your organization wants to put substantial resources into an area that is not a core competency. The definite conclusion here is that you shouldn't. Resources are too scarce to invest substantially in fields outside core competencies.

> A key part of the whole Winning Market Leadership Process is to focus when investing organizational resources so that they are deployed against the core competencies. Therefore, if a non-core requirement can be satisfied outside your organization by means of a strategic alliance or through outsourcing, that is the direction you should consider.

Plans should be made to buy rather than make what it takes to meet the requirement, or to obtain it through a joint venture or some other strategic alliance, and costs of this step should be estimated. If the answer is "No," you must either drop the opportunity (as you can't satisfy a key requirement for success), or rethink it. If capability to meet this requirement is so rare that you can't access it, you should consider a major investment to make it a core competency of your own. Needless to say, this would be a strategic issue that would very likely involve examining a whole portfolio of potential opportunities beyond just the one you are currently examining. Issues such as these will be more thoroughly covered in Chapter 7.

Let's return briefly to the QLT Phototherapeutics example. Figure 5-5 provides a summary of key requirements for success of the venture and fit.

Key Requirement	Core Competency	Can Be Satisfied	Can Be Outsourced	Fit
1. Biotechnology R&D	Yes	Yes	N/A	Yes
2. Laser & Fiber Optics	No	No	Yes	Outsource
3. Regulatory Expertise	No	No	Yes	Outsource
4. Marketing Expertise	No	No	Yes	Outsource
5. Sales Resources	No	No	Yes	Outsource
6. Cash	No	No	Yes	Joint Venture

FIGURE 5-5: QLT Phototherapeutics: Fit with Key Requirements
for Success in Photodynamic Therapy for Cancer

In this case, only the basic biotech research capabilities (Requirement 1) could be considered to be related to the corporation's core competencies at this stage. That is not to say that there weren't other requirements which might have been core competencies in larger, more experienced organizations—marketing, clinical trial, and sales force expertise, in this situation. QLT would indeed have been very happy to develop core competencies in these areas, but they were a long way from doing so. At the time, they had only two other business units (manufacturing generic pharmaceuticals and basic diagnostic kits), each with low revenue and profit. Acquiring the resources necessary to develop one of these other competencies was clearly beyond QLT's grasp at this point in their history.

For the areas which don't relate to a current core competency, the next question is whether these requirements can be satisfied now. Sometimes, resources to meet requirements for non-core competencies exist at the time the opportunity is being considered, and sometimes they don't. In the case of QLT Phototherapeutics, none of the other requirements (2 through 6) could be met internally. As the table makes clear, some major shortfalls existed between the requirements for success in bringing photodynamic therapy to market and QLT's existing competencies. Their core competency in biotechnology research and development would not be sufficient to see them through to market success. In fact, without considerable assistance from outside sources, they were very unlikely to reach the market at all. Fortunately for them, their core competency in biotechnology was so strong that they were an attractive partner. They subsequently signed a joint venture with American Cyanamid which provided them with the competencies and resources they were lacking. After a long and costly struggle, they reached the market in 1995 and were just beginning to generate significant positive cash flows in the late 1990s, although the company was not yet profitable.

Next Step: Understanding the Competitive Challenge

In this chapter we have examined the ability of the firm to respond to an opportunity, and through its response to create long-run competitive advantage by committing resources to its core competencies. The next chapter introduces competitive analysis.

Key Questions for Executives and Managers

- What are the critical strategic resource and competency requirements for competitive differentiation and success in this opportunity? What specific strategic activities will have to be done with excellence?

- When you look at the critical strategic requirements to create competitive differentiation, can you meet these requirements now? Where are the major missing competencies?

- Do you know what your core competencies are? Can your strategic response to this opportunity employ them? If so, which ones, and how? What competitive differentiation will be produced? If you are not employing any of your core competencies, why do you think you can gain competitive differentiation?

- Will your strategic response to this opportunity build on an existing core competency? What leverage will this gain in competencies provide for you in other opportunities?

- Do you have any constraining incompetencies—strategic activities that you do poorly and can't easily improve? For example, trying to get into a low-cost production opportunity when you are a high-cost manufacturer.

- What level of resources will be necessary to create and sustain the critical core competencies in this particular opportunity? Does this opportunity represent a place where the resources should be committed to these core competencies? Will these core competencies have applicability in other opportunities in the future?

- Of the strategic activities necessary to capitalize on this opportunity, which should you do internally, and which should you outsource? For each strategic activity that you perform yourselves, what competitive differentiation can you gain by improving a specific core competency?

- When you look at your competitors in this opportunity, do they have the opportunity of creating core competencies that will overwhelm yours and the opportunity? How might they do this if they decided to try?

CHAPTER SIX

Understand the Competitive Challenge

Introduction

At this stage in the planning process you will have screened a number of market opportunities to determine whether they are potentially attractive and profitable for the strategic business unit (SBU). Undoubtedly, some that looked quite attractive at a superficial level will have turned out to be much less attractive after a thorough investigation of the market forces affecting the market segment and after understanding likely buyer/choice rejection in the market chain. The internal assessment and the fit of the remaining opportunities to the resources and competencies of the company may also have led to some other opportunities being eliminated or being graded as less attractive.

At some stage in the planning process, you must develop a thorough understanding of the competitive environment so that you can better assess your SBU's ability to win a substantial share of the profitability represented by a particular market opportunity. Choosing opportunities also means that you are choosing competitors and the competitive environment in which you will be trying to win market leadership. In assessing the competitive environment, you should be careful not to assume that it is a "zero-sum" game. Sometimes, there are some real opportunities to shape the competitive environment, so that some, or all, of the players are better off, including you.[1] By working with your market chain partners and those with products or services that complement your product, you may be able to increase the profit "pie" associated with a particular opportunity.

> Some companies clearly put a high priority on gaining a thorough understanding of the competitive arenas in which they compete, while other companies don't. One leading Japanese company has several hundred people in the United States focused on competitive and market analysis, and these people funnel important competitive intelligence back to the business units in Japan.

The purpose of any competitive analysis is to develop a thorough understanding of the competitive environment surrounding a market opportunity. The market and competitive forces analysis discussed in Chapter 3 should give you a good understanding of the potential profitability of the market opportunity. The analysis of the competitive environment, combined with your earlier analysis of your resources and competencies, will help you to determine your ability to win a substantial share of the profitability in the opportunity. As a result of the competitive analysis you should be able to:

- better predict the future moves of competitors or potential competitors,
- understand their areas of vulnerability so that you can potentially exploit them,
- better predict their reactions to your future moves, and
- generate, through benchmarking, ideas as to how you might improve your own activities.

In fact, if you have an excellent understanding of the competitive environment, you may not only be able to predict future moves, but also be able to "shape" them, so that either you, or you and some of your competitors, benefit. In one case, a U.S. chemicals manufacturer heard that a European company was about to invest in one of its high growth, profitable markets. In response, the U.S. company

---

[1] Adam M. Brandenburger and Barry J. Nalebuff, "The Right Game: Use Game Theory to Shape Strategy," *Harvard Business Review* (July–August, 1995), pp.57–71.

restructured its prices for the various grades of product in its product line. This resulted in the European competitor designing its production facility to produce the most "profitable" products in the line. Once the European competitor had built the facility, the U.S. manufacturer readjusted its prices, making the products the European manufacturer had committed to less profitable. This undoubtedly influenced the European company's future investment plans, while allowing the U.S. producer to continue to earn attractive returns on its key products.

As a side benefit of a competitive analysis, you often learn a great deal about your competitors' operations. Sometimes these competitive "benchmarks" can be used to improve your own operations. For example, you may find that the way a competitor has organized its sales force and distribution system makes it much more effective at selling its products into a highly segmented market.

Process of Competitive Analysis

A useful process for conducting a competitive analysis is shown in Figure 6-1. On the left-hand side of this diagram are some of the major issues a company must address if it is to develop a thorough understanding of its competitive environment. On the right-hand side are aligned some of the tools that can be useful in addressing such issues. In this chapter we will focus on these issues and how the various tools can be used to develop an improved understanding of the competitive environment, so that the SBU team can develop useful action plans. Rarely will you need to use all the tools. The challenge is to find the most appropriate tools that will give you useful insights in a timely manner. Often just a quick cycle through each of the tools will help you select the right set for a particular situation and in that way ensure you are not "blindsided" by a potential competitive action or reaction.

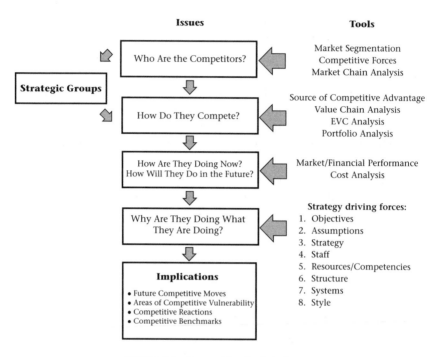

FIGURE 6-1: Competitive Analysis Process

Issues in the Competitive Analysis Process

Identification of Competitors

At this stage in the planning process the current, potential and indirect competitors should be clear. The market segmentation analysis, the development of an understanding of the market chain, and the market forces analysis should have given the SBU team a good understanding of the competitors the SBU will face in the market and the potential competitors that could choose to move into the market.

The indirect competitors, which represent the alternative ways or substitute ways to meet the same customer need but with a different technology, will also have been identified as part of the market forces analysis. The products and services produced this way represent a particular concern if they are on a rapidly improving price-performance curve relative to our product, and if they are produced by profitable companies that have the resources to aggressively market them. Thus videoconferencing services, which are both on a rapidly improving price/performance curve and marketed by large, profitable telephone companies, should be a major competitive concern for airlines and airframe manufacturers, such as Boeing and Airbus.

> The focus on indirect competition and substitutes is an important one today, since the biggest competitive threats in many technology-intensive markets do not come from direct competitors. Rather it is the competition from other market chains (and their webs) that may be attempting to meet the same customer needs with products and services based on very different technologies.

The list of current, potential and indirect competitors can be a very long one. However, often much of the competitive analysis task can be simplified by organizing the competitors into strategic groups. A strategic group is a group of companies that compete in the marketplace in similar ways. For example, in many of the major airline markets in the world, there are two broad strategic groups of airlines: the large full-service airlines that are often members of global alliances, and the smaller, often regional airlines that compete largely on the basis of low fares. The former group includes such airlines as American Airlines, British Airways, and Singapore Airlines. The latter group includes Southwest Airlines and EasyJet. Similarly, semiconductor companies can be divided into two broad strategic groups, those that operate their own fabs (semiconductor manufacturing facilities) and those that don't.

Often, part of the competitive analysis can be done at the level of the strategic groups, since the companies in each group frequently have similar strengths and weaknesses and similar strategies, use similar market chains, and may very well react in similar ways to environmental changes or competitive moves. This method may allow an SBU team to do much of its analysis based on five strategic groups, rather than twenty-five individual companies. At some point, when it becomes clear which of the competitors are strategically most important, it will probably be necessary to move down to the level of the individual competitors. But this need only be done for these significant competitors.

How Do They Compete?

Basic Strategy

As we will discuss more fully in Chapter 7, companies generally follow one of two basic strategies: cost leadership or differentiation. A company competing with a cost leadership strategy attempts to provide "acceptable" products to its target customers at low prices. A company following a differentiation strategy attempts to differentiate its products and services from those of its competitors by being a leader in developing innovative products and services that better meet the needs of its customers or by forging a tight, intimate relationship with its customers that its competitors will find difficult to penetrate (sometimes called customer intimacy).[2] Hewlett-Packard and 3M are classic examples of companies that have played a product leadership game very effectively in some of their businesses. Conner, a leading supplier of disk drives for personal computers in the early and mid-1990s, developed an intimate relationship with Compaq Computer and was able to differentiate itself from its competitors through this strong relationship.

In addition, companies can sometimes effectively exploit other sources of competitive advantage to buttress their basic strategic approach. These would include speed to market (a particular strength that MCI was able to exploit at several times to compete with AT&T in the U.S. long-distance telephone market), market access, brand equity, and economies of scale or scope.

Value Chain Analysis

An important tool for understanding how competitors compete is value chain or business system analysis. The value chain or business system describes the collection of activities that an SBU performs to produce, market, deliver, and support its products and services. These collectively determine the value it will create for its customers and its costs and cost structure. While there are various ways of describing the value chain or business system, the generic

---

[2] This discussion is based partly on the work of Michael Treacy and Fred Wiersema, "Customer Intimacy and Other Value Disciplines," *Harvard Business Review* (January-February 1993), pp. 84–93.

one developed by Michael Porter is widely used (see Figure 6-2). In this model, Porter divides a firm's activities into two kinds: primary activities, which involve the creation of the product, the logistics activities pre- and post-sales, marketing and sales, and the various service activities associated with the product; and support activities, which include technology development, procurement, human resource management, and the firm's infrastructure. Collectively these activities create customer value and result in the company having a particular cost structure. The customer is willing to pay a certain amount for this customer value package and this, less the total cost of creating the value, is the firm's margin.

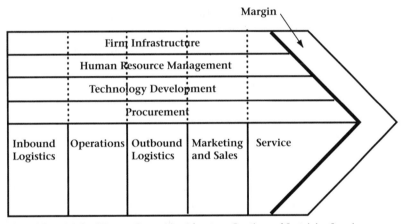

Adapted from Michael Porter, *Competitive Advantage: Creating and Sustaining Superior Performance* (New York: Free Press, 1985).

FIGURE 6-2: Value Chain

It is crucially important to understand how each of the SBU's key competitors or strategic groups of competitors create value and incur costs, because this can have important implications for identifying areas of vulnerability and likely actions and reactions. Clearly a company that outsources important activities, such as the development of significant pieces of its technology, is dependent on the ability of its suppliers to keep abreast of technology. Dell Computers faced this situation in the notebook computer market in the early 1990s, when its supplier of technology for this product line failed for a time to keep up with IBM and Toshiba, Dell's main competitors in this segment. Dell ended up failing to capture a significant share of this rapidly growing segment of the computer market during this time. It later reentered the market and has been very successful.

Economic Value to the Customer Analysis

Economic Value to the Customer Analysis (EVC analysis) is a useful tool for comparing an existing or proposed product to a competitor's product. In EVC analysis, you try to move beyond just comparing the cost of two products to a customer to looking at the customer's life-cycle ownership costs of your product and a competitor's offering.

A typical EVC analysis is shown in Figure 6-3. If you assume your competitor's current product is shown at the left of the diagram, you can see that the life-cycle ownership costs for a particular customer is $1,000, including purchase price, start-up costs (such as installation and training), and post-purchase costs (such as energy costs and maintenance costs). If you are able to develop a new product (Product X), which provides the same benefits to the customer, but has lower start-up costs and post-purchase costs, a fully rational customer would be willing to pay up to $600 for Product X. Usually, we would not charge the full $600, but somewhat less, giving the customer an incentive to switch to our new, and probably less proven, product. If another potential new product (Product Y) provides greater benefits to the customer than the competitor's current product and you can quantify these benefits (shown as incremental gross margin to the customer of $300 in Figure 6-3), then the fully rational customer will be willing to pay up to $700 for Product Y. Usually this type of analysis should be done on the basis of quite small segments, since the value of the product could vary from one group of customers to another. For example, if our product is much more efficient in its use of energy than competitive products and energy is a significant cost component, our EVC will be higher in geographical markets where energy costs are higher.

EVC analysis is extremely useful in helping you determine how your products compare with competitors' products and provides important information on how you might position your products relative to competitive offerings. For example, Dantec, a small Canadian high-technology company that makes sophisticated systems for controlling industrial drying processes, uses EVC analysis to justify its prices, which are higher than those for less sophisticated systems.

Dantec is able to demonstrate that a customer, by using its technology, can run its production process so that it produces a food product very close to its moisture specification. This can significantly lower its production costs. Essentially, Dantec's system allows the customer to sell a product with the maximum amount of water in it! This economizes on the more expensive grain, sweetener or meat that would be found in a product.

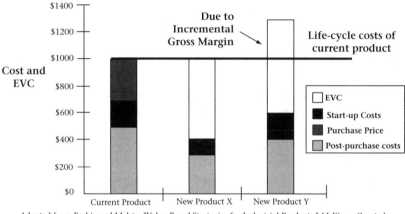

Adapted from Forbis and Mehta, "Value-Based Strategies for Industrial Products," *McKinsey Quarterly* (Summer 1981), pp. 35-52.

FIGURE 6-3: Economic Value to the Customer

Portfolio Analysis

In order to get a better understanding of a competitor's vulnerabilities and likely future actions and reactions, it is often useful to build a picture of the competitor's business and product portfolio. A careful examination of the portfolio can often provide information about the importance and attractiveness of the business or product line the SBU is, or will be, competing with, compared to the competitor's other businesses and product lines. In addition, a careful study of the portfolio can help the management team understand the financial and other resources the competitor may be able to draw on to support the contested business or product line.

For example, in 1996 Dell Computer Corporation entered the server segment of the PC market. Its entry into this segment of the market seemed to have been motivated by two things: the opportunity to earn attractive profits in this segment of the market and the need to negatively affect the profits Compaq was earning in the segment. By the mid-1990s, the server segment of the PC market was by far the most profitable, since the market and competitive forces in this segment of the market were much weaker than in the desktop or even the notebook segments. Compaq controlled well over 30% of this segment globally and it was believed to be the most profitable part of its PC business. Dell believed Compaq was using the profits from this business to support its efforts in the desktop and notebook segments, and Dell felt it had to do something about it. As Dell assistant vice president Hilly Fuchs said, "Compaq can and does use excess server margins to compete against us in desktops and notebooks.... To neutralize that, Dell needs to be in the server market."[3]

A classic example of how a competitor's portfolio of products can effectively restrict its freedom to move competitively occurred when Amdahl entered the mainframe computer market in the late-1970s. At that time the mainframe computer market was dominated by IBM. Amdahl was founded by Gene Amdahl, who had been a lead designer for IBM on the IBM 360 series of mainframe computers. Amdahl believed that by the mid-1970s a number of large organizations had sophisticated information technology staffs. He was thinking of companies such as AT&T, Citibank, and General Electric. Most of these organizations also either bought their computers from the manufacturer outright or leased them from third parties. Amdahl was convinced that the costs of marketing, customer support, and manufacturer-financed leasing for this segment were very low.

Historically, the barrier preventing companies from switching from one mainframe computer supplier to another had been the operating system, since most customers had made huge investments in software that could not very easily be moved from one company's operating system to a competitor's. He decided to introduce a line of IBM-compatible equipment priced about 20% below IBM's and with equivalent performance.

Amdahl believed that even though he was using more advanced technology than IBM, his manufacturing costs would be higher, since he lacked IBM's volumes and experience. But he knew that in setting prices for its large mainframes, IBM took into account the

---

3 "Dial Dell for Servers," *Business Week*, September 16, 1996, p. 102.

"average cost" of marketing, customer support, and financing across all purchasers of its large mainframes. By targeting very narrowly the most sophisticated group of IBM customers, Amdahl knew that his actual costs would be much lower than IBM's average costs. This gave him the opportunity to underprice IBM and still make a profit (see Figure 6-4).

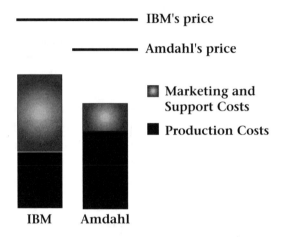

FIGURE 6-4: IBM's and Amdahl's Cost Structures and Prices

The main issue for Amdahl was how IBM would react. In the short run, IBM had little freedom. Almost all the short-term moves it might make would hurt IBM as much as or more than Amdahl. For example, if IBM decided to drop the price on the IBM 370 model most directly competitive with Amdahl's machine, it would also have to reduce the prices of all the neighboring models in order to maintain its price performance curve.[4] At the time this would have cost IBM hundreds of millions of dollars in lost profits. The tactic of using FUD (fear, uncertainty, and doubt) about Amdahl's future prospects to discourage customers from buying the Amdahl product would also be less effective, because the most sophisticated users (Amdahl's target) are the least influenced by this tactic. One

---

[4] Many manufacturers who have a closely related line of products array them on a price performance curve. Thus, a customer buying a model with 20% more performance than the model below it in the line will pay a certain price premium, say 15%. When the models in the product line are plotted on a log-log graph of price and performance, the line connecting them is called the price-performance curve. If the data is plotted on a log-log graph, the curve often approximates a straight line.

approach open to IBM was to start introducing new technology at an accelerated rate. This would make it expensive and difficult for the smaller, resource-constrained Amdahl to keep up. But even here, IBM was limited in what it could do in the short run, since many of its computers were rented or leased and it did not want this rental and lease base to become obsolete prematurely, because again this would have a significant negative impact on IBM's financial results. Ultimately, IBM did start accelerating the rate of technology introduction, but not until it had reduced the size of its rental base. It also increased the price of the operating system software and lowered the price of its hardware, making it less economical for customers to switch to Amdahl.

This example illustrates the fact that IBM, despite all its power and resources, was quite limited in its ability to respond to Amdahl in the short run. For Gene Amdahl it meant that he had three or four years to get established in the market before the full competitive power of IBM could be brought to bear on him.

How Are They Doing Now? How Will They Do in the Future?

In doing your competitive analysis it is important to understand how well your competitors in a market opportunity are doing. This information can be very important to you, since it can indicate how strenuously a competitor will defend its market position, and the resources it may have to counter your moves. This analysis should not be a static one. Rather you should also attempt to predict how your competition will do in the opportunity over time. An important aspect of this is trying to understand how your competitors' costs will change over time.

Market Share/Financial Performance

As a couple of the examples earlier in this chapter have suggested, it is important to track the market and financial performance at the company, business unit, and product line level. Performance can have a major impact on a competitor's likely moves and its vulnerability to your moves. An understanding of Compaq's financial performance in the server business motivated Dell to enter this segment of the PC market.

Cost Analysis

Cost analysis is an important tool that can help a company estimate the financial performance of its key competitors. In many industries, companies routinely buy new products produced by their competitors, tear them down, reverse-engineer them, and estimate the production costs. When the findings are combined with data on the competitor's logistics, marketing and selling costs, and the margins it gives to other players in its market chains, an SBU is often able to accurately estimate a competitor's costs and profitability.

In process industries, such as chemicals, the issue becomes one of estimating the capital costs and operating costs of a competitor's production facilities as well as its raw materials costs. Again, when these data are combined with information on logistics and marketing and selling costs, costs and profitability can often be measured quite accurately. Marketing and selling costs can be estimated by monitoring the competitor's use of advertising media and its promotional expenditures and by determining the size of a competitor's sales force and its average compensation.

In the case of major strategic moves, companies have invested well over a million dollars in estimating the costs and profitability of all the major competitors in a market. In one case, a large competitor in a commodity segment of the chemical industry estimated the costs and profitability of all the North American players in this segment of the industry before it made a billion dollar investment to try to move into an undisputed leadership position in the product segment in North America. From its analysis, it realized that one of the smaller players in the industry was in a very precarious financial position and was probably on the verge of leaving the market. This player was not an attractive acquisition target for the company doing the analysis, but it was potentially very attractive to one of a couple of European competitors, who were rumored to be considering entering the North American market. The company decided to reduce the competitive pressure it was exerting on this player in the short run to allow its profits to rise, so that it would be less tempted to leave the market. It instructed its salespersons to let this competitor win business from it at certain accounts that both companies were targeting, giving a temporary boost to its competitor's profitability.

Experience curve analysis can be a useful tool for projecting existing cost positions into the future. Experience curve analysis is based on the considerable amount of evidence that has been gathered by the Boston Consulting Group and others that shows that every time the accumulated experience of producing a product or service is doubled, the real (adjusted for inflation) cost of production[5] can be lowered by a certain percentage, often between 10 and 30%.[6] An important word in this statement is "can"—the experience curve merely provides the potential for cost reduction.

Managers and other employees must take the necessary steps to turn the potential into a reality. We are all very aware of the power of the experience curve in new, fast-growing industries, such as many segments of the electronics industry. Here, early in the life cycle of a new type of product, such as a cellular telephone, we see many doublings of accumulated experience in a couple of years resulting in rapidly falling prices. In more mature industries, such as many basic chemicals like polyvinyl chloride, it may take more than a decade to double accumulated experience, making the impact of the experience curve on costs and prices much less visible and often hidden by the much bigger changes occurring in the raw materials costs.

Thus, if a competitor is aggressively pursuing experience-based cost reductions, you should recognize that its costs are not constant and, in fact, could be changing quite rapidly. It is important for the management team to know how aggressively a competitor is pursuing these cost reductions.

Indicators of aggressive efforts to take advantage of the potential benefits of the experience curve include frequent redesign of the product to reduce its costs, investment in the latest production equipment, and management and employee incentive systems that are tied to the results of cost reduction efforts. This kind of information might be available from a variety of sources, including monitoring changes in the competitor's product, discussions with some of the competitor's key suppliers, interviews with former employees, and press reports.

---

[5] Really the cost of doing the value-added, unless a company is able to take advantage of its suppliers' experience curves.

[6] Pankaj Ghemawat, "Building Strategy on the Experience Curve," *Harvard Business Review* (March–April 1985), pp. 143–149.

Analysis of Strategy Driving Forces

A number of factors influence the strategy and tactics of a competitor. An understanding of each of these strategy driving forces, and particularly changes in any of these forces, can help a company identify areas of vulnerability and predict a competitor's future actions. In some cases these forces not only drive a competitor's strategy in a certain direction, but also inhibit it from moving in other directions. For example, a company's structure and systems may make it slow moving and unable to respond quickly enough in a fast-changing market. We will briefly review each of the strategy driving forces in turn.

Objectives

The objectives of a company can have a significant influence on its strategic and tactical moves. Some companies view themselves as the market or technology leader and will sometimes go to great lengths to maintain their leadership position. In its battles with Kodak in the instant photography market, Polaroid continually tried to maintain its technological leadership position. Other companies have very concrete financial objectives that significantly affect their market behavior. For example, a company that brags about having 10 years of year-on-year improvements in quarterly financial results is likely to go to extraordinary lengths to maintain this record, even if it means some sacrifice in short-run market share to maintain profitability.

Assumptions

A company's behavior in the market is also influenced by its assumptions—assumptions about the market, about itself, and about its competitors. For example, a company's decision to invest in a particular business or market is usually influenced by its assumptions about its size, growth rate, and profitability. There is evidence that in some cases companies have tried to discourage competitive entry by repeatedly and publicly stating that even though they are doing a lot of business in the market, they are finding it difficult to earn a reasonable profit.

A leading financial services firm that introduced a new technology-based service requiring massive investments in new systems "moaned and groaned" publicly about how difficult it was to make money with the new service. At least one observer considered this to be a conscious tactical move.

Apparently, other competitors, who had a much smaller base of customers over which to amortize the systems development cost, were discouraged from entering the market by this negative information. Ultimately, most were forced to enter, regardless of the profitability, because the innovator was capturing many of their customers and most of these customers were bringing their other, much more profitable, business to the innovator.

Strategy

Some companies are remarkably consistent in employing the same strategy over and over in the various markets in which they compete. For many years Texas Instruments (TI) was famous for using experience curve based pricing strategies to penetrate new markets for its semiconductor products. Often, this strategy involved initially selling the new products below cost, but counting on the power of the experience curve to reduce costs rapidly, so that ultimately the product would be profitable. By pricing aggressively, TI was frequently able to capture significant market share rapidly, and the low prices caused rapid market growth. When the strategy worked well, TI ended up with the dominant market share in the targeted markets. At this point it was often achieving good margins as a result of taking full advantage of the benefits of the experience curve. Many Japanese and Korean firms have followed similar strategies.

Structure

A competitor's organizational structure can often give important clues about how quickly and how effectively it can respond to threats and opportunities in a given market. If an effective response requires that two or more business units work effectively together, the speed with which the response will occur will almost always be slower than when the response is the responsibility of one business unit alone.

Rolm, one of the successful early entrants into the electronic PBX market, was confident that AT&T would not be able to produce a comparable product to its PBX for several years, even though AT&T had vast resources committed to the project.   This was because Rolm's top management knew the difficulties that Bell Laboratories, Western Electric, and the Bell operating companies would have working effectively together given their different objectives and agendas.

Staff

An important determinant of a competitor's behavior is the kinds of people it has in key positions. What are their backgrounds? What sort of training and education do they have? Where have they spent their careers both in the company and externally? What accomplishments have propelled them to their current positions? Answers to these questions can provide useful insights. For example, in a crisis, the top management team often will fall back on the strategies and tactics with which they are most comfortable. A CEO with a sales or marketing background may focus on sales or marketing initiatives to solve the crisis, whereas an engineer might fall back on R&D as the solution, or an accountant look to cost-cutting as the solution.   This was evident at Polaroid over the years, where the response to almost any threat posed by Kodak to its instant photography business was technology-based.

Resources and Competencies

Clearly, with the considerable emphasis on core competencies today, an important shaper of competitors' behavior is their core competencies and their resources.   In anticipating competitive moves, it is important to monitor competitors' efforts to develop or improve resources and competencies. Often the earliest indicator of a competitor's efforts to develop new or improved competencies is its hiring activity. Thus, when Procter & Gamble began hiring scientists with a pharmaceutical background, it was an early indicator of its commitment to a new market. Patent activity can be another early indicator of a company's success at developing a new area of technological competency.

Systems

A very important determinant of behavior is a company's systems. The capital budgeting system, the cost accounting system, the management incentive system, and the performance review system can all have significant effects on a competitor's behavior in the marketplace. For example, the CEO of one semiconductor company was well known for a heavy focus on manufacturing yields and employed stringent yield targets against which performance was reviewed on a monthly basis. As a result of this element in the performance review system, the design engineers used very conservative designs, which would allow high yields. The very conservative designs meant that the company was not competitive in many product segments and ended up focusing on small opportunities that didn't attract other competitors. This information was quite useful to some of its competitors.

Style

Many companies have a particular style of behavior that is sometimes driven by the personality of the CEO. Some companies are slow and bureaucratic, and others tend to "shoot from the hip." Some companies are extremely combative and will respond aggressively to any challenge. Motorola encountered this trait when it challenged Intel in the microprocessor market some years ago. Intel's top management mounted a campaign called "Operation Crush" to ensure that Intel won as many design competitions as possible.[7] The most senior executives of Intel, including the CEO, got involved in this campaign to ensure its success.

As the above examples suggest, it is important that companies monitor each of the driving forces for each of their chief competitors. In particular, the SBU team involved in the competitive analysis should be alert to changes in any of the areas, such as the appointment of a new CEO, since this may presage a significant change in the competitor's actions in the marketplace. As mentioned in Chapter 1, the appointment of Steve Jobs as interim CEO of Apple Computer in 1997 was followed by a number of significant changes in Apple's strategy.

---

[7] William Davidow, *Marketing High Technology* (New York: Free Press, 1986).

Pulling the Competitive Information Together

Today, the growth of the Internet has dramatically increased the quantity (if not always the quality!) of competitive information available to managers. Many companies post a large amount of useful information on their Web sites. Search engines and the availability of a variety of online data sources allow researchers and managers to rapidly assemble huge amounts of information on their competitors.[8] The challenge is to make sense of all the data and to turn the facts and figures into useful and useable information. The framework shown in Figure 6-1 can be one useful organizing tool.

Much of the information gathering for competitive analysis can be a relatively low-level activity, but the analysis of the raw data and the development of the implications for strategy require the skills of experienced managers.

When a company faces a few chief competitors, some companies assign teams of managers to role-play these competitors. Each team is provided with all the information available on the assigned competitor and is asked to digest it and decide what it would do if it were in the competitor's shoes. This information can then be taken into account as the SBU team decides what it will do.

When several SBUs in the company face the same competitor, a high-level, cross-functional, and cross-SBU team may be necessary to get the full value of the competitive analysis by taking into account the moves that might be made at the portfolio level.

Actions-Consequences-Evidence (ACE) Framework

One simple model that can help a team pull its analysis together for decision-making purposes is the ACE framework.[9] This involves laying out (perhaps in a decision tree format) the possible actions (or reactions) of a competitor, the consequences of each of these actions on the SBU's performance, and the evidence that the competitor might pursue this specific course of action. A partially completed example is shown in Figure 6-5. Clearly, if the framework is to give helpful results, a thorough competitive analysis is required to gener-

[8] Adam L. Penenberg, "Is There a Snoop on Your Site?", *Forbes* (May 17, 1999), pp. 322–325.
[9] Framework developed by Professor Mark Vandenbosch, Richard Ivey School of Business, The University of Western Ontario, London, Canada.

ate the information on likely actions, consequences, and evidence. It is also important to consider "worst case" actions and to spend time considering if any of the competitors can and will implement these actions. There will always be uncertainty in any analysis of this sort, but a good competitive analysis can greatly reduce it. Sometimes this framework will point out the need for some very specific information in a critical area, where the value of the information is likely to be very high. In such a case, a redoubling of efforts to get the essential information will potentially have a very high payoff.

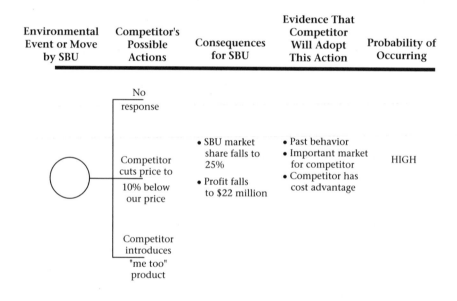

Environmental Event or Move by SBU	Competitor's Possible Actions	Consequences for SBU	Evidence That Competitor Will Adopt This Action	Probability of Occurring
	No response			
	Competitor cuts price to 10% below our price	• SBU market share falls to 25% • Profit falls to $22 million	• Past behavior • Important market for competitor • Competitor has cost advantage	HIGH
	Competitor introduces "me too" product			

FIGURE 6-5: Application of the Actions-Consequences-Evidence (ACE) Framework

Next Step: Making the Tough Choices

With a thorough understanding of the competitive environment in which an opportunity is embedded, you must now make a series of tough choices. These choices are of two types. First, there are choices to do with a particular opportunity. If the opportunity looks reasonably attractive and the SBU looks like it could develop a winning strategy, there will often be some strategic issues that must be resolved in order to finalize the strategy. Second, there are choices related to which combination of existing and potential opportunities the SBU should pursue. Rarely will an SBU have sufficient resources to pursue all of the viable opportunities. This leads to tough choices.

These are the key areas we will tackle in Chapter 7.

Key Questions for Executives and Managers

- Have you identified the key current and potential competitors you will face in the market opportunity? Have you actively thought about key indirect competitors who may meet the same customer needs with different technologies and market chains? Can you place the competitors into strategic groups to help simplify the analysis process?

- Do you understand how each of the key competitors or strategic groups compete?

- How are they doing now? How do you expect them to perform over the planning horizon?

- Do you have a good understanding of the strategy driving forces for each of your chief competitors? Why are they doing what they are doing? Have there been any important changes in these strategy driving forces that could signal a change in strategy?

- What are the implications of all this for future competitive moves, areas of competitive vulnerability, and competitive reactions? Can you use the action-consequences-evidence model to help predict actions and reactions?

CHAPTER SEVEN

Make Tough Strategic Choices

Introduction

By now your management team will have done a good deal of rigorous analysis on many of the current and potential opportunities in the business arena. Through careful segmentation of the market and evaluation of the market forces affecting the various market segments, you will have drawn up a list of potentially attractive opportunities. For the most attractive of these opportunities, the team will have laid out the market chains and tried to develop a good understanding of buyer choice/rejection behavior along the market chains. This analysis will likely have led you to drop some possibilities from further consideration. Having developed a good understanding of the opportunities, you will have begun the process of assessing the fit between the opportunity and your SBU's or company's resources and competencies. And, finally, the team will have attempted to develop a thorough understanding of the competitive environment in which each of the remaining opportunities exists.

The next step, making the strategic choices, is probably the most crucial step in any strategic market planning process. The strategic choices your team has to make are at two levels. At the level of the individual opportunity, the team has to pull all the information together to see if a strategic market plan can be developed that will propel the SBU to leadership in that opportunity. A second level of choices is at the level of the portfolio of opportunities. Your SBU is picking not only individual opportunities, but also a portfolio of opportunities that will be balanced and synergistic.

In order to make these tough strategic choices, your team will have to pull together the analysis for each of the opportunities under consideration, define the strategic issues, do some strategic thinking, and make the choices. It is a time to step back from the detail of each of the opportunities and to develop a holistic feeling about each of the opportunities under consideration as well as the portfolio of opportunities upon which the success of the SBU will be based. This is an excellent opportunity for the team to add their collective soft or "gut" feelings and intuition to the hard analytical data that will have been developed in the planning process. If done well, this part of the planning process is a powerful way for the team to continue the process of building a shared commitment to say yes to a few selected opportunities and to say a strong no to other opportunities.

An important part of the strategic thinking process is reviewing your SBU's past performance. It is always useful to step back and ask yourselves about your successes and your failures and to try to understand why you surpassed your objectives in some areas but fell short in others. This often has major implications for the selection of the opportunities you will pursue and the strategies you will adopt.

Often during this process it will become clear that the selection of an opportunity or the strategy for attacking an opportunity are highly dependent on the validity of a few significant assumptions. If the team can't reach agreement on these important assumptions, this may signal the need for gathering additional data and doing some highly focused marketing research. This is often the point where market research has its highest payoff. You are not tempted to do research on a bunch of vague research questions that might or might not provide useful input for decision making. Rather, you have a few very specific questions about important assumptions that will help you make important choices. This research should be very decision oriented and is often very useful.

Strategic Issues

What Is a Strategic Issue?

In any strategic market planning process, a large number of issues are likely to be identified. Many of these issues will be linked. A critically important task is for the management team to identify what are the truly strategic issues or challenges that must be dealt with. As discussed in Chapter 1, a strategic issue is one created by internal or external developments and that:

- has potential for a significant impact on the organization's future performance,
- is controversial in that reasonable people can disagree on how to deal with it, and
- has strategic consequences in that the resolution of it may mean implementing a change in strategy.

In the early 1990s Compaq faced a number of difficult challenges. Its personal computers were increasingly viewed by many customers as high-priced and over-engineered. The corporate market was reeling from the impact of the recession and was buying fewer personal computers. Historically, this had been a key market for Compaq. The market itself was undergoing some fundamental changes. There was a rapidly growing commodity segment of the market that tended to buy its personal computers from low-cost channels such as computer superstores and direct marketers. The other growth area was the high-end servers, which were employed in local area networks in organizations. Compaq's traditional distribution channel, computer dealers, was too expensive to access the commodity segment of the market and often lacked the technological expertise to install high-end servers in local area networks. A number of competitors, such as Dell, Packard Bell, and some of the Asian suppliers, were in the process of exploiting one or more of these market discontinuities, and Compaq was becoming increasingly uncompetitive in the important profitable growth segments of the market. The strategic issue facing Compaq's top management was whether the company should make a fundamental change in its marketing strategy to address these issues.

If Compaq had been using a strategic market planning process similar to the one proposed here, it would have seen the emerging crisis at least two or three years earlier. It would have recognized the changing segmentation of the market and the changing attractiveness of the different segments. New market chains were clearly developing and important changes were occurring in buyer behavior. Compaq's market chain had a poor fit with the new growth segments of the market, so even if it had competitive products it was not capable of reaching the customers in these segments. On all sides, the competition was intensifying. Clearly, it was a time for new choices, but it was not until the company suffered its first major quarterly loss that it replaced its founding CEO and began to respond more effectively to the changing market.

In the late 1990s Compaq faced a second crisis in the personal computer market as Dell's direct marketing model helped Dell gain leadership in many of the profitable growth segments of the market. This was one of the factors that led to the resignation of its second CEO in April 1999.

How Many Strategic Issues?

Organizations seem to be able to deal successfully with only a small number of strategic issues in any strategic market planning cycle. Most experienced strategists believe that the number of strategic issues being dealt with by one team of managers should not exceed five or six in a particular planning cycle. Attempting to deal with more than this number of issues at one time often means that the organization devotes insufficient resources and thinking to each one and usually fails to resolve the truly critical issues successfully.

Types of Strategic Issues

In many planning situations, two types of strategic issues emerge in the planning process. The first type are issues associated with a particular opportunity. Usually they are tied to the development of a strategy to take advantage of the opportunity and counter the threats identified in the analysis for that particular opportunity.

The second type of issue is one that cuts across several or all of the market opportunities under consideration in a particular business arena. In high-technology businesses, one frequently recurring issue is the choice of opportunities to pursue and the priorities among them. These choices are based on balanced consideration of the attractiveness of the market opportunity and the ability to win market leadership in it.

This chapter will provide some tools and concepts for dealing with both types of strategic issues.

Developing a Winning Strategy for an Opportunity

As we have argued earlier, the key to success in technology-intensive businesses is identifying those market opportunities that are likely to generate high profitability for the market leaders and then to develop a strategy to become the market leader. Generally, in technology-intensive markets, the company that is the market share leader captures a disproportionate share of the profitability in the market. For example, in the large jet engine business General Electric captured 72% of the profits in that market from 1992 to 1996. This left only 28% percent to be split between the other two major players, Pratt and Whitney and Rolls-Royce.[1]

Two major approaches to winning market leadership are cost leadership and differentiation.

Cost Leadership

A company following a cost leadership strategy attempts to deliver "acceptable" products at the lowest possible cost. Sustainable competitive advantage is achieved by aggressive management of all the key cost drivers, including experience curve factors. In order to maintain a leadership position, a company must aggressively control its costs throughout its value chain and in its market chain or chains. For a couple of years, Texas Instruments was very successful at doing this with light-emitting diode (LED) digital watches. In the PC software business, Borland executed this strategy quite successfully in

---

[1] "Defying the Law of Gravity," *Business Week*, April 8, 1996, pp. 124–126.

the late 1980s and the early 1990s. Many computer users viewed Quattro Pro, its spreadsheet product, as being highly competitive with Lotus 1-2-3 or Microsoft Excel. However, the Quattro Pro product was priced aggressively in the market, selling for less than $100, considerably below the prices of Lotus 1-2-3 and Excel. Many observers felt that Borland was able to price its products so low and make a profit because it did a good job of managing its costs in its early years.

As the Quattro Pro example indicates, cost leadership does not mean "cheap" products with outdated functionality. In order to be competitive with the offerings of other competitors using differentiation strategies, the product and any associated services must come close to matching those of the differentiation leaders. The cost leader's products might be able to lag a little in the latest functionality or the best customer service, but they can't lag by much for long before the customer believes that the company no longer offers value.

Companies adopting a cost leadership strategy face a number of major risks. There is always the danger that the bases for cost advantage are lost to a competitor. For example, if a major reason for your cost advantage is that your product is assembled by low-cost labor in Mexico, your advantage could be threatened if your main competitor happens to have its products assembled in a country where the currency is devalued. This happened to some companies in assembly-intensive industries when several Asian currencies were devalued in 1997. Suddenly, these companies found that competitors based in Thailand or Indonesia had significantly lower costs than they did and thus a key source of competitive advantage was threatened.

In other cases, the cost advantage that a company has achieved is the result of a strong position in a particular technology. If a competitor leapfrogs over this technology with a new technology that is either lower cost or provides substantially greater customer value, a company's market position can erode very rapidly. This happened to Texas Instruments in the 1970s in the digital watch market. Texas Instruments had a high market share as a result of aggressive pricing based on a strong cost position in the LED technology. However, when liquid crystal display (LCD) technology appeared and offered customers a substantially better product, TI's market position declined rapidly and the company had to take a large write-off in early 1983 when it got out of the digital watch business.

A second risk of a cost leadership strategy is that two or more companies may be equally successful in executing the strategy and these companies end up in an unprofitable price war. This is always a danger unless you have a clear sustainable advantage on one or more of the key cost drivers in a particular business. If you do, this is likely the result of a core competency that contributes to achieving a low-cost position.

The third risk is that you provide your customers with very low-cost products but fall far behind the leaders playing a differentiation game with regard to product functionality or service. Then, even though your prices are much lower, the customer may not see the value in your product. This has happened to a number of companies in the personal computer business, who offered very low-cost products based on old-technology microprocessors.

Differentiation

A differentiation strategy involves providing unique and superior customer value in either product leadership or customer intimacy.[2]

A company that commits to a product leadership strategy must be the market leader in providing new or better functionality or service to its target customers. In order to do this successfully, the company must be very good at sensing latent or emerging customer needs and developing new products or services to meet these needs in a timely manner. Product leaders must also be willing to ruthlessly make their own existing products obsolete.

An example of a business unit that has done this very successfully is the microprocessor unit at Intel. In this business, Intel has proved to be a successful product leader. It rapidly and continuously introduces improved products within a particular product generation, and every two to three years it introduces a new generation of technology. It has been very successful in getting its most important customers, the personal computer manufacturers, to adopt its newest and latest technology. In order to speed up the adoption of its new technology at both the manufacturer and end-user levels, it aggressively advertises the benefits of its new technology over its previous technology. It also provides a great deal of support to its customers,

---

[2] Michael Treacy and Fred Wiersema, "Customer Intimacy and Other Value Disciplines," *Harvard Business Review* (January-February 1993), pp. 84–93.

the personal computer manufacturers, with reference designs, motherboards, and even semi-complete systems, in order to allow them to adopt its new technology as rapidly as possible.

Customer intimacy represents a second and very important differentiation strategy in technology-intensive industries. Companies using this strategy often develop a symbiotic relationship with one or a small number of customers within a given market segment. If the company is supplying a crucial component or subsystem that is a major source of differentiation in the customer's product, the relationship may be with only one customer, ideally the market leader. In other cases, where the company has more power or is supplying an industry standard product, it may be able to establish this relationship with a number of customers. When companies successfully adopt a customer intimacy strategy, it is sometimes difficult to tell where one company ends and the other begins as the two organizations become so interdependent.

Dell Computer has been extremely successful at building intimate relationships with many of its large corporate customers. One of its tools is Premier Pages.[3] For each of its large customers, Dell builds a set of Web pages, which are often linked to the customer's intranet and which allow approved employees to configure PCs online, to pay for them, and to track the order status. The PCs will usually arrive preloaded with the customer's standard software and even with the customer's asset tags already attached. Dell can also keep track of a customer's PC inventory and even generate lease management reports, if the PCs are leased. These programs can save large customers millions of dollars per year and make it inconvenient for the customer to switch to another PC supplier.

> Often a customer intimacy strategy creates differentiation not by producing a better product or service for the customer, but by making the whole process of choosing, buying, and using the product or service very simple and painless for the customer. Although this strategy might sound quite mundane, in many industries it effectively removes a lot of potential headaches for the customer and can provide tremendous customer value.

---

[3] Eryn Brown, "9 Ways to Win on the Web," *Fortune,* May 24, 1999, pp. 112–125.

While it may be theoretically possible for a company to adopt both product leadership and customer intimacy strategies simultaneously, in practice most business units do not seem to do it for extended periods of time. This seems to be because the two differentiation strategies need quite different resources and capabilities that may be in conflict. However, even a company strongly committed to product leadership may have to develop very close and intimate relationships with a customer or customers in a market segment in order to move a new technology across the chasm between the early adopters and the early majority. Generally companies that adopt a customer intimacy strategy are less likely to be leaders in the introduction of breakthrough technology and are more likely to play a key role in a market only after a new technology has moved beyond the innovators and early adopters and into the mainstream market.

If a company is successful in differentiating its product and/or service from its competition, it should be able to command a premium price. The price premium should exceed the cost of delivering the incremental benefits. Clearly, a differentiation strategy does not allow a company to ignore costs. The company must strive to achieve cost parity with other competitors in the market in all areas that do not directly contribute to differentiation.

Strategic Breakpoint

When you differentiate a product or service you may or may not create sufficient incentive for the customer to choose your product over the customer's existing or other new choices. The strategic breakpoint refers to the degree of differentiation you must achieve to create in the customer a powerful motivation to choose your product over the alternatives. If you create a powerful motivation, you have achieved a real competitive advantage. As shown in Figure 7-1, the relationship between the differentiation a company is able to achieve and competitive advantage is not always a simple one. Often, if a company is only marginally better than its competitors in delivering a benefit to its target customers, there will not be much of a competitive advantage and little significant change in market share. But, at some point if the differentiation achieved is with respect to an important benefit for the target segment, the differentiation will have a significant competitive advantage and hence improved market share. You then have the necessary conditions for a strong positioning statement—a product that both meets the customer's needs and does a better job of meeting those needs than any competitive offering. Finally, at some point, increased differentiation compared to competitors will have diminishing marginal returns.

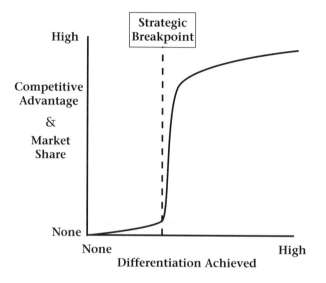

FIGURE 7-1: Strategic Breakpoint

When ABB (before it became ABB) entered the power equipment market in North America in the early 1970s, this market was mature and dominated by such formidable competitors as General Electric, Westinghouse and McGraw-Edison.[4] Then, as a result of the rapid rise in oil prices in the mid-1970s, the market declined dramatically. After conducting a great deal of market research on U.S. purchasers of this kind of equipment, ABB realized that warranties were an important buying determinant for several of the market segments. At that time no competitor offered a warranty of greater than one year. In order to differentiate itself from its competitors on this important attribute, ABB decided to introduce a full five-year warranty on its equipment. In order to be able to do this in an economical way, the company had to make major changes in how it

---

[4] This example is based on Dennis H. Gensch, Nicolas Aversa, and Steven P. Moore, "A Choice-Modeling Market Information System That Enables ABB Electric to Expand Its Market Share," *Interfaces* (January-February 1990), pp. 6–25.

designed and manufactured its products. Within a year of introducing the new warranty, ABB managed to increase its market share from 8% to 15% in a very difficult market environment. One could argue that if ABB had made the warranty on its equipment 18 months, it would have achieved some differentiation, but it might not have achieved real competitive advantage and hence a significant increase in market share.

This notion of a strategic breakpoint has important implications for new product development. One can argue that sometimes a good new product development strategy is to focus on a compelling benefit that target segments are seeking and try to make sure that you clearly differentiate yourself on this benefit. That is, you try to get beyond the strategic breakpoint for that particular attribute. In some high-technology markets where there are significant switching costs, this might require not a 20% improvement in performance, but perhaps a 200% or 300% improvement or more! If you are able to get beyond the breakpoint, the strategy may be much more effective than trying to beat your competitors by a little on a number of different attributes. By adopting a more focused new product development strategy aimed at achieving a dramatic improvement in performance on a key attribute, both the time to market and the cost of developing the new product may be dramatically reduced.

Determining the degree of differentiation you need to achieve to reach the strategic breakpoint is not an easy task. Hard economic analysis from the buyer's perspective (Economic Value to the Customer Analysis) might let you determine how much differentiation you will need to achieve before a fully rational customer will switch to your product.[5] How far beyond this you need to go may require managerial judgment or market research.

Risks of Adopting a Differentiation Strategy

One clear risk is that you create differences that customers don't value. This is a major risk in a technically oriented organization, where engineers and scientists want to see their technological advances incorporated in products, even if they don't provide any real value to the customer.

---

5 John L. Forbis and Nitin T. Mehta, "Value-Based Strategy for Industrial Products," *The McKinsey Quarterly* (Summer 1981), pp. 35–52.

A second risk in many technology-intensive companies is that the managers and engineers focus too much on the core product in trying to differentiate their product. Sometimes non-product ways of differentiating may create greater customer value and may be much more sustainable in the marketplace. For several years, National Semiconductor had great success with a semiconductor product called "Simple Switcher." The product itself was quite similar to those of competitors, but Simple Switcher did have superior software that made it easier for the customers' design engineers to design the component into their systems. It also came with performance guarantees and standard magnetics, which were also seen to be significant benefits by many of the adopting engineers.

The third risk is that a company will differentiate its product on dimensions that will become less important to customers over time. After-sales service and support has often made North American companies successful in differentiating their products in the North American market from those of European or Asian competitors. However, with greater emphasis on total quality management and product reliability, after-sales service and support is becoming irrelevant for many product lines. For example, the top-of-the-line storage devices manufactured by IBM are designed and manufactured to deliver millions of hours of service between failures. If customers are convinced that these products can deliver this level of reliability, they will put much less emphasis on after-sales service and support.

A fourth risk in employing a differentiation strategy is that the company will be successful in creating significant differentiation but at such a cost that the customer is unwilling to pay the premium for the differentiation created.

A final risk that has destroyed some technology-intensive companies is their failure to continue to invest to maintain a differentiation edge over competition. Companies become the market leader in a business, but then take the profits and invest them outside their core market, resulting in the core product falling behind that of competition. This may be an appropriate strategy in a mature or declining market, but seldom in an embryonic one, unless the company has no potential to continue to be competitive in the market. The leader in the personal computer word-processing market in the early 1980s was a product called WordStar which was manufactured by Micro Pro. After achieving leadership, it focused its R&D energies elsewhere to try to replicate its early success in the word-processing market in other application areas for personal computers.   Meanwhile, WordPerfect Corporation was investing heavily in developing the WordPerfect software.   When Micro Pro responded by introducing a second-generation product called WordStar 2000, it bought the computer code base from another company.   The file format of the original WordStar and the new WordStar 2000 were incompatible.   So rather than customers upgrading automatically from WordStar to WordStar 2000, they also looked at other options.   By that time, WordPerfect was generally viewed as a superior product, so many of these customers switched to WordPerfect and WordStar faded from the scene.

Sustaining the Competitive Advantage

In today's fast-moving technology-intensive markets, it is very difficult to sustain competitive advantage.   Like Micro Pro, a company can rapidly move from market leader to an "also ran."

In order to sustain competitive advantage, a company should have a clear understanding of its strategy for gaining and sustaining competitive advantage and it should adhere to that strategy, unless there has been a major change in the market environment or the organization's competencies.

Competitive advantage is more likely to be sustainable if it is based on several linked sources of advantage.   Almost all the companies that manage to sustain competitive advantage over long periods do not rely on just one source of competitive advantage, but rather on a core competency or competencies.   Tandem's dominance of the fault-tolerant computer market for over 20 years was the result of a unique systems architecture, and continuous improvement in the hardware and software associated with fault-tolerant computing, and a worldwide support and professional services organization that was effective at working with customers to help them exploit Tandem's technology.

Some sources of competitive advantage are relatively easy to imitate.   Technology is increasingly one of these.   In many technology-intensive businesses it is hard to maintain any long-term competitive advantage through technology alone.   Technological advances tend to erode quickly as competitors reverse engineer successful products and as leading engineers and scientists are hired by competitors.   Often more durable sources of competitive advantage may be non-technology sources, such as the use of a unique market chain or strong and intimate relationships with important customers.

As we saw in the WordStar example, a company must be willing to invest continuously in improving and upgrading its sources of advantage and to ruthlessly render its existing products obsolete.

Convergence of Cost Leadership and Differentiation

When the generic strategies of cost leadership and differentiation were clearly articulated by Michael Porter in the 1970s, one could readily identify companies that were pursuing one or other of these strategies. As shown in Figure 7-2, today many leading companies seem to be converging in the top right-hand corner of the matrix. That is, some of the companies that are the differentiation leaders in their market segments are also close to being, or are, the cost leaders. Companies like ABB, Compaq, and Hewlett-Packard in printers seem to be able to lead their markets or are very close to the market leader in achieving differentiation, while being very cost competitive at the same time. In many highly competitive businesses, where there are no strong barriers to competition, companies must strive to achieve this convergence, so that they leave no openings for aggressive competitors.

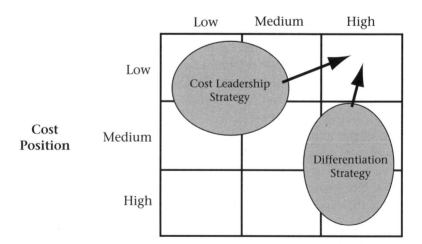

FIGURE 7-2: Convergence of Cost Leadership and Differentiation Strategies

Selecting the Portfolio of Opportunities

As we mentioned at the beginning of this chapter, one of the strategic issues is deciding which opportunity or opportunities to pursue. This typically involves ranking the various opportunities that have survived the various assessments and made it to the strategic thinking stage, and, if more than one opportunity is to be pursued, ensuring that the selected opportunities make an attractive and complementary portfolio.

Balancing Market Attractiveness and Ability to Win

Clearly, the most attractive opportunities are those involving profitable market segments where the business has the ability to gain or retain market leadership. Unfortunately, things are usually not quite that simple. Often a company or SBU will have identified some attractive and profitable market segments, but its analysis of the market requirements, its competencies, and the competitive environment suggest that it has almost no ability to win. Unless it can come up with creative ways to overcome the deficiencies in its resources and competencies, it doesn't make sense to choose such an opportunity. It may be possible to acquire some of the skills and resources and perhaps develop a new required competency by hiring individuals with needed skills, using a strategic alliance, or even making an acquisition. Similarly, there is no point in entering an unattractive market segment with very limited potential for profit generation, even if the company or SBU has the capability to become the market leader and dominate it. Businesses are often faced with making some fairly complex tradeoffs in order to rank the opportunities according to the return they will receive for the resources committed.

It is important that all businesses select markets that are small enough relative to their resources and capabilities to achieve a dominant leadership position (say a market share of 40% to 50% or more in a developing market segment) within a reasonable time. It makes no sense at all to target a market in which the business unit is not large enough to be able to grow fast enough to capture the dominant market share. All the company will be doing is creating demand that other companies may have the capacity to satisfy.

For a smaller company, the best markets or market segments to target are sometimes ones that are relatively small, perhaps not "glamorous," but that for a variety of reasons will attract few competitors, helping to sustain a reasonable level of profitability. If a business can become the market leader in such a market segment, it can do quite well. ASM, a relatively small manufacturer of ion implant equipment for the semiconductor industry, executed such a strategy quite successfully in the late 1980s and early 1990s. While Applied Materials and Eaton, two of its formidable and larger competitors, targeted the high-current 8-inch wafer market, ASM targeted the less glamorous medium-current 8-inch wafer market. As its large competitors focused on the larger and superficially more attractive market segment, ASM was rapidly able to achieve a market leadership position in the medium-current market and earn high profits.

Displaying the Portfolio of Opportunities

A number of different portfolio mapping approaches have been proposed for summarizing and presenting the various opportunities a business is, or might be, considering. The GE/McKinsey portfolio model shown in Figure 7-3 is one of the more popular ones and picks up the two major dimensions involved in the choice of a set of opportunities, namely market attractiveness and business strength. Some of the factors that might underlie each of these dimensions are shown in the figure. Clearly, the relative weights that should be placed on each of these sub-factors will vary from situation to situation. Existing businesses are usually plotted on this matrix as circles, with the area of the circle proportional to current SBU sales. For opportunities that are currently being pursued, you will have much more hard data to plot a business opportunity's market attractiveness and your relative strength in that opportunity. For potential opportunities, the positioning will be more speculative.

Where the business opportunities are positioned in the matrix provides some rough guidelines about the general investment strategy for the various opportunities. Those in the three upper-left cells are classified as invest/grow. This suggests that the SBU should invest aggressively in these businesses to try to develop these businesses, providing a winning strategy can be arrived at. For those opportunities down the diagonal, the generic suggestion is that the SBU make selective investments but manage these business opportunities for earnings. Presumably none of the new opportunities will be positioned in the harvest/divest cells, since such opportunities would have been screened out at earlier stages of the planning process. However, some of the existing market opportunities that the SBU is pursuing may fall in these cells and the generic strategy recommended for these businesses is divestiture or harvesting. In harvesting a business, a company stops investing in it and tries to maximize the cash flow as the market share inevitably declines.

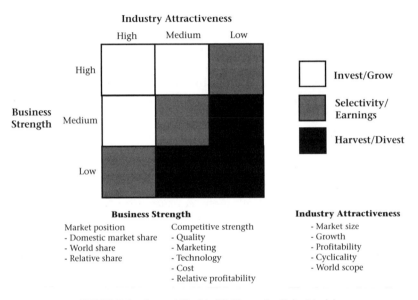

FIGURE 7-3: General Electric/McKinsey Portfolio Model

Originally, portfolio models had a heavy focus on cash flow balance. That is, a company would use the cash flow from its harvest/divest businesses and its selective investment/earnings businesses to fund its invest/grow businesses. However, most companies should be able to access external sources of funding to support attractive business opportunities. Thus, the use of portfolio models to help think through cash flow balance issues is valuable only to companies that are unable to access external funding at a particular time. Today, the most valuable uses of the portfolio tool are to display the set of business opportunities in a way that encourages a productive dialogue about priorities and choices, and to act as a rough guideline for establishing performance expectations and strategy objectives for each of the business opportunities. Explicitly recognizing that the different opportunities are in markets at different stages of development, and require different levels of resources and different mixes of competencies, encourages management to select objectives that make sense given that opportunity's particular positioning in the matrix and strategic role. For a new opportunity in a fast-growing attractive market where you have the requisite competencies, the primary objective might be capturing market share with much less emphasis on return on assets employed. In a more mature business opportunity where only a few selective investments are warranted, the focus might be on maximizing the return on assets employed.

Viewing the opportunities under consideration as a potential portfolio forces the decision makers to consider the resources that will be generated and consumed by each of the opportunities. In addition, any resources external to the strategic business unit that it might be able to draw on should also be considered. For example, General Electric's Major Appliance business was able to use technical and manufacturing skills from GE's Aircraft Engines business to develop and manufacture a new high-technology compressor that required extremely precise manufacturing tolerances. In looking at resource generation and resource consumption issues, financial, human, and physical resources, such as manufacturing capacity, should be considered too. In many technical companies, limited access to engineering and scientific talent, as well as marketing talent, can be a major constraint on the number and type of opportunities that should be included in the final portfolio. Ideally, the opportunities included in the portfolio should exploit potential synergies, should help further develop the SBU's core competencies, and move the SBU in its chosen strategic direction.

As mentioned earlier, "maps" of aspects of an SBU's business can present powerful overviews and lead to a variety of useful insights. A management team can develop maps that might be useful to them in making their critical choices. In some research and development-intensive businesses, a useful map is one that tracks the SBU's investments in research and development, and relates them to the values they are designed to create for the customer and the technology requirement (see Figure 7-4).[6]

---

[6] This section is based partly on Steven C. Wheelwright and Kim B. Clark, *Revolutionizing Product Development: Quantum Leaps in Speed, Efficiency, and Quality* (New York: The Free Press, 1992).

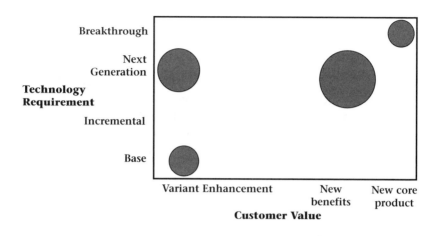

FIGURE 7-4: Map of Portfolio of an SBU's Research and Development Activities

In this map the diameter of the circles is proportional to the R&D investment. This map allows the SBU management team to capture a snapshot of how they are spending their R&D dollars, while pursuing a particular portfolio of opportunities. The team might become quite concerned if all the R&D investment was going into the base technology to produce new products or services that were merely variants of the current product. However, in the example in Figure 7-4, the company seems to be putting most of its R&D into a next-generation technology which promises significant new benefits to its target customers. In addition, it has a small R&D investment going into trying to develop a breakthrough technology which could lead to a new core product.

Making Clear Strategic Choices

In many technology-intensive businesses (as in other types of businesses), executives often don't make the tough choices and try to pursue too many opportunities simultaneously. A major reason for doing some clear strategic thinking at this stage in the planning process is to enable the management team to make the tough choices and say yes to a few opportunities and no to the rest of the opportunities.

Ironically it is often the companies with the most attractive opportunities that have the most difficult time making the tough choices. In the mid-1990s Machine Vision International had strong capabilities in all four of the core technologies underpinning vision systems for robotic applications. The company chose to pursue a wide range of machine vision opportunities in automotive, electronics, food processing, aerospace and several other industries. Each application posed significant engineering challenges. In addition, the marketing and sales process required for the different industries was also quite varied. As a result, both engineering and sales costs got out of control, leading to severe cash flow problems and a loss of investor interest. The company was unable to pull out of a downward spiral and was forced to close down its operations.

A more positive example was described in Chapter 4. Documentum carefully selected one opportunity and then focused all its resources on developing a complete solution for its target segment. It rapidly achieved a profitable leadership position in its targeted opportunity.

Unfortunately, managers almost universally shy away from making the hard choices, and they justify the lack of hard choices on a variety of grounds. Sometimes they are afraid of putting all their eggs in one or a couple of baskets. In other cases, management might be unwilling to say no because the opportunity is one the CEO or some other key executive is particularly enthusiastic about. Sometimes it is because management wants to encourage experimentation. This is a laudable goal, but it is too easily carried to excess; the SBU could lose focus and start losing its competitive position. Another important reason in many organizations is that the top management team is afraid of "turning off" the individual or team that is championing a particular opportunity. So, instead of saying no, top management says maybe and gives the team some but not enough resources, almost ensuring an ultimate failure. And finally, the management team may not have a clear vision of where it wants to take the SBU. Without a clear direction it is difficult to prioritize all the opportunities.

The failure to make hard choices about which opportunities to pursue can be particularly troublesome in the case of a new technology that has achieved some success with the innovators and the early adopters. Up to this point, the company may have been able to sell a product that is incomplete in many respects. But as the company tries to move the product into the mainstream market, it encounters more and more difficulty with customers wanting complete solutions, not partial solutions. The tendency here is to go out and talk to random groups of customers and get their wish lists about what is required for a complete solution. With the long wish list in hand, the engineers and others in the company may go to work methodically trying to deal with all the customer requirements. Unfortunately, these composite lists are often long and have many conflicting items. At the end of a year of working through the list, the company has likely not developed a complete solution for any one market segment, so again adoption of the new technology by the mainstream market has not happened. If the company had picked one attractive segment and focused all its efforts on its wish list, that segment would probably be adopting the product already.

Too often the management team—by putting off making the tough choices, such as the one above—ends up spending resources on many opportunities, with the people working on these opportunities becoming more and more committed to them, making an ultimate no even more difficult. If you don't make the tough choices, you will find yourselves in the spiral shown in Figure 1-4 in Chapter 1 where you end up totally underwhelming the competition.

Next Step: Managing Critical Relationships

Having made the tough choices about which market opportunities to pursue and having developed the broad outline about how you are going to win in each opportunity, you now have to begin to detail the winning strategies.

In many technology-intensive businesses, building effective relationships with market chain members and others in your broader market web is critical for success. The next chapter deals with understanding the various types of relationships that might be important to you and how to develop the critical relationships that can help you win in your chosen market opportunities.

Key Questions for Executives and Managers

- Have you identified the key strategic planning issues that must be resolved in this planning cycle both for the particular opportunities under consideration and at the broader level of the portfolio of opportunities?

- Have you reviewed your past strategies and the results you have achieved? Do you understand the reasons for your successes and your failures?

- Have you been sufficiently creative in developing your strategic options?

- Are you managing your portfolio of opportunities appropriately? Are you giving high enough priority to the opportunities that offer the best chances of success? Are you being brutal enough in withdrawing resources from low priority opportunities?

- Are you making the tough choices, or are you waiting for the market to make the choices for you?

CHAPTER EIGHT

Manage Critical Relationships

Introduction

Assuming the opportunity you are considering is still on your list, having survived your stringent examination and benefited from your strategic thinking, you now need to flesh out a strategy to win market leadership. Frequently, relationships with market chain members and with organizations and individuals beyond the market chain are important to strategy in technology-intensive businesses. No strategy for winning market leadership is complete until critical market-based relationships have been identified, and plans, people, and resources put in place to manage them.

We deal with relationships at this stage in the book because they are so fundamental to success in a business opportunity that they can be the single determining factor in a decision. It may be a "no go" decision if competitors have unassailable positions in key relationships, such as with distributors; if capabilities and resources cannot be developed to manage critical relationships; or if relationship management costs are too high. There is no sense completing the rest of a strategy to win until the relationship issues have been examined.

This chapter deals with building competitive advantage through relationships, and managing these critical relationships as a fundamental part of your strategy for winning market leadership. We start by answering the question of why relationships are critical in technology-intensive businesses. We next develop a framework which captures the external relationships of concern in what we call a "market web." We go on to detail the nature of some of the relationships within the market web and the implications for managing them successfully.

Why Are Relationships Critical?

In technology-based businesses, market chains are often long, complex, and evolving. Building strong relationships with market chain members, both on the supply side and on the customer side, can determine whether you win in an attractive market opportunity.

Building these relationships in technology-intensive businesses is important for a fundamental reason. With the blurring of competitive advantage around the technology itself, with pricing strategies responsive to competitive moves, with distribution channels providing access to most end users, gaining competitive advantage through these dimensions of a marketing program is becoming more and more difficult. True, it is possible to gain advantage through, for example, having a lock on a distribution channel making it difficult for new market entrants, or by developing brand equity as have Intel and Microsoft. However, in many instances, companies are left attempting to develop competitive advantage through the nature and strength of the relationships they build—gaining collaborative advantage.[1] Collaborative advantage is the linking of capabilities between organizations to create value for the end user, and strategic leverage for market chain members.

Having upstream relationships with suppliers is one way to use collaboration to advantage. Creating close and strong ties with suppliers to the point of sharing information via electronic data interchange (EDI) and extranets, developing joint marketing plans, and exchanging employees can have a number of effects. The value to the customer is enhanced through lowering costs, increasing distribution efficiencies, creating new products, and realigning value-adding roles. Going down the market chain, collaborating with market chain members closer to the end user allows you to tap into

---

[1] Rosabeth Moss Kanter, "Collaborative Advantage: The Art of Alliances," *Harvard Business Review* (July–August 1994), pp. 96–108.

knowledge, trends, and emerging needs understood by those closer to the end user; a combination that can guide innovation. For example, Cisco has very effectively harnessed the Internet to better serve its customers.[2] Software at its Web site allows customers to configure and price products and submit orders. Once the order is placed, customers can track the progress of their orders online. After the products are delivered, much of the technical support is available online. Besides creating significant value to the customer, this system allows Cisco salespersons to focus more energy on deepening their understanding of customer needs and building positive relationships with their customers.

Relationships not directly on the market chain can also have a critical impact on success. For example, maintaining constant communication with those who influence a customer's decision-making behavior can be crucial. This might mean working with companies or associations that are setting technology standards, or working with consultants who can influence adoption rates. Collaborative advantage can also be gained through alliances with companies that have complementary products to yours so together you can offer a solution that is greater than could be attained by each of you working apart. Forming co-marketing alliances and horizontal selling alliances with complementors can leverage your strategy in the marketplace and increase your flexibility. Intel has connected with over 500 complementors, with some connections involving direct investment, to ensure that leading-edge applications will require the power of Intel's future generations of microprocessors.

Consciously looking for these and similar kinds of opportunities can be vital in global markets where partnering, joint ventures, and alliances of all forms give you flexibility to develop appropriate collaborative efforts in different market conditions. For example, joint ventures are strongly encouraged, and sometimes demanded, in countries such as India and China.

The fundamental precept to remember is that relationships in various forms can make the difference between market opportunity

---

2 Shawn Tully, "How Cisco Mastered the Web," *Fortune*, August 17, 1998.

success and failure. Identifying critical relationships and managing them is essential. Ideally, this collaborative advantage can be developed to the point of creating barriers to others' market entry. A number of different types of relationships have been mentioned, but is there a way to frame these in an organized fashion? We believe that the concept of the "market web" does this.

The Market Web

Our challenge is to capture all the relationships that need to be managed in your opportunity, at the same time making sure the resulting framework encourages you to ask the appropriate questions when it comes to managing relationships. To meet both objectives, we use the concept of a "market web," similar to a spider's web with the strands of the web being relationships.

At the centre of the market web is the market chain, which consists of you as the focal company and a number of relationships upstream and downstream from you. Surrounding the market chain are a number of "off-chain" relationships which augment the market chain and turn it into a web. These can contain relationships with individuals, organizations, and associations that need to be managed since these players are capable of affecting the decision-making process of a market chain member and, perhaps most importantly, the end user. For example, a car dealership can influence where a first-time car buyer gets car insurance. The insurance company may actively work on developing relationships with dealers to have the business steered in its direction.

The *form* of these relationships, both on the market chain and off the chain, can range from loose and distant, such as in a transactional relationship, to tight and close, as in a strategic alliance. Somewhere on this continuum are value-added partnerships which are surfacing in more and more webs and are therefore discussed as part of this chapter. The question is, should any of the relationships in your web be formed as value-added partnerships, and what leads to successful relationships of this form?

The *nature* of the strands in the web can become quite complex, with many relationships containing a number of dimensions. For example, two companies may sell to each other, buy from each other, compete with each other, co-develop products, and jointly sell to other companies. Managing these multidimensional relationships can be a challenge, but companies that figure out how to do it, and how to leverage the potential synergies across the dimensions are on the way to developing collaborative advantage. It becomes even more challenging with "sticky" strands in the web. Sticky strands would occur when you form alliances with companies with whom you also compete. Just like spiders, superior companies know these strands are sticky and manage them so as not to get caught in their own web.

A Generic Market Web and an Example

Figure 8-1 captures the essence of a market web. Here we see market chain strands, off-chain strands, and knowledge and influence strands defined as follows:

Market Chain Strands

- **Buyer-Seller Relationship:** A relationship between the focal company as seller and a downstream company as buyer.
- **Supplier Relationship:** A relationship between an upstream company as a supplier to the focal company.

Off-Market Chain Strands

- **Complementor:** A synergy between companies such that the presence of one company in the marketplace complements the presence of the other to the benefit of both companies. For example, the better Microsoft Windows does in the marketplace, the better Windows application providers do and vice-versa.
- **Co-Marketing Alliance:** An alliance between companies, typically at the same level in the market chain, to jointly execute parts of a marketing program, for example, jointly sponsoring and developing a marketing campaign.
- **Horizontal Selling Alliance:** An alliance between companies, typically at the same level in the market chain, to sell together, for example, making joint sales calls.
- **Collaborative Product Development:** An agreement between companies to jointly develop new products.

Knowledge and Influence Strands

- **Learning Alliance:** A relationship between companies whose purpose is to inform each other of trends, emerging needs, and changing market conditions to each other's benefit.

- **Influence Relationship:** A company's relationship with an individual, another company, or an association where the aim of the relationship is to communicate with and influence those who can in turn influence a decision.

Note that any of the market chain and off-chain relationships could be value-added partnerships, to be discussed later, and that any of the relationships could be multidimensional with companies being in buyer-seller, collaborative product development, co-marketing alliance relationships, and competing all at the same time.

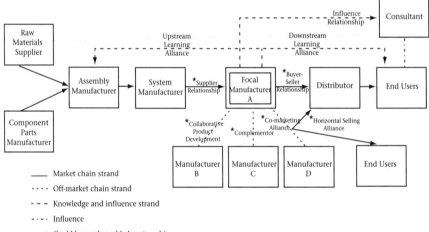

FIGURE 8-1: A Generic Market Web

Figure 8-2 shows the market web involved in the relatively simple situation of a systems integrator, S-S Technologies' Integrated Systems Group (ISG), that bundles together software and hardware to provide turn-key solutions in the factory automation arena.[3] Here we see traditional market chain relationships (1, 2). Going beyond these, ISG has formed learning alliances with upstream suppliers and with leading-edge customers to stay in touch with rapid changes in

---

3 This example is based on Ivey case study No. 9A94C006, *S-S Technologies Inc. (B) – Marketing* (London, Canada: Ivey Management Services, 1994).

user needs and technology platforms which will shape their business (7). Another company under the S-S Technologies umbrella is also critical to ISG with regard to selling complementary products, a move that expands both companies' markets (3), and being involved in joint product development (6). We also see a value-added partnership formed with key agents selling into the small end-user market(*). There is an interesting "coopetition" relationship with Andersen Consulting, where the two companies worked together to close a major contract at Canada Post (4), but also compete in an ongoing way in other situations. Looking up the market chain we see that suppliers to ISG work in concert in their selling efforts (5). Finally, there are a number of parties that can have a substantial impact on ISG through influencing suppliers, agents, and end users. Associations and consultants, for example, influence the decisions of end users. In this case, ISG needs to identify these potential influencers and actively develop relationships with some of them (8).

Even in this relatively simple context, a number of strands are complex, multidimensional, and critical to ISG—they require management. In the case of S-S Technologies, this exercise resulted in people being added to the marketing department to manage the critical relationships. Before the analysis, the assumption had been that great products and services would carry the day.

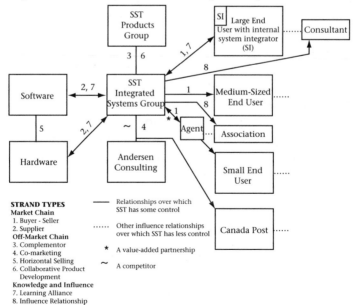

FIGURE 8-2: Market Web for S-S Technologies' Integrated Systems Group

A Managerial Perspective on Market Webs

The picture of a market web makes sense; however, what are you to make of it as a manager pursuing market leadership? Four implications arise which need your attention and decisions:

1. Leveraging market webs can help you create sustainable competitive advantage through superior value.
2. You have to clearly define your company's value-adding role in the market web. What should you be doing rather than what should other members of the web be doing?
3. Market webs should evolve over time as conditions change and opportunities come up. It is up to you to manage this evolution.
4. You must identify the critical relationships in the web, and allocate resources to ensure that they are managed effectively.

Market Webs as Value-Creating Systems

A fundamental and critical notion of market webs is that they are value-creating systems. Your challenge is to identify the market web that will create superior value and to focus on the vital relationships in that web that must work to make your strategy successful. Developing the market web is a strategic exercise. It is not a matter of capturing just the players and relationships involved, but what relationships should be there and what relationships must be changed. The web can be used to create unique competencies, which are difficult to duplicate in the marketplace and difficult to buy, and therefore start to look a lot like a core competency.

An additional consequence of thinking about market webs is that competition in the marketplace becomes competition among webs, as opposed to among individual players or even market chains. Each web is attempting to get the same fly, and it is the web that is best built and best managed that achieves its objective. In many instances, if you stick to traditional company-to-company competitive analysis, you might discover that you appear to be stronger than similar members in other market chains. By looking at the web, you might conclude that each member of a competing market web is not as strong as the competing members of your market chain or web. However, it is the linkages and the relationships in the competing web that can push you into an uncompetitive position.

Using market webs to help make decisions forces you to think clearly through your value-adding role in the web. Identifying all members of the web and which can best do what in the value-creation process allows you to clearly delineate your value-adding role. Clearly articulating and understanding your role, compared to others' roles, can help take you to marketplace success. For example, Astra Pharma realized that they had a potential winner in the anti-ulcer drug Prilosec. However, they also realized that rapid entry into the U.S. market was imperative, and that they did not have the capabilities to bring this about with Prilosec. By Astra Pharma adding Merck into the web for clinical testing, registration, marketing, and sales of products, Prilosec rapidly became the market leader in the United States.

Evolution of the Market Web

Market webs are not static. As competitive conditions change, as market web members change their objectives and loyalties, and as new products and services go through the adoption life cycle, the web needs to change. In the PC printer business, new members were added to the market chain over the adoption life cycle. As consumers became more comfortable with the technology and their ability to install printers and print drivers, these printers started to show up in big box retailers and wholesale clubs, such as Costco, and even in drug stores. In many technology-intensive industries, standards-setting bodies emerge and you may need to start building relationships with these bodies to be able to make decisions on your technological roadmap or to influence the emerging standards. Intel is represented on most software standards committees, giving it a voice in shaping such things as the Internet. This involvement also provides a forum for promoting PCs as the technology of choice for corporate and home buyers as opposed to lower-end devices that do not require Intel processors.

The managerial implication of this is that you have to maintain a fine balance between building strong, open relationships in the web that jointly create value, and having all market web members sensitive to the fact that relationships may need to be added or broken as things change.

Managing Critical Relationships

After identifying all existing relationships and changes in relationships that could create a stronger web, you need to pick out the handful of relationships that must be carefully managed. This means identifying the critical relationships, and then identifying specific managers, other people, and resources within your organization that are required in these relationships.

Defining Critical Relationships

The following questions may help sort out which relationships are critical and which require less attention:

- Is the relationship critical to creating value for the end user?
- Is the relationship in the core market chain and directly connected to you, for example, is it a supplier relationship? A customer relationship?
- Is the relationship with a complementor who is crucial to creating the products/service bundle?
- Would strengthening this relationship have a significant positive impact on customer choice/rejection behavior?
- Would this relationship result in learning what is critical to further developing your market opportunity?
- Would strengthening this relationship result in outstanding competitive advantage?

In order to make better decisions on, and better manage critical relationships, you need to understand the nature of the various kinds of relationships or strands in a market web. Although they are not cleanly separable, we see three categories of strands in market webs:

1. **Market chain strands**, which are part of the market chain, and its associated flow of goods and services

2. **Off-market chain strands**, which extend the market chain into other companies with which you are involved, for example, in joint marketing and product development activities

3. **Knowledge and influence strands**, where you build relationships to learn and to influence choice/rejection behaviors

You also need to see how a number of these relationships could be in the form of value-added partnerships, and how a number of the strands can be "sticky" and challenging to manage.

Market Chain Strands

As highlighted in several places in this book, market chain relationships involve those relationships from raw materials suppliers right through to end-user customers. This captures the flow of the product/service and associated value developed for the end user. The most important relationships in the market chain are usually customer relationships and supplier relationships.

Customer and Supplier Relationships

In a book on strategic market planning, we cannot address all that is involved in building customer relationships through superior selling, relationship management, and sales management. What is important is to give a brief overview of a relationship process that is critical to success in technology-intensive businesses: managing key accounts.

Managing Key Accounts[4]

In technology-intensive businesses, often a small number of customers represent a large portion of either current or future business, and the profits this business generates. How should you identify such important accounts? How do you manage them? Choosing key accounts is not just a matter of looking at sales volume or account profitability. Customers can be critical to your success for a number of reasons, including these: they have a global scope; they play a leading role in developing new technologies in an emerging market; or they are in segments of a market you plan to address in the future.

Once one of these key accounts has been identified, you need to allocate time and effort to developing a solid account or relationship plan for these customers. This means allocating management and sales force time to understanding the customer's business inside out,

---

[4] Robert B. Miller and Stephen E. Heiman, *Strategic Selling: The Unique Sales System Used by America's Best Companies* (New York: Morrow and Company, 1985).

for example, their challenges, their objectives, their profit dynamic, their marketplace, and their key success factors. Based on this in-depth understanding of a key customer, you can identify significant opportunities within the account for you to enhance customer profitability, leading to long term success.

In implementing this approach to key accounts, some tactical issues also need to be considered, such as the role of the customer in developing this account plan, the best way to access significant decision makers within the account, and finally the process for gaining resources in your company to be able to initiate and develop the opportunities within key accounts.

Don't forget that the concepts outlined with respect to managing key customers also apply up the market chain, with suppliers. If everyone in the market chain sees these concepts and ideas and accepts the concept of the market web for developing competitive advantage, all members of the market web will be open to collaborative thinking and to leveraging each other's strengths in order to win business from competitive market webs.

Off-Market Chain Strands

Managing critical relationships goes beyond the market chain. You also need to think about the set of relationships that surround your market chain and that may be equally important in winning market leadership. These are the relationships that build the web and are in many cases formed between members at the same level in the market chain. In our experience, it is those organizations that complete the market web with an array of off-chain relationships that can achieve market leadership. What is the nature of these relationships and in what forms do they emerge?

Formal and Informal

We often think of alliances as entities with strong agreements about governance, resource commitments, expectations, goals, and conflict resolution mechanisms, as in the case of joint ventures. What we observe, in addition to these formal agreements to do something, are less formal arrangements to enhance market presence, reduce costs, and/or add value. The formal agreements are not as important as the will to make things happen in the marketplace.

There is a role for formal alliances such as joint ventures, however, strengthening the market web through less formal, but potentially more responsive alliances needs to be considered in your relationship strategy. Three alliances that can play critical roles in technology-based markets are collaborative product development alliances, co-marketing alliances, and horizontal selling alliances. The question for you is how these types of alliances can add value to the end user, thwart competition, and enhance the strength of your market web.

Collaborative Product Development Alliances

Collaborating in product development can generate a number of benefits for technology-intensive businesses. First, the crucial time to get a product to market can be potentially reduced. Second, leveraging core competencies and technologies through another firm's different competencies occurs. Third, cost and risk can be reduced based on joint investments in projects. Finally, joint product development might build the market's attractiveness by taking a significant competitor out of the market—for example, if Rolls-Royce and BMW got together to build an aircraft engine, there would likely be one less competitor in the market, which could increase the overall profitability of the market.

However, collaborative product development alliances are not without their problems. A prime difficulty in technology-based companies is control over technology. Sharing technology can be dangerous, and a successful collaboration must be built on trust and commitment more so than on agreements. There are numerous examples of technology-based firms successfully collaborating to develop products—for example, Motorola, Apple, and IBM getting together to develop the Power PC microprocessor; Intel and HP building the Merced microprocessor.

Co-Marketing Alliances

Microsoft used its alliance with IBM for the MS DOS operating system in the early 1980s to catapult itself into the dominant PC software firm. Apple Computer, Aldus Corporation, and Adobe Systems worked together in 1984 to develop the desktop publishing market. Allen-Bradley, a division of Rockwell Automation, manages more than 80 partnerships focused on assembling a complete portfolio of products for its distributors. As part of the co-marketing effort, Allen-Bradley gathers its alliance partners annually for a trade show for its distributors. These are examples of co-marketing alliances—alliances formed to execute one or more aspects of marketing strategy between firms.

Evidence suggests that elements for success include:

- Careful project selection based on the market opportunity and resources required;
- Careful partner choice looking for compatibility in interests and working styles, and roughly similar resource endowments and market positions; and
- Relationships that are structured to balance any power imbalances going into the alliance.

Co-marketing alliances often emerge in markets where there is a lot of technological uncertainty, since alliances allow connectivity across complementary products without requiring firms to move beyond their core competencies. One of the most successful co-marketing alliances has been Astra Pharma's and Merck's involvement with the U.S. launch of Prilosec which was described previously. More generally, we see a number of hardware and software companies allying to take advantage of market opportunities. The challenge for you is to creatively identify such co-marketing alliance opportunities and to make them happen.

Horizontal Selling Alliances

Horizontal selling alliances are a relatively new strategy adopted by technology-based businesses where complementary sales organizations join forces. Their sales representatives work as selling partners to provide integrated solutions to specific customers. This is a form of a co-marketing alliance focused on the selling task. These alliances can present both organizations as having superior solutions compared to competition. This happened, for example, in the case of IBM salespeople teaming up with Sybase to sell RISC/6000 workstations and database solutions.

Your challenges, if you discover a role for selling alliances in your market web, are twofold. First, issues that loom large between organizations include the choice of partners, structuring agreements, and designing ongoing control mechanisms. However, the greater challenges exist in neutralizing differences between the selling partners who actually generate the sales in the field. Sales representatives may come from very different organizations whose goals, objectives, planning horizons, and reward systems may be very different. Many companies fail with selling alliances at the ground level. Trust between the selling partners is vital to success, but developing trust between reps with different agendas is difficult.

Knowledge and Influence Strands

Aside from the relationships discussed so far, you need to identify and strategically manage at least two other types of strands in the market web: knowledge strands, where you learn things; and influence strands, where you attempt to influence those who influence decisions in the market chain.

Knowledge Strands: Learning From Others in the Web

A key to market leadership in technology-intensive markets is keeping up. Coping with the rate of change, the amount of information, and the resulting ability to foresee future directions based on evolving and emerging technologies is critical. Keeping on top of all these issues can become difficult when you are located at the upstream end of the market chain. In this situation, it is essential to understand new needs emerging down the market chain right to the end user. In addition, knowledge rests with other marketplace players such as associations, standards-setting bodies, and complementors.

Unless your company makes a conscientious effort to keep up with these emerging needs, technologies, and other insights, it becomes disadvantaged. You need to form learning alliances to continuously stay in touch with what is happening at several points in the market web. This is especially so with members in the market chain who have the potential to influence market evolution. For example, given the large impact that Intel has on how end-user products evolve, keeping in touch with Intel in a proactive, formal-ized manner makes sense if you are located anywhere in Intel's per-sonal computer market web.

In forming a learning alliance, you have the opportunity to cul-tivate the most demanding end users and non-users to get to the peo-ple with the ideas. If you can work with these people, share information, and gain their confidence, you will be in a position to leverage the requirements of the most demanding end users into meeting the needs of less demanding customers. For example, Medtronics requires its salespeople to stay in close touch with the arrhthymia luminaries in leading cardiology centers to be able to stay on the leading edge. In a similar manner, SGS-Thomson is able to design systems-on-a-chip incredibly quickly partly because it works closely with top customers to gain know-how about systems-on-a-chip.

Effectively using such relationships requires a well developed ability to sense what is an important development and to analyze its potential impact on your organization. The learning alliances become the eyes and ears of the organization. Unless these learning alliances are constructed and actively developed, the required learn-ing will not happen.

Influence Strands: Affecting Choice/Rejection Processes

A carefully designed market web includes relationships between you and other individuals and organizations that can affect the choice/rejection process at any stage in a market chain. For example, industry associations can influence how a market chain member makes decisions. Individuals and organizations that could affect choice/rejection would include: consultants, standards-setting asso-ciations, systems integrators, industry leaders, distributors who are not in your market chain but could influence a customer's choice concerning your product, and Wall Street analysts who can influence your company's image.

Intel's sales reps call on software vendors, information technolo-gy buyers, and retail outlets selling their CEO's vision of a PC on every desk and in every household—a proactive attempt to influence influencers. Microsoft identified 22 categories of market influencers who would be critical in the development and roll-out of Microsoft

Windows NT and developed an infrastructure to build relationships with these groups.

You need to decide what to do with these influencers, how to keep in touch with them, and who should be responsible for managing relationships with these influencers. The unpredictable adoption-rate curves discussed previously are often the result of organizations not recognizing the key influencers of choice processes down the market chain and not developing plans to interact with them.

Value-Added Partnerships: A Key Relationship Form

Value-added partnerships emerge when two or more firms agree to fundamentally change how they do business, to integrate and mutually control some of their joint business systems, to become interdependent, and to share in the resulting benefits. You can apply the concept of value-added partnerships to downstream customers and upstream suppliers, and to off-market chain relationships. The basic concept is a recognition on the part of partners that the success of each firm depends in part on the other firm, with each firm taking actions to provide a coordinated, interdependent effort focused on jointly satisfying requirements in the marketplace. The impetus to form such partnerships is often found in external competitive pressures that neither you nor another company can overcome alone. Value-added partnerships are outward focused—they are based on shared strategies as to how to win in the marketplace.

In market chains, these kinds of partnerships are in contrast to more traditional relationships. Traditionally, to a large extent, power and conflict have been the operating forces between market chain members. Even the concept of "a channel captain" suggests that the person who has power controls the market chain. Power can come from a number of sources, including: unique products, information and control over information which other market chain members may not have, size, and power due to a set of managerial skills not possessed by other market chain members. Typically, power imbalances are leveraged by the more powerful market chain member to organize and coordinate market chain activities and strategies.

One argument for moving toward partnerships is that it is more and more difficult to win the power and control game. For example, strong manufacturers who have maintained power and control through size and product uniqueness are losing these advantages. Distributors and retailers are becoming more knowledgeable and, increasingly, they also have access to information that was traditionally in the hands of manufacturers, thus picking up power and control. End users are smarter and have many more choices, giving them power. When you look at the structure of many market chains, you see a number of players with close to equal power. This emerging scene of power shifts in many technology-intensive markets suggests that perhaps market web/market chain members working together as partners are more efficient and effective than market web members focusing on attempting to control and influence each other.

Let's recognize that this is not always the case, though. If forces in your market that we discussed in Chapter 3 are in your favor— weak suppliers, or weak customers, for example—you may still be in a position to exercise power and win via the old rules. We see examples of this in Microsoft and Intel when they have exercised power to the point that they were challenged in the courts. We might argue that Intel has been able to maintain a dominant position, and thus maintain power over market chain members, through a number of moves. For example, working with the end customer to develop brand recognition through Intel Inside gives Intel power as they own, to a certain extent, the end customer. In addition, Intel has the ability to move downstream, and moves downstream when it builds motherboards and even complete computers. These and other sources of power allow Intel to manage their market chains through more traditional mechanisms.

Partnering Success Factors

If forming value-added partnerships in parts of your web makes sense, what are the factors that lead to productive partnerships? The chief success factors are market-based, organization-based, people-based, and relationship-based.

Market Factors

From a **market** perspective, partners choose each other based on compatible positions in the marketplace. One partner positioning itself in the marketplace based on low price would be incompatible with a partner attempting to position itself based on superior quality. Success also depends on choosing partners that can fill gaps in your value-adding role and vice versa.

Selecting partners requires tough choices. You cannot go to a large number of market chain members at the same level in the chain and claim to be partners with them all. Making the choice of whom to approach as a partner is difficult because historically many companies have not made choices—in fact, the opposite has often happened. A manufacturer has often gone to a number of distributors or other downstream members, using the argument that no matter who wins the battle downstream, the manufacturer will win. In the value-added partnership picture, however, these choices are required. You cannot dedicate the time, effort, energy, and investment required to establish and maintain strong market chain partnerships without making choices.

There is evidence of market chain members making such choices and gaining substantial market leadership positions. For example, Novartis, a major agricultural chemical manufacturer (formerly Ciba-Geigy), made some tough choices when selecting distributors for the launch of a major new product in western Canada. By focusing on one distributor, an outstanding market-launch strategy was developed with commitments on both Novartis's and the distributor's part to make this a success. The final choice was based on common objectives and a common perspective on how both organizations wanted to be positioned in the marketplace. The strategy has been dramatically successful, resulting in large revenues and large increments in market share.

Organization Factors

The partnering **organizations** themselves are the second source of key success factors. Your organization must be "ready" to engage in partnering, if partnering can enhance the strength of your market web. There must be a willingness to collaborate and to reject past behaviors based on power and control. Evidence of these factors is often found in your ability to foster good relationships internally. Partners must share certain cultural similarities, ethical standards, and norms and values to be successful in the partnering game. Finally, at the organizational level, top management must be committed to partnering since it requires patience and resources to create these partnerships.

Organization-based attributes are part of the reason for the success of the Ford-Mazda alliance. Ford had traditional strengths in marketing, distribution, and market access, whereas Mazda's strengths were more in engineering, manufacturing, and technology. A partnering of these strengths led to such things as the Mazda 323 complementing the Ford Escort and so on down the product line. Keeping top management involved, meeting often and usually informally, using a matchmaker to bring the organizations together, appointing a monitor of the relationship, and anticipating cultural differences were important in this partnership.

People Factors

The essence of partnering, however, is **people**. Formal contracts do not make successful relationships, people do. The people involved in your partnering process must, as individuals, be ready to accept this new mode, willing to develop trust with their counterparts, and willing to commit to the relationship. As well, there must be multiple levels of communication between partners to ensure ongoing success.

Relationship Factors

In addition, certain characteristics of the **relationship** itself as it evolves are important. Joint planning, joint development of marketing strategy, investment in specific assets that are valuable only within the relationship, and implementation of systems of milestones and measurement, are often found in successful partnerships. Mechanisms must be in place for effectively resolving conflict, and both sides must be willing and able to modify structures, systems, processes, and interfunctional teamwork as the relationship matures. This is true both between the partners and within each of the partners' organizations.

What does this all amount to? You need to look for opportunities to include partnering in your market webs where it can add real value. You then have to work hard to develop these partnerships since you may be working from a history of inherent mistrust and lack of commitment. You also need to keep your eye on the many key success factors involved with partnering.

Managing "Sticky" Strands in the Web

To manage market webs in a superior fashion, you need to realize that some of the strands in the web are multidimensional and complex, and become tricky to manage in a consistent and coherent fashion. The most obvious case of this is managing a relationship with a customer who is also a competitor—coopetition. For example, look at the relationship between one software business unit at McDonnell Douglas and Digital Equipment Corporation (DEC). At one stage in McDonnell Douglas's evolution, it decided to set up a separate profit centre that would sell the software developed by the company. The vice president of this organization described the complexity of the various relationships between the McDonnell Douglas unit and DEC in the following way. In the first instance, McDonnell Douglas sold software to DEC, the next day McDonnell Douglas was purchasing hardware from DEC, on the third day DEC and McDonnell Douglas were competing for a piece of business where both were selling similar software. On the fourth day, DEC and McDonnell Douglas were in a horizontal selling alliance where DEC hardware was being bundled together with McDonnell Douglas software to meet the specific needs of a customer.

Canon and Hewlett-Packard have an enduring technology alliance building laser printers with HP PC know-how and Canon's superb laser engines. But they also compete fiercely in the ink-jet and laser printer markets to the point of almost wiping out margins in the ink-jet market through a price war in 1996. This relationship has been described as an uncomfortable mutual dependence.

How, in general, do you go about managing such complex "sticky" strands in the market web? One option for managing complex relationships is to stay away or get out. When such relationships are encountered, a reaction on the part of many firms is to find a way out. However, avoiding or leaving a multifaceted relationship can be costly. For example, in 1984 GM purchased a 50% stake in Daewoo Motor Company and invested $100 million in a Daewoo factory in Korea to manufacture the Pontiac LeMans for GM. However, in 1988 when Daewoo started competing with GM in selling small cars to Europe, GM's European division protested and GM pressured Daewoo to sell only 3,000 cars, then withdraw from the European market. Next Daewoo created a new sedan that it wanted to sell in the United States and other markets but GM refused to allow it.

The result was GM trying to sell its stake in Daewoo and losing its major manufacturing base in the growing Asian market.[5] This way of leaving the relationship may not make a lot of sense unless there are legal reasons why some of the dimensions of a relationship must be separated.

The next approach would be a divide-and-conquer strategy where the dimensions of a relationship are cleanly separated with different people involved in each dimension. The drawback here is losing the synergies that can be gained by pulling these dimensions together and sharing information across the dimensions. The third response is to creatively decide how to manage these multidimensional relationships. This may be through structure, or it may be through communications and control systems. In many cases, it is through the appointment of a senior executive to manage all dimensions, make sure that synergies are gained, and see that issues such as collusion and tied buying are avoided. Kodak found that they were in such a relationship with Philips in Europe and that their relationship involved many of the dimensions discussed above. Their solution was to appoint a senior executive in the Kodak organization as vice president, Philips. His business card actually read "Vice President, Philips" and his mandate was to manage the sticky relationship between the two organizations on a global level.

When you are faced with such relationships, which are common in technology-intensive markets, you have to make a strategic decision about how to deal with them. This is especially true in the case where a customer becomes a competitor, or where you become a competitor to your customer. In this specific situation, you might consider attempting to use your position of power, if you have one, to discourage competition. For example, in 1996 Motorola decided to use only a limited number of its distributors for its new high-end StarTAC phone and it would allow them to carry the product only if they put up StarTAC displays and promoted the product. This attempted use of power partially backfired since the stipulation created conflict with the distributors' own attempts to brand their services. Alternatively, you might build other positive dimensions of the relationship to discourage the competitive dimension, or you might set up an agreement which indicates to your customers that if

---

[5] Barbara A. Carlin, Michael J. Dowling, William D. Roering, John Wyman, John Kalinoglou and Greg Clyburn, "Sleeping with the Enemy: Doing Business with a Competitor," *Business Horizons* (September–October 1994), pp. 9–15.

they meet certain targets over certain time periods, there may not be a need to compete with them. For example, one manufacturer of telecommunications equipment gave its distributors exclusive rights to distribute its products in their geographic markets as long as they achieved certain goals. If they failed to achieve the agreed upon objectives, the manufacturer could add additional distributors.

Relationships and the Market Opportunity

Let's tie our discussion of relationships to two areas of winning market leadership. The first is the role of relationships in opportunity assessment. The second is the role of managing and implementing relationships in the context of a complete winning market strategy.

The Opportunity

Certain market opportunities which have appeared to be attractive until this stage may all of a sudden become unattractive when relationships are considered—a late surprise in the planning process. Opportunities become unattractive because of the overwhelming issues associated with designing and managing a winning market web. There may be difficulty getting key players committed to relationships, a lack of experience in managing such relationships, or a lack of resources to maintain and develop such relationships. However, it is better to discover this now than to proceed with an opportunity only to fail because of relationship challenges.

A large U.S. company withdrew from an opportunity based on relationship issues. Historically, the nature of the customer relationship had been very transactional, focusing on selling supplies. As technology changed to computer-based integrated information systems, the company discovered that they were a long way from having the capabilities to manage the complex, cross-functional sales teams that were required to build relationships with customers in the new context. Even though they had invested millions in developing new technology, they decided, because of the relationship issues, to cease selling to end users, and to sell the technology on an OEM basis to other manufacturers.

At a higher level, if a number of opportunities you are considering start to look unattractive because of market web issues, you need to face up to the more fundamental issue of developing capabilities around managing relationships so that you can tackle future opportunities.

The Winning Strategy

We have dealt with the issue of building and managing critical relationships in its own chapter because of its fundamental importance to technology-intensive businesses. This is a somewhat artificial separation since developing relationships is a key component of completing the winning strategy to attack attractive market opportunities.

Next Step: Completing the Winning Strategy

Having identified the critical relationships and developed a strategy to manage them for each opportunity, you are now ready to complete all the other elements of the winning strategy for each opportunity as discussed in Chapter 9.

Another dimension of a winning strategy is superior implementation and execution. In most technology-based opportunities, an individual cannot manage any one relationship. It is more likely that a team of people from your company will be involved in any given relationship. This requires assembling the team, which is often an informal team, developing cohesion within the team, and ensuring that the organizational support, for example, the reward system, is in place to make the teamwork happen. Some of these issues are addressed in Chapter 11, which focuses on the implementation of strategy, others are picked up in Chapter 12, when teams are looked at in the context of marketing planning systems.

Key Questions for Executives and Managers

The important questions emerging from market web management are:

- Have you identified clear ways in which relationships can create value and deliver competitive differentiation through collaborative advantage?

- Have you designed a powerful market web with market chain strands, off-market chain strands, and knowledge and influence strands? Do you have a path for its evolution?

- Have you carved out a clear value-adding role for your company in the web? Can you play a strong role in guiding your web—being at the strategic center?

- Do you know which of the strands in your market web are absolutely critical to success in your opportunity?

- Have you asked penetrating questions about each of these critical strands, such as why is this relationship critical, what dimensions are there in each relationship, what is the current status of the relationship, is it strong and close or weak and distant, are competitors better positioned in certain relationships?

- Has responsibility for the management of these critical relationships been assigned to individuals and teams within your company?

- Do you have, and have you allocated, the capabilities and resources to effectively manage the critical relationships? If not, have you decided what to do about it?

- Are there plans in place to build and evolve critical relationships?

- Do you see the potential for developing market web management into a core competency?

CHAPTER NINE

Complete the Winning Strategy

Introduction

Through the process of strategic thinking (Chapter 7), you have identified and worked through a number of the major issues associated with your opportunity. Managing relationships has also been isolated as being critically important to a winning strategy (Chapter 8). The focus of this chapter is on completing the strategy. Even at completion, though, asking key questions does not stop as conditions change and competitors make moves. However, completing the winning strategy will allow you to move ahead and consider profitability, cash flow, and implementation issues.

A Framework

What are the elements of a complete winning strategy? Figure 9-1 outlines the scope of the issues that need to be considered. Our Winning Market Leadership Process indicates that by this time you have chosen an opportunity, and completed an assessment to see how this opportunity fits with the strategic business unit or company's portfolio of opportunities. The link between the work you have done, and what you need to do, is the development of a clear position for your product or service in the market in which the opportunity exists. This is where completing your winning strategy starts.

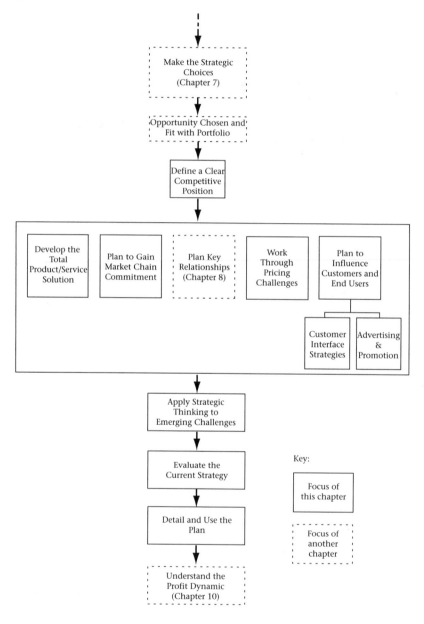

FIGURE 9-1: Complete the Winning Strategy—A Framework

Once this clear position has been identified, completing the plan involves defining the total product/service solution, planning how to gain the commitment of market chain members to your plan, continuing to refine the relationship work already done in the context of the market web, working through a number of pricing challenges, and developing a plan to communicate with customers and end users.

Once you have made these more tactical decisions, you again need to apply strategic thinking to new challenges that emerge. This leads you to evaluate your completed strategy. We will propose a set of criteria and tough questions to help with this assessment. Finally, the plan needs to be assessed with regard to how it can be continually updated in rapidly changing market conditions, and how the plan can be useful to people in your company. This chapter is intentionally unbalanced in the attention given to specific issues. Our aim is to spend more time on areas that present special issues for technology-intensive businesses.

Define a Clear Competitive Position in the Opportunity

The opportunity for which you are developing market leadership is defined by a combination of target markets to pursue, applications and functionality to provide, technologies and capabilities to use as a platform, and the role that your organization plans to play in adding value. The decisions you make about these elements should lead you to position yourself well in the marketplace. Positioning on the surface looks relatively straightforward—it is about making your product or service easy for the customer to choose. You must decide how your solution is a great fit with your customers' needs and demonstrate that to customers in the targeted segments. You have to decide, and then demonstrate, why your solution is a better fit with their needs than any competitive offerings, either direct or indirect. If you can develop a positioning statement that captures these advantages, you end up with a clear focus regarding your opportunity.

We have discovered that many managers think they know how they are approaching a market but are unable to provide clear answers to three simple questions:

1. Who are you pursuing?
2. What do you offer of value?
3. How are you differentiated from competition?

If you can't answer these basic questions succinctly as in an "elevator speech," there is no way in which you can develop a winning strategy. You require a clear position to be able to complete the product/service solution, to develop prices, and to decide on a communications strategy. The positioning statement becomes the link between your chosen opportunity and the tactical decisions to be made with respect to your marketing program.

Tandem Computers, now part of Compaq, was very successful in positioning itself in the highly competitive computer market. By linking multiple processors, Tandem provided a computer system that had extremely high reliability. High reliability is critical in many applications, including real-time transaction processing. By continuously investing in improved hardware and software, for many years Tandem was able to maintain a lead over competitors like IBM in what became known as high-reliability fault-tolerant computer systems. Tandem used the slogan "The Non-Stop Computing Company" to position its products in its target customers' minds. Non-stop computing was clearly relevant to their needs and differentiated Tandem from its competition.

If you, like Tandem, are able to capture your positioning in a "bumper sticker" statement, and can broadly communicate it to all those involved in the strategy, you will find a distinct consistency and focus. A clear positioning statement is the foundation of strategy.

Complete the Total Product/Service Solution

So far you may have conceptualized the product or service to offer. A winning strategy requires that you go beyond this core technology/functionality to conceptualize the total product/service solution tailored to the needs of the segments your product or service addresses and differentiated in a sustainable way from competition.

You must think about augmenting the core technology with surrounding service such as assisting customers with product design, integrating your logistics with customers' logistics, offering warranties, and providing after-sales support. The result should be a sustainable competitive advantage and increased profitability. Figure 9-2 (which was used in Chapter 4 to show how the whole product evolves over the adoption cycle) demonstrates how a pharmaceutical company might conceive of the total product/service solution at a specific time for a given target market. At its introduction, the pharmaceutical compound alone may not be enough to generate enthusiasm among innovators or technology enthusiasts. The firm may need to augment the offering with detailed pharmacological information—that is, information on the chemical mechanism that makes the drug work. Later, the total product/service solution might have to be reconfigured to include training sessions, and references to other physicians, to attract the segment of mainstream physicians.

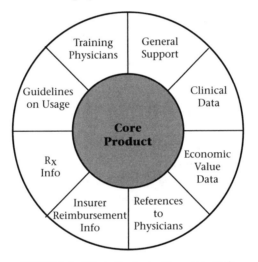

FIGURE 9-2: Whole Product - Pharmaceuticals

When considering the total product/service solution, it is important to conceptualize it from the perspective of end users, market chain members, and other stakeholders. Even if the solution looks ideal from the end-user's perspective, if market chain members do not see added value in your offering compared to a competitor's, adoption will not occur. The pharmaceutical example also points to how the total product/service solution may be viewed differently by different stakeholders. For example, insurance companies and government payors may not view the offering as complete if it does not contain economic value data.

A critical issue to think through at this stage is the impact on the profit dynamic over time if you augment the core product or service. Many companies, in evolving their total product/service solution, increase their service costs to the point that the opportunity becomes unprofitable. This can happen in an insidious manner when customers continue to ratchet up the features and services they expect as part of the core offering. This feature and service "creep," along with price squeezes, can result in negative cash flow. If this does happen, you need to reassess the kinds of customers you are attracting, the ability of the sales force and other communication vehicles to communicate the value proposition, and the ways you have augmented the core product in an attempt to reduce costs.

Other questions emerge when completing the total product/service offering. First, what will your balance be between standardization and customization? If your technology plans call for a fairly rapid evolution of new-generation products, customization can become a nightmare, as each new generation will require recustomization. Second, product line breadth and depth issues need to be sorted out for the opportunity. How many products do you want to have in your product line? Third, a debate must be held with respect to industry standards compared to proprietary technology. If the direction is toward industry standards, a process must be developed to place bets on one or a few emerging industry standards. Trying to bet on all emerging standards stretches finances, people, management attention, and product development time. Fourth, you must constantly look for opportunities to integrate high-contribution services into your product offerings. Not all services become part of the standard product offering. Some can be profitably sold to segments of customers. For example, in the aircraft engine business, smart companies are constantly looking for opportunities to provide additional services to generate additional cash flow streams.

Plan to Gain Market Chain Commitment

In pursuing market leadership, managers tend to focus, and rightly so, on the value proposition to the end user. What is often not given as much attention is how the proposition looks to members of the market chain. A critical stage in completing the winning strategy is planning how to gain commitment from the various members in your market chain. It is critical to take their perspective. How does the total product solution offering appear to them? How will this offer affect their profitability and their differential advantage in the marketplace? How will the total product/service solution allow them to enhance adoption at the next level of the market chain?

Basic Issues

Market chain members will commit to supporting your venture if they see in this opportunity "strategic leverage." The essence of this concept, which is explored in detail in Chapter 10, is that market chain members need to be shown how your proposition will affect their profit dynamic or profit model. It could affect their profit dynamic by allowing them to reduce costs, enhance revenue, provide differential advantage to beat competitors at their level in the market chain, or enhance their overall bundled offering.

Intuit demonstrated this type of understanding and commitment to its retailers by pricing its software, such as Quicken, so that it was cheaper when bought at a retail store than if bought directly from Intuit. This policy encouraged customers to go to the retail store, which gave the retailer an opportunity to up-sell and cross-sell and generate cash flow and profitability. It also gave Quicken an overwhelming presence in the retail store, which encouraged new users to choose Quicken since it appeared to be the most popular brand of personal finance software.

There must be enough contribution margin in your proposal to allow a market chain member to deliver its value-adding role and to make money. That is, the strategic payoffs from adopting and aggressively pushing your product must exceed the resources the market chain member must commit to adopt and sell your product.

The level of support a market chain member requires needs to be identified. Questions such as these should be addressed:

- Is support readily available?
- Is it available during the hours that a market chain member requires?
- Is it responsive?
- Does the support team understand the issues that market chain members face?

An additional issue to consider is exclusivity. Market chain members may want exclusive rights to your offering in a given geographic area for a given period of time. What happens if exclusivity is granted and the market chain member does not provide the support necessary for success? Going hand-in-hand with any form of exclusivity are agreements and targets to be met on the part of market chain members. These capture the "we give, we get" of the situation.

The acid test for determining if your proposal does add value to market chain members is to put yourself in their shoes. In that position, if you were offered a proposition such as the one you have formulated, would you choose it? What is missing? What would make you reject this offering or not give it enough attention to encourage rapid adoption down the market chain?

It takes only one level of the market chain to not be on board for you to end up in a losing market position. At National Semiconductor, a fax/modem/data board for PCs was launched into retail distribution through large computer retailers. Customers had to install the board on their PCs themselves or have someone else, such as the retailer, do it. The retailer's sales force also had to become intimately familiar with the product and its application. With the margin structure, and several competitive offerings, there was little incentive for the retailer to focus on National's board and it was not successful.

Work Through Pricing Challenges

No plan is complete until a pricing strategy has been developed. Initial prices must be set for new offerings, and you must plan how prices will change over the adoption life cycle as well as over the entire period from launch to death. The assumption here is that you do have control over pricing decisions, which may not be the case. A powerful market chain member or competitor may be in a position to dictate your price. In this situation, your challenge is to see if, at that price, you can meet your corporate objectives such as cash flow and profitability. The framework in Figure 9-3 captures some unique issues regarding the pricing challenges that many technology-intensive businesses face.

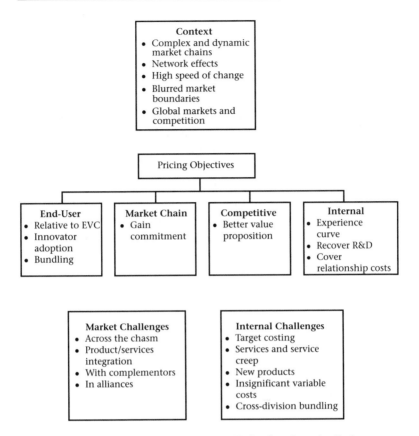

FIGURE 9-3: Pricing Challenges in Many Technology-Intensive Businesses

The Impact of Context

Several pricing issues in technology-intensive businesses arise from the context in which these businesses operate. Technology-intensive businesses face some unique challenges that affect the entire planning process, and specifically affect the pricing of products and services. In the face of shortened product life cycles, pricing becomes absolutely critical to success. There is often a narrow window in which to recover high R&D costs, to cover costs associated with managing relationships in extensive market webs, and to generate cash flow to meet corporate objectives.

Product commoditization, where competitors can rapidly copy your offering, also raises challenging pricing issues. After launch, it may not be long before customers and users start to see that there are equivalent or similar offerings in the marketplace. The first question they raise is: Why should we pay a premium for your offering? In some situations, this puts pressure on getting a large positive contribution from your opportunity early and on managing costs through the adoption life cycle, so as products are commoditized, there still may be a positive contribution. In other situations, such as in the software business, where fixed costs are high, variable costs low, and costs for customers to switch are high, you may go to the other extreme and price low to establish yourself as the market leader. If you are in a market where network effects are key, you may even consider giving away software in order to build a dominant position. Profits must then come from upgrades and related products. Netscape was one of the pioneers of the Internet business model of giving away software to build market share. At one stage it had an 85% share of the Web browser market.

Pricing Objectives

Pricing in technology-intensive businesses involves a fine balance between end user, market chain, competitive, and internal objectives. The relative emphasis given to each of these four sets of objectives will change over the life of the opportunity.

End-User Objectives

When you are setting pricing objectives with the end user in mind, it is paramount to understand the role price plays in the end-user's decision to adopt a product or service. Is price the major factor in the decision process or is it relatively low on the list? Thinking through the customer's choice/rejection process, as we did in Chapter 4, is critical.

One objective in establishing prices from the end-user's perspective is to set the price relative to your understanding of the Economic Value to the Customer (EVC).[1] As discussed in Chapter 6, this is the price a rational end user should be willing to pay so as to be indifferent between the current approach to solving a problem and the one you are proposing. For example, if you are offering reduced

---

[1] See John L. Forbis and Nitin T. Mehta, "Value-based Strategy for Industrial Products," *The McKinsey Quarterly* (Summer 1981), pp. 35–52.

life-cycle costs by providing lower maintenance costs and by having a more reliable product, the end user should be willing to pay a price premium. However, this EVC will not likely be the final price, as the end user will need an inducement to switch to your solution and will also use other price reference points and benchmarks when making the decision. For example, a company developed a metal pad to place in the helmet of pile-driving equipment. From the perspective of economic value to the customer, a price of $900 can be justified since the new pad increases productivity and decreases downtime. However, the current cost of simple asbestos pads in this application was $3 to $4. This large perceived gap made it impossible to charge $900 even though the end user should be indifferent between this and the current cost of $3 to $4 per pad.

A second objective in pricing relative to the end user is to establish a price that induces innovators to be attracted to your offering. Without getting the innovators on board, the adoption process grinds to a halt. As one approach, beta customers may be given the product, not only to provide feedback on it, but also to build commitment to it and to induce switching.

Finally, you need to consider the issue of bundling versus unbundling of products and services. Are the end users to whom you are appealing more interested in having an integrated product/service solution, i.e., are they willing to pay a bundled price for products and services, or are they more interested in paying for those components of the total solution which they deem necessary?

Market Chain Objectives

From a market chain perspective, pricing decisions must be such that the ongoing commitment and enthusiasm of market chain members is maintained. In some technology-intensive businesses, a different perspective might have to be taken on meeting market chain objectives. Over time, as a product becomes more commodity-like, you may not have the margin dollars available to meet existing market chain member needs. In this case, the market chain needs to be reconfigured to incorporate lower cost channel members. For example, PCs and printers have moved from specialty computer stores to computer superstores, big box retailers and discount department stores.

Competitive Objectives

Pricing versus competition is easily defined yet difficult to execute. The objective is to create a better value proposition than the competition can offer. By a value proposition we mean "the what you get for what you give."

$$\text{Value Proposition} \ = \ \frac{\text{Get}}{\text{Give}} \ = \ \frac{\text{Results Produced} + \text{Process Quality}}{\text{Price} + \text{Access Costs (time, effort)}}$$

The "get" is first of all the results produced by the total solution of products and services. Second, it is the additional benefits the end user experiences from interaction during the sales and service delivery process. With Saturn automobiles, for example, the soft-sell approach and the celebration that each customer experiences when receiving delivery of the car is the process quality in the value proposition. The "give" is the end user's spending of dollars, time, and effort over the life of the purchase.

> In our experience, managers are more adept at thinking about the denominator and are tempted to reduce price over time. They might be further ahead by paying more attention to increasing the numerator, i.e., the quality or the value-added services provided.

Internal Objectives

Key to managing price from an internal perspective is knowing what your corporate targets are, and how these might evolve over the life cycle of the product/service. Are you interested in maintaining specified profit margins over time? Achieving market share goals? Pricing in concordance with the experience curve? Achieving certain cash flow profiles over the life of the project? Clear commitments need to be made about the priority of potentially conflicting internal objectives. Certain objectives are more thought provoking in technology-intensive businesses.

One important issue is pricing relative to the experience curve. The experience curve reflects the percentage reduction in cost that can occur with each doubling of cumulative production and is typically in the range of 10 to 30%. In technology-intensive businesses, where many products are early in their life cycles, we find many doublings of experience in a short period of time, hence rapid declines in cost. Deciding how to evolve prices as these costs reduce is a challenge. Figure 9-4 shows how a company in the semiconductor business approached this issue. Price was set below costs early on to encourage adoption and gain market share. In the second phase, the company holds a price umbrella to get a fast return on investment. However, this practice encourages competitors to enter the market because of the perceived opportunity to generate profits under the umbrella. In phase III, competitive pressures cause the company to lower prices at a rate that is in fact steeper than the experience curve in order to protect its competitive position. Finally, toward the end of the life cycle, price becomes less volatile with the price curve paralleling the experience curve. Another company in the same situation that was more willing to wait for its return on investment might reduce its price in line with experience curve cost reductions. While less profitable in the short run, this action would discourage competitive entry and might result in a higher market share and higher profits over the product life cycle.

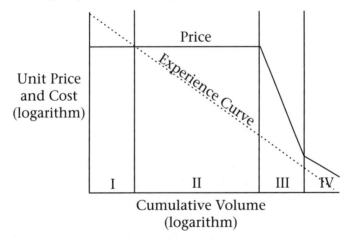

FIGURE 9-4: Pricing Relative to the Experience Curve[2]

A second issue relates to the investment in research and development associated with the opportunity. Given shortened life cycles and the commoditization of technology-intensive products, the temptation is to recover R&D costs quickly. The downside of this

---

2 *Perspectives on Experience* (Boston: Boston Consulting Group, 1970).

approach is that it would encourage a high initial price, which might discourage innovator adoption and result in a low market share.

A third issue to emphasize in technology-intensive businesses is the cost of relationships. As you discovered in the previous chapter, there are numerous key relationships that must be managed to achieve a winning market leadership position. In establishing a price, the cost of developing and maintaining these relationships must be considered. These costs rise probably more quickly in technology-intensive situations due to the messy and extensive nature of market webs.

The challenge is to continuously balance the four sets of objectives. The company that successfully manages this delicate balancing act over the life of an opportunity evolves prices in a way that gains market chain commitment, satisfies end users' search for value, differentiates itself from competitors' value propositions, and meets internal objectives. Beyond objectives, what other pricing challenges might you face in your kind of business?

Other Challenges

Market Challenges

There are a few market challenges associated with pricing that may be greater than most others. The first is evolving a pricing strategy to get across the chasm that often exists between the acceptance of your offering by earlier adopters, and the goal of gaining broader acceptance. Crossing the chasm requires that you have a total product/service solution in order for the early majority or pragmatists to adopt. As the home market for PCs evolved, Compaq developed the Presario line to appeal to users looking for an all-in-one packaged solution that would be easy to install and operate. Such a solution appealed particularly to the late majority or conservative segment of home users and was quite successful. The challenge is deciding what should go into the bundle and how to price this entire bundle, rather than pricing specific components.

A variation on the bundling challenge is how to set prices in those instances of product-service integration. For example, how does Xerox determine what to charge a customer on a per copy basis? The price would have to recognize Xerox's investment in equipment, anticipated service costs based on reliability estimates, and future costs of parts and labor. A similar problem is posed to companies like GE who are willing to commit to maintaining an airline's aircraft engines for a certain amount per hour flown over a 10 to 20-year period. If the products and services were sold separately, the product would typically generate a one-time cash flow, whereas the services component would generate cash flow over an extended period of time. As you will see in our discussion about the profit dynamic associated with these situations (Chapter 10), it is complex.

Two other pricing issues arise in the context of the market web. The first is how to set your price relative to the price of components coming from complementors. For example, if you are a software supplier, how do you price your product relative to the cost of the hardware that an end user might need to solve a problem? Another instance where the market web generates pricing issues is pricing within alliances. If you enter a horizontal selling alliance, the issue becomes how the two organizations decide on a pricing strategy which appeals to market chain members and end users, and at the same time allows both organizations to satisfy their internal objectives. This decision may be difficult if the two companies have different internal objectives. One may be interested in immediate cash flow whereas the other may be more interested in longer-term return on investment.

Internal Challenges

Managers in technology-intensive businesses need to be acquainted with a number of additional internal challenges. First, you might want to consider some form of "target costing" in price setting. Establish what end users and market chain members expect as a price for your total product/service offering, then set cost objectives for the components that go into the solution. A difficult issue in technology-intensive businesses is determining expectations with technologies that may be so innovative it is difficult for them to be expressed. Assessing the economic value to the customer (EVC) of current and potential solutions may help in this situation.

As mentioned earlier, a second issue to be recognized internally is that of feature and service creep. As your product/service moves from innovators and early adopters toward the majority in the adoption cycle, expectations rise regarding services. An issue here is tracking the incremental features and services you are adding to the bundle, and attempting to ensure that appropriate pricing decisions are made to cover them. A better response may be to look to members of the market chain to enhance the bundle if they can do so in a more efficient and effective way.

The third internal challenge is that of pricing new products. If the opportunity involves a product relatively similar to that existing in the marketplace—i.e., it is low on the newness dimension—both you and your customers have a reference point which guides the pricing decisions. If a product is very different, however, the question becomes how much buyers will pay for perceived differences in functionality, technology, or appearance. Crude as it is, the intuitive approach to setting prices for new products is probably the most common one used. This does not excuse you from structured attempts to estimate demand, determine market requirements over the product's life cycle, estimate EVC, estimate costs over the life cycle, or estimate competitors' entry capabilities and probable entry dates.

An additional challenge in technology-intensive business is pricing products and services where variable costs are insignificant. In the software business, it costs next to nothing to produce one more CD-ROM or to allow a customer to download a file from the Internet. In this case, one option is to set a low price just above variable costs. The implications may be insignificant cash flows and insignificant funding available for future opportunities. On the other hand, such a low-price strategy could play well in a market exhibiting network effects and may result in a high market share, which can then be leveraged with profitable upgrades and add-on products. Microsoft with its "deep pockets" has executed this strategy very effectively in several markets. In these cases you must really conceive of the entire opportunity, and related opportunities, from start to finish to ensure the appropriate pricing decisions are made.

A final internal challenge associated with pricing arises when customers expect bundles of products and services that cut across your divisional or SBU boundaries. Because a division or SBU may be measured on its own dollar contribution or profitability, there may be an unwillingness to give up margin in one division to ensure the selling of the bundled offering. For example, a large newspaper in New York went to the marketplace looking for a bundled offering across a number of product lines such as overhead projectors, professional film, printing plates, equipment, and so forth. The only organization that was able to meet this request was a Japanese organization accustomed to cutting across internal silos to put together such packages. North American organizations could not resolve the internal dynamics associated with meeting such a request. Transfer pricing does not get around this issue as each division making a component of the package wants a margin and the division dealing with the customer wants an incremental margin as they bundle the transferred product together with other products. These double margins often make the bundled solution unattractive.

To recap, there are a number of substantial and unique challenges associated with pricing in many technology-intensive businesses. The challenge for you is to work these through and recognize which are the key issues in your opportunity.

Plan to Influence Customers and End Users

No marketing strategy is complete until you have made decisions on communicating with both market chain members and end users. The objective is to develop effective communication strategies to influence choice/rejection within the market chain and at the end-user level. In technology-intensive businesses, influence is exerted by developing outstanding customer interface strategies, and through advertising, promotion, and public relations.

Customer Interface Strategies

Communication with market web members and some end users is usually direct. It typically involves salespeople and people from other functional areas, enhanced by Web-based systems. An implication of this complexity is that influencing can be expensive. This requires that you identify critical segments of end users and specific members in key market chains to whom you will direct your communication resources.

You need to identify the different "customer interface strategies" applicable to different segments of market chain members and end users. Interface strategies are the decisions you take to combine salespeople, people from other functional areas and divisions of your company and other organizations, and systems/technologies to create a powerful interface between your organization and a market chain member. Interfacing with powerful market chain members is critical. A computer manufacturer's choice of semiconductor suppliers is critical to the success of the semiconductor manufacturer, so the computer manufacturer often holds a lot of power. This influence is becoming more evident as large customers such as Compaq and DEC merge. Developing the right interface is key for the semiconductor manufacturer.

An additional trend which makes planning a customer interface strategy critical is that of customers asking suppliers to coordinate their efforts across product lines, divisions and geographic boundaries to ensure a consistent offering and interface. When customers demand these kinds of things, it is imperative that you understand what has to go into this integrated interface to satisfy such customers.

Rockwell International demonstrates resourcefulness in creating market advantage through interdivisional and cross-functional cooperation. Cross-functional teams and new organizational configurations around core business processes have created an atmosphere where cross-divisional issues can be addressed. Success and learning from cooperating in past situations has allowed Rockwell to win a number of additional contracts because of the kind of interface they were able to pull together—the kind of interface that leads to long term supplier/customer bonding. Outcomes have been impressive. Between 1986 and 1996, Rockwell lost $4 billion in government business as defence spending declined but replaced it with $4 billion in commercial business.

To guide your thinking about customer interface strategies, a range of them is illustrated in Figure 9-5. The kind of interface required can be assessed by looking at the complexity of the customer's need for information and integrated solutions on one dimension, and the customer's need for a relationship on the other. For example, a customer who has complex information and systems need, but low relationship need, requires an interface that delivers systems and solutions. Customers with relatively simple needs, and customers who do not place a high value on relationships, can be approached on a much more transactional basis. The extreme is where customers demand systems and solutions because of the complexity of the situations they face, and place a high value on the kinds of outcomes that can result from strong relationships. In these cases, you need to think about developing strong partnering interfaces.

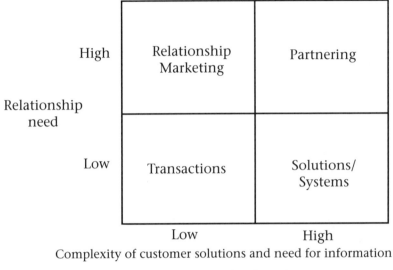

FIGURE 9-5: Customer Interface Strategies

Baxter Health Care has developed a strategy of customer-focused teams whereby the nature of the team varies by customer segment. Some of their interface strategies go as far as delivering supplies right to hospital floors and actually running hospital departments. It is this creative development of customer interfaces that has led to Baxter Health Care's reputation of being leading edge.

The Role of Technology

Aside from identifying the people configuration required at the interface, you need to think about the role of technology at the customer interface. Internet marketing implies a very different role for technology and people, telemarketing can become a strong component of an interface strategy, and you can even go as far as a virtual interface strategy such as in virtual banking. Today extranets are forming that allow customers and suppliers to interact by extending their intranets into each other's organization. This enabling technology enhances the interface and may provide substantial competitive advantage, as Intel, Cisco and Dell, among others, have realized.

Advertising and Promotion

Do advertising and promotion matter? In our experience, technology-intensive businesses tend to underplay the role of advertising and promotion. They believe that product innovation and outstanding relationships with members of the market chain will carry the day. However, another belief often expressed is that the closer your organization is to the end user in the market chain, and the more end users there are, the more important advertising and promotion become. For example, if you are a PC retailer, advertising to consumers and corporate customers may be essential.

Advantage Through Advertising

A great example of innovative advertising—although it flies in the face of accepted wisdom—is the creative approach that Intel, relatively far upstream in the market chain, first took in the early 1990s to develop consumer loyalty at the end-user level. The Intel Inside advertising campaign shows end users demanding Intel chips. Cisco and Nortel Networks have attempted something similar with their "Cisco Powered Network" and "How the World Shares Ideas" campaigns. These campaigns are targeted at boards of directors, senior executives and the broader investment community. Since technology commitments are moving into the boardroom, both Cisco and Nortel Networks are creating awareness of their network equipment through corporate advertising strategies.

You should also consider the opportunity to create primary demand for a new product. Primary demand stimulation may be done in conjunction with complementors. For example, a joint advertising campaign between an electronic game manufacturer and game software provider might demonstrate to consumers that the latest generation of video game technology can provide a superior entertainment experience compared with earlier game technology.

Advantage Through Promotion and Public Relations

Promotion and public relations can be important components of a winning strategy. Public relations can be directed at influencing standards-setting associations, for example. Making sure that associations are aware of innovations, and are promoting your overall corporate image, can be part of a winning strategy.   Another approach to building a strong public image is through using executives in these public relations and promotional roles. A number of technology-intensive organizations have developed executive partnering programs. These programs formally identify the role that senior executives should play in dealing with associations, alliance partners, standards-setting associations, etc.

In general, do not discount the importance of advertising if you are upstream in the market chain. Make sure that opportunities for promotion, public relations, and publicity are leveraged, especially with members of the market web that are not specifically part of the market chain. Review the role that executives can play in enhancing your organization's image.

Apply Strategic Thinking to Emerging Challenges

At this stage you have given it your best shot to complete a winning strategy for this iteration of the planning process. Based on a clearly defined position in the marketplace, you have developed the total product/service solution, planned how to gain market chain commitment, reviewed key relationships, faced challenges associated with pricing in technology-intensive businesses, and developed communication plans both for customers and end users. It is time to apply the same kind of strategic thinking encountered in Chapter 7 to any issues that surfaced in completing the winning strategy. This task reinforces the iterative nature of our planning process and encourages you to be on guard for major strategic issues at any time. What are some of the strategic issues that you might have found in completing the winning strategy?

You might have discovered:

- a fundamental issue with the positioning you are attempting to develop. If you are doubtful as to whether the position you have developed is a clear winner, you need to revisit your understanding of competition and how you can differentiate yourself, and you need to go back to a more in-depth understanding of customer and end-user needs.

- that the total product/service solution is far different from the core product that you thought was the foundation of your opportunity. The question then is: Can you in fact develop the total product/service solution in a way that can create value for customers and end users, and in way that generates acceptable profitability for you?

- in thinking about getting market chain commitment and working out some of the pricing challenges, that there are more substantial barriers to adopting your offering than originally anticipated. This forces you back to re-estimate the adoption rates proposed, and to think ahead to the implications for the financial outcomes of the opportunity.

- that you have underplayed the importance of relationships and communicating with customers and end users. This discovery will cause you to review the inherent capability of your organization to execute these communication plans and gain market chain commitment.

- a sense that difficulties will be encountered as you attempt to move from the adoption of your product by early adopters or visionaries, to the adoption by the mainstream early majority or pragmatists. Enhancing the core offering to include all the value-adding services needed by the pragmatists creates challenges, which need to be addressed.

- the need to introduce next-generation technology much earlier than anticipated. The concept of eating your own lunch before a competitor does requires strategic thinking. When is it right to introduce the next generation while the current generation is still generating significant positive cash flow?

It is important to review these types of issues to ensure that they have been addressed in the strategy.

Evaluate the Current Strategy

It's time to discover whether the current strategy you have developed is as powerful as it can be for this iteration of the planning process. This exercise involves asking three fundamental questions, which form the foundation of our Winning Market Leadership Process. This gets us back to Chapter 1 and the following figure.

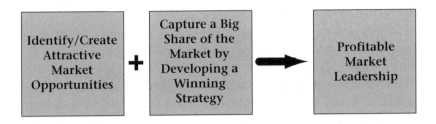

The fundamental questions to revisit are:

- Are you going after an attractive market opportunity?
- Can you win with your proposed strategy?
- If you win, will it be worth it?

What happens if you discover that you do not have great answers to these questions? You need to return to those areas in the Winning Market Leadership Process that need further probing to lead you to positive, confident answers to the fundamental questions. We've included pointers to specific chapters in our discussion to get you to where you might need to probe further. After looking at these three basic questions, we also propose a couple of other characteristics of a powerful and complete strategy.

Are You Going After an Attractive Market Opportunity?

An attractive opportunity shows total profit potential, has the market forces working in your favor, and passes the test of the underlying assumptions still being valid.

Profit Potential and Market Forces

By total profit potential, we mean someone can make money in this opportunity. This is quite different from assessing revenue potential and market growth, which can be misleading indicators of a good opportunity. Attractive total profit potential doesn't mean that you will be the winner or the market leader, but it does mean that the forces in the marketplace make it attractive (see Chapter 3). The profit pie is large enough for you to consider participating.

Assumptions Are Valid

When developing your winning strategy, you made a number of assumptions about the environment, the market, your own capabilities, competition, and other areas, as you worked at making decisions. It is now time to check these assumptions to make sure they are up to date. Are they reasonable? Have you tested your strategy against the sensitivity of some of your assumptions? For example, what if you've assumed a certain growth rate? Is this still a reasonable assumption, and what would happen if this growth rate were off by 25%?

Another key area to check out is the potential reaction of competitors. Since you've started your planning iteration, competitors have also been planning and making changes. Are the early assumptions with respect to competitive actions, reactions, and interest in this opportunity still legitimate (Chapter 6)?

Can You Win with Your Proposed Strategy?

Even if you decide there is an attractive opportunity, you need to confirm that the complete strategy you have developed can lead to a market-leading position. Can you beat competition to gain a large enough share of the profit pie to meet your objectives? A winning strategy meets basic marketing criteria, is consistent, and is feasible.

Basic Marketing Criteria

Every strategy must be focused, provide true customer value, and develop sustainable competitive advantage. Focus means choosing whom to serve, and perhaps more importantly whom not to serve in the marketplace. Roy Vagelos, CEO of Merck claims, "The only way to make the kinds of complex bets that you must make in an information intensive business like Merck is by balancing two metrics: risk and focus."[3] Inherent in his definition of focus is choosing market segments to serve, functions/applications to provide, technologies/competencies to bet on, and value-adding roles for you to fulfill (Chapter 3).

---

[3] Nancy A. Nichols, "Medicine, Management, and Mergers: An Interview with Merck's P. Roy Vagelos," *Harvard Business Review* (November-December 1994), pp.104-114.

By true customer value we mean offering something of importance for which customers are willing to pay. It also means having a way to get customers to reject their current solutions to problems, so they will be in a position to choose you and your value proposition. Get tough with yourself, as people often think they are providing value, but from the customer's and end-user's perspective they are not (Chapter 4). Value can also be seen in getting beyond a strategic breakpoint and creating something that really excites customers (Chapter 7).

By sustainable competitive advantage we mean something that you can do better than your competitors, and that you can maintain over time. This success often implies you are leveraging core competencies (Chapter 5).

Consistency

Your complete strategy must have integrity and consistency. First of all, your strategy must be internally consistent. It must be consistent across market chain selection, key relationships developed (Chapter 8), communication programs, the product service/offering, and pricing. The strategy must also have integrity and consistency over time. You should be able to see your strategy unfolding and evolving as the market changes. If you see potential disconnects in strategy over time, they need to be addressed now.

Feasibility

A check of the feasibility of your strategy requires thinking along two dimensions. The first dimension is feasibility given your available resources and competencies. If you determine that your strategy is not feasible, you must go back and look for additional resources and competencies to allow the strategy to unfold, or reassess the strategy itself, given the constraints on resources and competencies (Chapter 5).

The second dimension of feasibility is having a strong sense that the strategy can be implemented within a desired period. It is not just a matter of having the resources and skills available, it is a matter of whether they can be marshaled in a timely and efficient manner to meet your objectives (Chapter 11).

If You Win, Will It be Worth It?

Chances are that if you have identified or created an attractive opportunity, and if you have convinced yourself you can win market leadership, going for it will be worth it. "Worth it" is a combination of generating cash flow and profitability relative to company objectives, matching returns to possible vulnerabilities and risks in the opportunity, and being of strategic value to the company.

Potential Returns

An important question to ask is whether reasonable estimates of potential returns meet your company's objectives. This procedure requires an assessment of the amount and pattern of the cash flow over the life cycle of the opportunity. Even though total returns may look attractive, if the pattern of returns does not tie in with corporate objectives, your strategy may need revisiting (Chapter 10). The potential returns must also be judged against marketplace objectives such as market share goals and objectives concerning market leadership.

Vulnerability

Now is the time to thoroughly assess the risks inherent in the opportunity and in your strategy. How robust is the strategy to changes in key assumptions? Are there any new threats that have arisen since starting the planning process? An additional area to question is the ability of the strategy to change as the marketplace evolves in somewhat uncertain directions. Is there a certain robustness to the strategy? Inherent in looking at vulnerability is identifying "risk points" to be carefully managed. GE Capital does an outstanding job of this, which many observers feel has been a key to its success.

An interesting example of assessing risks and vulnerability was the purchase of MEDCO, a pharmacy benefits management company, by Merck for $6.6 billion in 1994. Merck, a pharmaceutical company, decided there was a great opportunity to change its value-adding role by getting into the pharmaceutical distribution business and prescription drug management. The opportunity arose because of changes in the health care environment putting more emphasis on drug and disease management, as opposed to producing new and innovative drugs. Senior executives were aware of the risks inherent in investing $6.6 billion.

A number of actions were taken to attempt to contain this risk. For example, a concerted effort was made to blend some of the management from MEDCO with the management of Merck to make the organization seamless in its functioning. If the purchased organization were not fully integrated with Merck, the synergy required to take advantage of changes in the marketplace would not occur. This "risk point" became a focus of management time and attention.

Strategic Value

You need to confirm that the opportunity you are addressing, and the strategy you are pursuing, is consistent with the strategic direction of your organization. You need to know that the opportunity you are firming up fits with the portfolio of opportunities your organization or strategic business unit wants to pursue.

In certain instances, this third dimension of "worth it" may carry more weight than potential returns from the opportunity. You may decide to pursue an opportunity because it will lead to other lucrative opportunities. The inherent question is whether your company would be better off in the longer term by pursuing this opportunity than it would be if it didn't.

Other Considerations

A powerful strategy also shows the following characteristics: decisions are explicit and can be put into action, and the strategy meets the "gut feel" test.

Decisions Are Explicit and Can Be Put into Action

A solid strategy is based on a foundation of explicit decisions which can be put into action. Key decisions have not been avoided, people are not left to guess what decisions have been made, and decisions can be acted upon. The most fundamental decisions that need to be made explicit are those dealing with the dimensions of the opportunity. Have you clearly identified market segments to pursue, functions and applications to be delivered, technology platforms and capabilities upon which to build these functionalities, and the value-adding role that your organization and others will play in this opportunity? Other key decisions should also be made explicit. Ask yourself the question: Are there big areas that remain hazy and left for others to fill in as they perceive the situation?

"Gut Feel"

After judging your strategy against the three fundamental questions, your strategy must pass the "gut feel" test. Call this managerial intuition based on experience. The strategy that you have developed must excite you, and the people around you, for it to be successful. If this strategy cannot light fires under people, we suspect there is something wrong. A great strategy inspires, instills confidence, and excites people.

Developing strategy is not a simple task. The three fundamental questions can be asked at any stage of your planning process as a mechanism to check on how you are doing. A complete winning strategy should generate strong positive answers to these three questions and reflect the other considerations of explicit decisions that can be acted on, and passing the "gut feel" test.

Detail and Use the Plan

We have all had this experience. A plan is developed. At the end of the planning iteration, people are convinced the planning process is over. The plan gets put into a binder and sits on a shelf. The plan is not referred to because it is not visible or in a format that people can easily respond to. A great plan must be visible, must be shared, and must continuously generate enthusiasm. Through the iterative process of developing the plan and gaining commitment to it, hopefully you and other managers have developed a mental model of this plan—something that you and others carry around, something that you continuously refer to, and something that you continuously refresh as events and reactions of competitors unfold.

> You might take your plan and create posters and pictures that capture its substance. Simple things such as these are visible reminders of the essence of your strategy. Hard-hitting yet simplified versions of strategy can direct efforts. For example, in the early 1990s, Logitech, the large manufacturer of mice and other devices associated with PCs, refocused the organization and brought consistency to

organizational efforts by defining themselves as being in the "Senseware" business. This one-word slogan captured people's imagination and was useful in focusing efforts in R&D and other areas of the organization. Senseware captured the kinds of opportunities the company would pursue.

Detailing and using your marketing strategy is not so much about capturing it completely in a firm format which could end up on a shelf. It is about coming up with a creative format that allows people to continuously revisit the strategy, be inspired by it, and be guided by it when decisions are made.

Next Step: Understanding the Profit Dynamic

The real test of any strategy addressing an opportunity is the financial test. In the next chapter we discuss the translation of your complete winning strategy into the common denominator of cash. This chapter will focus on understanding the profit dynamic.

Key Questions for Executives and Managers

- Is the position that you will take in the marketplace for this opportunity crystal clear with regard to target market(s) and benefits to focus on to meet these customers' needs and beat competition? Do you have this focus, which is necessary to complete your winning strategy?

- Have you developed the total product/service solution? What services will be included as part of the basic offering, and which ones are to be viewed as incremental cash flow opportunities?

- Is the offering such that it will compel strong and unequivocal support from market chain members? Do they see strategic leverage in the proposition? Is each market member's value-adding role clearly identified?

- Have you revisited the relationships critical to your opportunity to ensure that you can manage and resource them?

- Do your pricing decisions reflect a balance across end user, market chain member, competitor, and internal objectives? Have you dealt with the unique pricing challenges in technology-intensive businesses such as pricing relative to the experience curve?

- Have you explicitly designed customer interface strategies to solidify the approaches to various end user and market chain segments? Do your customer interface strategies generate competitive advantage and enhance your ability to pursue your strategic path?

- Have you creatively considered the role of advertising, promotion, public relations, and publicity in your winning strategy?

- Have you applied strategic thinking to major issues that emerged as you completed your winning strategy?

- Does your strategy pass the test when you ask the three fundamental questions underlying a powerful strategy? Are you going after an attractive opportunity? Can you win with your proposed strategy? If you win, will it be worth it?

- Is your plan in a format that makes it a living plan? Encourages excitement and commitment? Is easy to revisit as conditions change?

CHAPTER TEN

Understand the Profit Dynamic

Introduction

In Chapter 9, you developed the strategy for your particular product or service opportunity. This strategy may evolve with further iterations of the planning process. The tentative strategy is now the basis for developing a thorough understanding of the profit dynamic, and developing answers to such critical questions as, "Are we going to make money if we follow this strategy?" and "Will we meet our profit and cash flow objectives?"

You may have a hierarchy of strategic objectives associated with this opportunity, but the primary objectives must be financial, and of these, the most critical one is cash flow. Ultimately the purpose of any strategy is to positively affect the cash flows of the corporation and generate economic returns that exceed your corporation's cost of capital. This process creates shareholder value. In some cases, the particular opportunity by itself might not be profitable,[1] but it should generate sufficient positive cash flows elsewhere in the organization to justify the investment of resources. For example, some North American and European companies, such as Kodak, have invested

---

[1] We will use the term "profitable" in this chapter to mean opportunities where the present value of the cash flow stream exceeds the cost of capital.

heavily in opportunities in Japan, even though these opportunities are not in themselves immediately profitable. However, the objective has often been to depress the profitability of Japanese competitors in their home market, so that they have less cash flow to support their activities elsewhere in the world. Thus, these North American and European companies hope that the poor cash flows from these Japanese opportunities are more than offset by higher cash flows in the rest of the world.

This chapter focuses on the profit dynamic, which allows you to decompose and explore the critical components of cash flow for product and service opportunities. Understanding the profit dynamic for a market opportunity requires an in-depth knowledge of each of the major cash flow drivers.

The objectives of this chapter are to help you conceptualize how different product and service opportunities can create cash flow; for your particular strategic opportunity, to identify the key factors for building cash flow; to analyze where the greatest opportunities for, and threats to, cash flow creation are in different situations, such as new product development and product-service integration; and to introduce strategic leverage, a tool which will help you explore the impact of your strategy on the cash flows for other key players in your market chain.

The Profit Dynamic

There are a wide variety of possible measures of financial performance, from revenue, cash flow and profit to measures of asset utilization (such as return on equity, return on capital employed, or return on net assets) and measures of shareholder value (such as economic value-added). Particularly in circumstances where large investments are made relative to the size of the company, risk must also be considered.

For your purpose in building a winning strategy for your market opportunity, a desirable measure should meet two critical criteria. First, it should be simple, so that it can be easily understood and communicated. Second, it is imperative that the measure you use not have any allocations of corporate fixed costs or investments. The measure we will focus on here is cash flow, specifically the incremental cash flows that your opportunity will generate for your company. After discounting this cash flow at your company's cost of capital, you will be able to tell whether it creates an economic benefit for your shareholders. While profit is usually closely related to cash flow, the two are often not identical. The accounting model used to calculate profit is an accrual model, which means that not all transactions used to measure profit are cash transactions. For example, some revenues may be accrued (accounts receivable) and some costs may be allocations of fixed costs or non-cash expenditures, such as depreciation.

Opportunities can be conceptualized as either product, service or integrated product-service opportunities (recall the discussion in Chapter 2). Most product opportunities have associated services opportunities that go with them (e.g., after-sales service and support), and similarly, most service opportunities have associated product opportunities. How you conceptualize your opportunity can have a major impact on how you manage the profit dynamic over time.

The Drivers of Positive Cash Flow: Total Margin Generated

The drivers of positive cash flow are shown in Figure 10-1, for two different situations. In the first situation (1), your product is sold on a unit basis, which applies to most products and some services (for instance, days of a consultant's time). Here, the number of units of the product sold in a given period multiplied by the dollar unit margin for the product is the total margin dollars for that period. The total margin on these units is the primary positive driver of cash flow. In the second situation (2), your sales aren't made on a unit basis, but instead, on the basis of contracts or jobs. This sort of situation is most likely to occur for services (e.g., maintenance agreements on a fleet of aircraft, or seismic data gathering and analyses on oilfields). In these situations, as shown in Figure 10-1 row (2), revenue dollars for a period multiplied by the percentage margin gives total margin dollars for that period. Again, total margin is the major driver of positive cash flow. Of course, both models of generating total margin can apply in some situations, where the purchases that are made are for integrated bundles of services and products. Jet engine sales that cover purchase of the initial engine plus 10 years of services on it is an example of an integrated product-service.

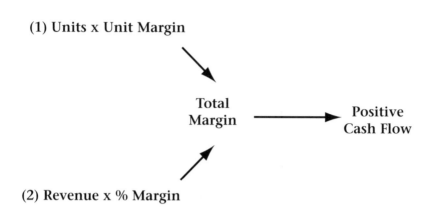

(1) Units x Unit Margin

Total
Margin ⟶ Positive
Cash Flow

(2) Revenue x % Margin

FIGURE 10-1: Positive Cash Flow Drivers

It is critical to note the connection between total margin and positive cash flow. In too many situations, managers see high revenue opportunities as automatically having high potential for profit and cash flow. This is clearly not necessarily true when you explore the profit dynamic. High revenue situations with very low margins could result in very low positive cash flow even before considering fixed costs and investments. As discussed in Chapter 3, the attractiveness of a market opportunity is not its revenue potential, but rather its ability to create large net positive cash flows for the players. Situations that don't produce much total margin and positive cash flow are unlikely to be highly profitable in the long run, and hence don't represent attractive opportunities.

Negative Cash Flow Drivers: Fixed Costs and Investments

As shown in Figure 10-2, there are two major negative cash flows in a product, service or product-service integration situation: fixed costs and investments. Examples of fixed costs are the salaries of individuals who are assigned to work on the market opportunity, and sales promotion. Investments are major outlays of cash which are committed to the market opportunity with the potential for longer-run returns, and frequently involve the creation or purchase of an asset. Research and development or building a manufacturing facility are examples of investments. In some cases, this investment may involve an immediate negative cash flow. In other cases, it may involve a series of negative cash flows required to fund the investment such as the interest on, or amortization of, debt which finances the investment, or annual lease payments. Viewed in this way, for your specific opportunity, the strategy has to create sufficient positive cash flow to more than offset the negative cash flows over the appropriate time horizon.

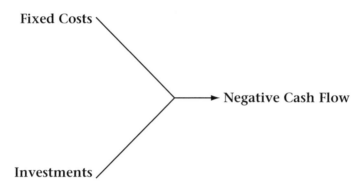

FIGURE 10-2: Negative Cash Flow Drivers

Cash Flow Profiles

Every strategic opportunity produces a potential cash flow profile as shown in Figure 10-3. A great profile is characterized by relatively few small negative cash flows, and many large positive cash flows. A poor profile is the reverse of this.

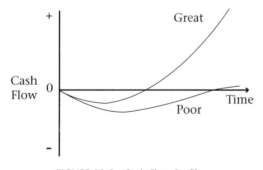

FIGURE 10-3: Cash Flow Profiles

Conceptually, cash flow profiling is a powerful and simple tool for a management team to probe the cash flow characteristics of an opportunity, particularly early in its planning cycle. Crude estimates can be made of positive cash flows over time (total margin dollars per year) and negative cash flows (fixed costs and investment costs over time), which can be further refined as better estimates become available. Viewing this data as a graphic "profile" with "real-time" data can be a powerful tool for the management team as it examines the sensitivity of the cash flows to changes in key drivers, and as it tries to communicate the financial impact of the opportunity to others.

We will now get into greater detail on managing the profit dynamic for an opportunity.

The Profit Dynamic

The basic profit dynamic is shown in Figure 10-4, and it applies to product and services situations where there are specific units produced and sold, and against which specific variable costs can be charged.

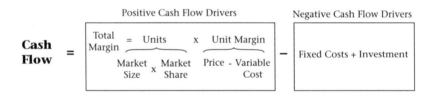

FIGURE 10-4: The Profit Dynamic

This is true of most products, and some services. There are six major independent drivers of cash flow:

Market Size (Units)	is the unit size of the served market segment(s).
Market Share (% of Units)	is your share of all the sales (in units) to the market segment(s) you are serving. Market size multiplied by market share yields **unit sales** of the product over the appropriate time horizon.
Price	is the unit realized price of the product or service.

Variable Cost	is the unit variable cost of producing the product or service, free of all allocations. **Unit margin** is price minus variable cost.
Fixed Costs	include all incremental fixed costs associated with the product for the appropriate period of time, free of all allocations.
Investments	include major investments made in support of the opportunity over its life cycle.

The profit dynamic focuses attention on the behavior of cash flows over the life cycle of an opportunity. The nature of the drivers can change significantly over time with major impacts on cash flow. Understanding the profit dynamic clearly lets you predict more accurately the impact of changes in strategy on the cash flow stream over the life cycle of the opportunity.

While the major cash flow drivers are conceptually well defined, ambiguity frequently is found in management practice about what some of them mean. Market share should be based on the served market rather than the overall market. If the overall market is used as the base, this could give a misleading picture. You could appear to have a very small market share, while actually you have a very high share in your served segments. This is particularly important because you are attempting to achieve market leadership in certain targeted segments, and usually the market leader will be able to capture a disproportionate share of the profitability in the opportunity.

A particularly important cash flow driver is unit variable cost. It is important that this cost be truly variable and that it not include allocations of investments and fixed costs, which some companies continue to do. Fixed costs are conceptually clear, but again some companies allocate some fixed costs. Fixed costs should ideally include only those incremental fixed costs specific to the opportunity and not those allocated from other sources. The same is true of investments.

For many opportunities, the quality of information on the major cash flow drivers varies. Usually, there is much better information about the negative cash flow components of the profit dynamic, which are more directly under your control, than about the positive cash flow components, which depend on customers' and competitors' reactions to your strategy. This has important implications for where you will focus your effort to improve the quality of the profit dynamic information, and where you will conduct sensitivity analysis to determine the impact of strategy changes on the profit dynamic drivers.

An Alternative Form of the Profit Dynamic

Sometimes, particularly when the market opportunity under consideration involves services, sales aren't made on the basis of units. For instance, consider a multi-million dollar contract for servicing jet engines. Here, it may make more sense to use a percentage margin rather than a unit margin. In other circumstances, sales might be made in complex bundles of different kinds of units, and again margins may be better considered on a percentage basis. In these situations, an alternative form of the profit dynamic is applicable, as shown in Figure 10-5.

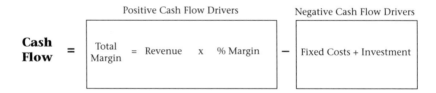

FIGURE 10-5: An Alternative Profit Dynamic

The difference between this form of the profit dynamic and the basic one, which was presented in Figure 10-4, is in the calculation of Total Margin. Now, in Figure 10-5, it is Revenue multiplied by Percentage Margin, where:

Revenue   is your dollar sales in the served market segments over the life of the opportunity.

Percentage Margin   is the contribution that will be earned on each dollar of revenue. Again, only variable costs should be included and there should be no arbitrarily allocated costs included in these variable costs.

The profit dynamic is usually applied on an annual or quarterly basis and then aggregated over the life of the opportunity with appropriate discounting. Sometimes, of course, sales might be in the form of large contracts that include substantial unit sales of products and substantial services contracts as well. Increasingly, organizations are recognizing the benefits to both buyer and seller of contracting for associated services at the same time as they purchase products. In complex situations like these, the overall profit dynamic to be employed might well be an aggregation of both unit-based and revenue-based versions of the profit dynamic.

Locating Key Sensitivities in the Profit Dynamic

The Unit Sales-Unit Margin Map

One of the real benefits of having a thorough understanding of the profit dynamic is that it suggests areas where you might focus efforts to improve total margin and cash flow. A tool that can help with this analysis is the unit sales-unit margin map shown in Figure 10-6. This allows you to map your opportunity or even a portfolio of opportunities on the basis of their unit sales, unit margins, and therefore their total margin and positive cash flow. Looking at the map, the best situation for any existing or new product opportunity is, of course, high unit sales and high unit margins, which means high total margin creation and positive cash flow. With a product with high total margin, the fixed costs and investments would have to be very high in order not to produce high net positive cash flow. But what happens if your opportunity doesn't fall near that "best situation" and instead appears to be in one of the Danger Zones shown in Figure 10-6?

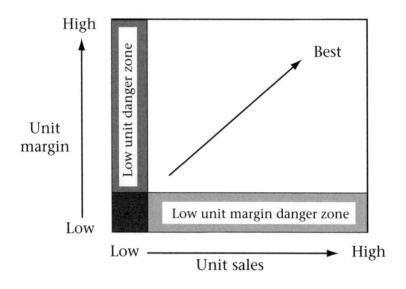

FIGURE 10-6: Unit Sales-Unit Margin Map

Opportunities in the low unit margin danger zone in Figure 10-6 have relatively high unit sales but low dollar unit margins. As a result, a relatively small drop in unit margin (if, for instance, variable costs are underestimated, or forecast prices can't be achieved because of customer resistance or competitive retaliation) can have a devastating effect on total margin production and therefore positive cash flow and profitability. This could be easily missed, if the focus in managing the profit dynamic is solely on building revenue.

Strategies for managing opportunities in the low unit margin danger zone should focus on managing price and variable costs for the product. One potential strategy would be to identify segments of the market that are less price-sensitive and to focus on them. Another approach would be to carefully manage discounts for large volumes, early payment, special promotions, etc., so that realized prices are maximized. Clearly, in such situations you should also concentrate on carefully managing all the elements of variable cost.

The low units danger zone in Figure 10-6 has opportunities that have significant unit margins, but relatively low unit sales. A relatively small decline in unit sales can result in a devastating drop in total margin and positive cash flow. In this danger zone, the emphasis in the strategy has to be on maximizing unit sales. In these cases the size of the market segments and market share achieved in these target segments are the critical variables that must be carefully reviewed in the development of the marketing plans. Thus, the areas of particular focus are different for products in the low units danger zone than they are for products in the low unit margin danger zone.

The Impact of Fixed Costs and Investment Changes on the Profit Dynamic

You should also pay careful attention to fixed costs associated with an opportunity, particularly if changing the fixed cost structure has the potential to significantly affect total margin generation. Sometimes small changes in fixed costs can generate major changes in total margin and cash flow. The temptation sometimes is to cut back on such fixed costs as personal selling or sales promotion, since each dollar saved will go directly to the bottom line and will improve the cash flow by an equivalent amount. However, if you reduce the fixed costs to enhance the cash flow, you must also carefully consider the effect it will have on the other elements of the profit dynamic, such as size of the served market, market share achieved, price realized, and level of variable costs. There are a number of examples of companies introducing high-technology products at high prices; they then economize on the marketing communication program (thus reducing the fixed costs) that is essential to convince customers the product is worth the high price. Sales fail to materialize and the venture is unprofitable.

In a similar way, the profit dynamic can be very sensitive to investment decisions. You might expect a particular set of investment decisions to generate a certain stream of total margin and positive cash flow. At that point the critical question to ask is whether a different set of investment levels would have a significant positive impact on total margin production through their impact on size of the served market, market share achieved, price realized, and level of variable costs. For example, investing in a world-scale plant can significantly reduce the variable cost of producing some products, but at the same time it may dramatically escalate the market share necessary to make them profitable.

New Product Opportunities and the Profit Dynamic

The profit dynamic for new product opportunities represents a special case. Compared to existing products, where estimates of market size, market share, realized price, variable cost, fixed costs, and investments have some existing historical basis, there is often enormous uncertainty as to how these numbers will unfold over time for a new opportunity, particularly if it involves a new-to-the-world product. The profit dynamic over time for a hypothetical new product is shown schematically in Figure 10-7. Investment costs, such as development costs, and fixed costs, such as relationship costs and other fixed costs, all represent negative cash flows that usually begin well before product launch. Total margin, the positive driver of cash flow, depends on the adoption rate for the new product and unit margins, and does not begin until after the product launch. The behavior of each of these individual profit dynamic components over time has a profound effect on long-term profitability.

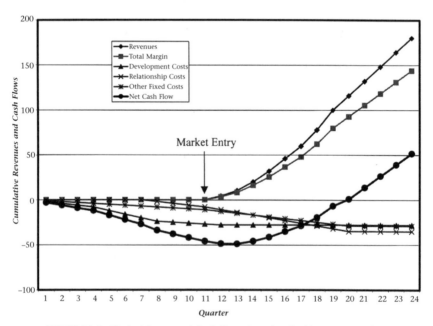

FIGURE 10-7: Typical Pattern of Cash Flow Associated with a New Product

The Critical Importance of Adoption Rate

The adoption rate for new products is a key driver of positive cash flow in the profit dynamic and is contingent on choice/rejection behavior along what is often a complex market chain. Estimates of adoption rates and hence sales forecasts for new products are frequently inaccurate, with sales often developing much more slowly than anticipated. This consequence is frequently a major contributor to weak financial results and new product failure. However, in addition to adoption rate, any of the other variables in the profit dynamic can have a major negative impact on cash flow projections, including the size of served market, market share achieved, price realized, variable cost, fixed costs and investments. All of these variables in the profit dynamic must be dynamically analyzed and tracked in "real" time in order to manage the potential profitability of a new product.

An example of the profit dynamic applied to a new product opportunity was the General Electric UDF (Unducted Fan) aircraft engine.[2] In the late 1980s, after a decade of work on the project and an expenditure of $50 million, GE's Aircraft Engine Business Group had to decide whether to complete the development of this radical new engine concept and bring it to market. To complete the project, they estimated they would have to spend at least another $560 million in R&D and invest at least $640 million in manufacturing facilities. The major advantage that the new engine offered airlines was a 40 to 70% lower fuel consumption over existing engines, an improvement that could generate annual savings to the airlines of $160,000 per engine. However, because the new engine would look and operate very differently from current engines, there was concern about how airframe manufacturers, such as Boeing and Airbus, and airlines would react to the UDF. This created great uncertainty for GE about the number and timing of UDF engine sales. In this complex situation, the strategic choice facing GE was whether to proceed with the new engine opportunity or to drop it.

---

2 This example is based on the case "General Electric Company: Aircraft Engine Business Groups" in Glen L. Urban and Steven H. Star, *Advanced Marketing Strategy: Phenomena, Analysis, and Decision* (Englewood Cliff, New Jersey: Prentice Hall, 1991), pp. 50–75.

Some of the major factors influencing the profit dynamic that GE managers had to consider in making their critical GO/NO GO decision were the following:

- Market Size. From the point of market entry in 1992 through the year 2000 and beyond, the market for engines of the size of the UDF engine was expected to be about 500 units per year, due to the growth in short haul passenger routes operated by major airlines and their partners. As a result, the total unit size of the market was very attractive.

- Market Share. In order for GE Aircraft Engines to gain market share, major airlines and airframe manufacturers would have to reject conventional fan jet engines and choose the UDF engine. Given the quite revolutionary nature of the UDF technology and its higher initial capital cost (but lower ongoing fuel costs), selling the UDF engine and gaining market share was expected to be difficult. In addition, because deals for engines often involve "all or nothing" negotiations with major airlines and airframe manufacturers, market share estimates were difficult to make and had high variance. Sales could even be close to zero if there were no major adoptions.

- Price. As a result of high variable costs, pricing the UDF engine would be difficult. Pricing at fan jet levels (about $4.4 million per engine) would produce large negative unit margins and negative cash flows in the first year or two, which might be difficult to offset later on. Pricing significantly above the fan jets would almost surely result in rejection because the fuel costs savings would not be enough to offset the higher initial capital cost of the UDF engine.

- Variable Costs. The initial variable costs of the UDF engine were expected to be significantly higher than price ($6.6 million on average for the first 100 engines), but they were expected to come down on an 80% experience curve.[3] Achieving high volume was critical to lowering unit variable costs. As a result of the price and the variable cost situation, unit margins for the first

---

[3] That is, every time the cumulative production of the engine doubled, the unit costs were expected to decline by 20%.

few years of production of the UDF engine would be negative or only modestly positive.

- Investments.   From 1986 to 1992, investments in the project would be huge. A minimum of $1.2 billion would be necessary for R&D and manufacturing over that period with the potential for even higher expenditures.

- Fixed Costs. The fixed costs of operating the plant to produce a UDF engine as well as the other incremental fixed costs GE Aircraft Engines would incur in going into the UDF engine business would be very high.

Based on the assumptions in the above discussion, the major cash flows underpinning the profit dynamic are shown in simplified form in Figure 10-8.

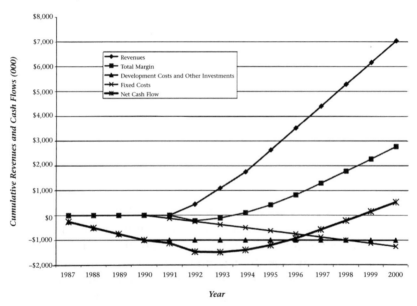

FIGURE 10-8: Projected Cash Flows Associated with the GE-UDF Engine

As Figure 10-8 makes very clear, based on the assumptions outlined, the profit dynamic for the UDF did not look very attractive and was in fact very risky. The total margin generated, because of the low unit margins and the difficulty of gaining share, could be very low initially. On the other hand massive investments would have to be made before the first engine could be sold. Thus, in present value terms the opportunity is unattractive, since at any reasonable discount rate the later positive cash flows will not offset the high initial negative cash flows. From an opportunity point of view, the critical issue for GE management was to look at the profit dynamic as a whole and try to determine if there were any strategic or tactical moves they could take that would make the profit dynamic more attractive. In this particular situation, it looked very difficult, and GE decided to reject the opportunity.

Applying the Profit Dynamic to Individual Customers

The profit dynamic can also be a useful tool for evaluating a potential relationship with a new customer. This exercise may be particularly critical in businesses where there are high switching costs and where big investments must be made before significant revenues and cash flows will come from that customer.

In some industries a few highly influential customers influence sales from many other customers. Consider the case of a company like Varian Medical Systems, which markets radiation therapy and treatment planning equipment for the treatment of cancer. If it wants to maintain leadership in its market, it must have a strong presence in most of the leading cancer treatment centers in the world, such as the M.D. Anderson Cancer Center in Texas and the Memorial Sloan-Kettering Cancer Center in New York. It is in centers like this that the oncology luminaries work, the seminal papers on radiation therapy are written, and future oncology specialists are trained. Yet because Varian's competitors also want a major presence in these accounts, it is difficult to generate positive cash flows from these accounts. In order to determine whether it is worthwhile to spend marketing, sales, and research and development funds on such an account, management must try to compare the cash flow streams that Varian would achieve under two different scenarios: one with the leading medical center as a customer and one without it. This analysis forces management to think not only about the cash flow impact of product sales, product upgrades, and service revenues from that medical center, but also about the product sales, product upgrades, and service revenues that might be expected to occur over the planning horizon from business at accounts that are influenced by the decisions of the leading medical center (see Figure 10-9).

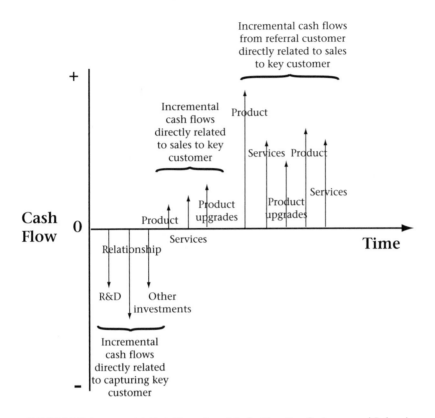

FIGURE 10-9: Incremental Cash Flows Associated with a Key Customer and Referral Sales that Result from a Satisfied Key Customer

The decision to pursue an account then becomes one of deciding if the incremental cash flows that will result from capturing the customer, when discounted at the company's cost of capital, are positive. Clearly, maintaining a highly satisfied customer is essential if the referral cash flows objectives are to be achieved.

Product-Service Integration and the Profit Dynamic

Integrated Product-Service Opportunities

An emerging reality for many companies is the potential for increased cash flow by developing integrated strategies for products and services, as illustrated in Figure 10-10 (recall the discussion in

Chapter 2). Consider a company that has traditionally sold "turnkey" production facilities and provided after-sales service for these facilities if the customer wished. The company's management, recognizing a trend to greater outsourcing among its customers, might see an opportunity to sell a fully maintained, integrated manufacturing facility that the customer pays for on the basis of $X per unit produced by the facility. In profit dynamic terms, it might believe that the development of an integrated product-service strategy will create higher long-term cash flows than the traditional product and service strategies would, if they were managed separately. The development of the winning strategy for such an integrated product-service opportunity would require the management team to develop a complete and integrated strategy for the product-service "package." This would involve going through the process described in Chapters 8 and 9.

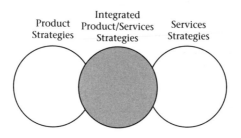

FIGURE 10-10: Strategic Marketing Planning:
Integrating the Product-Service Processes

Developing strategies for integrated product-service opportunities represents a considerable challenge for many companies. In many companies, different organizational units and managers manage products and services and make independent strategic choices. The product and services "sides" of organizations frequently operate with different, even conflicting, objectives, and with different performance measures for departments and important managers. Furthermore, these different parts of the organization frequently have separate and different internal cost infrastructures and accounting processes, so that making integrated strategic and financial choices is difficult.

The situation often becomes even more complicated when you turn to your customer, the potential purchaser of the integrated product-service package. The customer may be organized to buy your products and services separately or it may perform some of the services itself. A customer like this is not likely organized to buy integrated product-service packages. In this kind of situation, it may be difficult to see and demonstrate where improved performance and cost synergies can be realized by the customer who purchases an integrated product-service package.

Management of the Integrated Product-Service Profit Dynamic

The profit dynamic can be a useful way of summarizing the financial impact of alternative product-service strategies and identifying the ones with the greatest future cash flow potential. One of the advantages of conceptualizing the profit dynamic in cash flow terms is that the product and service cash flows can be managed together and the impact of trading one off against the other can be seen. By the same token, managing the product profit dynamic and service profit dynamic piecemeal can present major problems. For example, an organization focused solely on the product may have a strong incentive to get a product to market quickly, even if this creates problems with product quality and reliability. This move could have a major negative impact on the profitability of the service side of the organization, who may have signed long-term fixed-price service agreements with major customers.

Some of the potential challenges that an integrated product-service strategy presents to the product and service sides of organizations can be in resolving differences in objectives. Alternative objectives could be to maximize product cash flow, to maximize service cash flow, or to maximize the integrated product-service cash flow. These three objectives can lead to different strategic choices with very different combinations of total margin, investments, and fixed costs, and hence different patterns of net cash flow. In this situation, there are often some real advantages to looking at the product-service opportunity as an integrated whole. Products that may be unattractive by themselves may actually be very attractive, in both strategy and cash flow, if they are integrated with packages of services. Similarly, the converse is true: services that are unattractive may be attractive if they are bundled with the sale of products designed to be sold as part of an integrated product-service package.

In the next few years, we are likely to see more and more organizations overcome organizational barriers and inertia and develop more integrated product-service offerings that have the potential to significantly enhance the cash flows of the company.

Managing the Profit Dynamic in Market Chains: Creating Strategic Leverage

The profit dynamic is a powerful tool for demonstrating the impact of your strategic choices on the cash flows for that opportunity. We have also emphasized the importance of carefully managing the market chain for your opportunity. Strategic leverage is a concept that combines these two tools to look at facilitating the rapid adoption of products down market chains and to ensure the market chain members have an incentive to carry and aggressively push your products and services. Conceptually, strategic leverage is relatively simple. For any company in your market chain, the strategic leverage you create is the ratio of the strategic payoffs from their adoption and sale of your product divided by the resources necessary for them to make the adoption and to sell your product. These strategic payoffs and resources are defined in terms of the same generic product and service profit dynamics that have been discussed in this chapter. Essentially, strategic leverage asks the question "What impact is your opportunity going to have on the cash flow of the other members of your market chain?"

$$\frac{\text{Strategic}}{\text{Leverage}} = \frac{\text{Strategic Payoffs from Adoption}}{\text{Resources Committed to Adoption}}$$

Identifying Points of Strategic Leverage

For any other member of the market chain for your product or service opportunity, adoption and sale can have any or all of the following points of leverage:

- Market Size Leverage. Adoption of your product or service enables them to serve new segments or markets, thus increasing the size of their served market.

- Market Share Leverage.   Adoption of your product or service enables your customer to increase its market share in the markets they are serving.

- Price Leverage.   Adoption of your product enables them to change prices in their markets. If it enables a price increase, this potentially has a direct positive impact on unit margins. A price decrease may leverage unit sales.

- Variable Cost Leverage. Adoption of your product enables them to significantly reduce their unit variable cost.

- Fixed Cost Leverage. Adoption of your product enables them to significantly reduce their fixed costs of serving their target markets.

- Investment Leverage. Adoption of your product enables them to significantly reduce investments they must make to serve their target markets.

Clearly, whether the opportunity provides positive or negative leverage for the market chain member depends on the interactive effect of the six key drivers on that member's profit dynamic. Some examples of potential points of leverage for downstream members of the market chain (your customers) are shown in Figure 10-11. A similar set of points could also be developed for your upstream market chain members.

Market Size Leverage	Market Share Leverage	Price Leverage	Variable Cost Leverage	Fixed Cost Leverage	Investment Leverage
Provide product variants that help your customer enter new segments	Create greater end-user value than competition	Create greater end-user value than competition	Develop a lower cost means of distributing your product	Provide your customer with tools to help them improve their productivity	Reduce your order-delivery cycle time to allow your customers to reduce inventories
Identify new end-user applications that increase product usage rate	Help your customers improve relationships with their customers	Build brand equity for your product to reduce their customers' price sensitivity	Make your product easier for your customer to sell and install	Develop marketing communications program targeted at end users so customers can reduce their marketing budgets	Modularize your product, so that customer can meet a wide range of end-user needs from a limited inventory

FIGURE 10-11: Examples of Ways to Create Strategic Leverage for Customers

Strategic Leverage and Adoption Rates

The major reason for you to carefully analyze the strategic leverage you can create in your market chains is its potential impact on adoption and sales rates for your products and services, which as we have seen is one of the main drivers that influences your profit dynamic. The greater the strategic leverage, the more enthusiastic the market chain member is likely to be about adopting and aggressively selling your product or service. Adoption rates and sales will tend to be higher when:

- your strategy significantly affects a key driver of your market chain member's profit dynamic. For example, Triad, a leading supplier of hardware/software "solutions" for auto parts distributors, was often able to double the unit margins of its customers by developing software to help them improve their realized prices.

- strategic leverage can be created for more of the companies in your market chain.

Strategic leverage analysis can be a very useful tool for helping you systematically review how you can positively influence the adoption and sales rate for your products and services. It keeps you from forgetting about the effect your new product or service will have on other members of the market chain.

Next Step: Implementing the Strategy

Assuming that the profit dynamic for each opportunity you are considering looks attractive and that there is strategic leverage for each market chain member, you are now ready to implement your winning strategies. In the next chapter, we will look at some of the issues involved in successfully implementing winning strategies.

Key Questions for Executives and Managers

- Are your profit and cash flow objectives clear? It is critical in looking at any opportunity to have clear and widely shared profit and cash flow objectives.

- Have you carefully thought about each of the major profit dynamic drivers and do you understand which ones are going to have the greatest impact on cash flows for the opportunity? Specifically:
  - Market Segment Size. How large is the actual segment(s) of the market that you are focusing on after correcting for the coverage of the segments your market chain strategy will provide?
  - Market Share. Are market share estimates realistic given what you know about customer choice-rejection behavior and competitive reactions? Do they reflect likely lags in the adoption process?
  - Unit Price. Are your prices realistic given the competitive reality and are they consistent with your assumptions about adoption rates?
  - Unit Variable Costs. Are all elements of your unit variable cost estimates realistic?
  - Fixed Costs. Are the fixed costs associated with the overall strategy for the opportunity realistic? Have you considered all incremental fixed costs and are you ignoring any allocated fixed costs?
  - Investments. Are R&D costs and other investments realistic with regard to the amount and timing?

- Is the profit dynamic brought together in one place and scrutinized regularly and frequently by the management team? Is it updated as new information becomes available? Is sensitivity analysis used to understand how changes in key drivers will affect the overall profit dynamic?

- Is the profit dynamic analysis done consistently across all opportunities within the business units, so that top management can make the tough strategic choices about which opportunities to say yes to and which ones to say no to?

- Can we make any imaginative changes in strategy for the opportunity that might have a significant positive impact on the profit dynamic for the opportunity? For example, are there any integrated product-service opportunities that promise greater cash flow and profitability?

- Are we applying the profit dynamic analysis to individual key customers to determine if it is worthwhile to invest scarce resources in capturing them? In these analyses, are we capturing all the incremental cash flows that may be generated in other referral accounts by a strong, positive relationship with such a key customer?

- Are we creating strategic leverage for all the key players in our market chain so that they have a strong incentive to adopt and aggressively push our products and services?

CHAPTER ELEVEN

Implement the Winning Strategy

Introduction

In previous chapters, we have discussed your choice of a business opportunity, developed a marketing strategy for exploiting it, and evaluated its profitability. Now we move to consider how you will execute the strategy. Note that the focus of this chapter is internal, on the changes that will be required in behavior in your organization, if your new strategy is to be successfully put in place. External changes in the market chain were explored previously in the chapters on customers and relationships.

As we have discussed throughout the book, the Winning Market Leadership Process which we outline can be productively used for a wide variety of opportunities. At one extreme are relatively straightforward opportunities such as adding a new geographic segment, or a new application to existing ones for a product or service. Responding to an opportunity like this might call for only minor changes in strategy, and implementation could be relatively straightforward, requiring no radically different policies and procedures. At the other end of the spectrum, your opportunity could necessitate a major strategic departure from current practices, and implementing it could require revolutionary change in the organization.

In any case, until you implement it, the strategy cannot be adding value for your customers, your market chain, or yourselves. In fact, if you do not implement the strategy properly, very likely it won't be successful at all. We think of the success of a strategy, specifically the profit and cash flow it produces, as a *multiplicative* effect of the competitive power of the strategy and the effectiveness of its implementation, rather than an *additive* effect. In other words:

$$\text{Profit \& Cash Flow} = \text{Competitive Power of Strategy} \times \text{Effectiveness of Implementation}$$

This means, of course, that both good strategy and good implementation are necessary for strong strategic performance. Poor scores on one of the two cannot be entirely offset by strength in the other. A company's ability to implement a given strategy is directly related to its resources and capabilities.

Consider the case of S-S Technologies (SST), an Ontario company that manufactures and sells interface cards for programmable logic controllers (PLCs). It built a competency in managing the distributors who sold the product to manufacturers around the world. In the early 1990s, SST's own systems integration division developed one of the first software products which could simulate the start-up of a manufacturing operation in a very cost-effective manner, creating faster start-ups with fewer problems and major savings in engineering time. However, selling this simulation software entailed selling a new concept—simulation via software—which had to be sold at the level of the customer's manufacturing and engineering vice presidents. Skilled as they were in selling high-volume, low-unit-cost PLC interface cards, SST did not have a strong capability for selling a concept.

The same was true for most of their distributors, who typically had much more short-term interests in moving products and earning commissions than in investing their time in a developmental sell. Consequently, although the simulation product had high potential and high value to customers, it never became a significant success for SST. The major reason was a poor match between the company's capabilities and what was required for successful implementation of an effective strategy for the simulation software.

Strategy and implementation have a critical effect on each other.[1] These interactions are illustrated in Figure 11-1. For instance, the

---

[1] This discussion draws heavily on Thomas V. Bonoma, "Making Your Marketing Strategy Work," *Harvard Business Review* (March-April 1984), pp.68-76.

benefits of a good strategy can be negated by poor implementation (in the upper right cell within Figure 11-1, labeled "Problem"). The trouble arises because, if poor implementation is not recognized as the source of the indifferent market results, a perfectly good strategy may be altered in the quest for greater profitability.

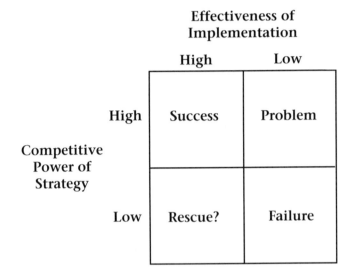

FIGURE 11-1: Interactions Between Strategy and Implementation

The upper left and lower right cells in the diagram are much less likely to pose questions about diagnosis, as the market outcome is clear. Both strategy and implementation are either strong (the Success box), or weak (the Failure box), and cash flow provides ample evidence of the fact. The Rescue? cell, however, is more ambiguous in the results it produces. In the best situation, effective implementation buys time and actually allows for correcting a weak strategy. This is the cell that many field sales forces would suggest they inhabit, constantly saving the day by correcting the mistakes in an ineptly produced strategy from headquarters. Of course, the result may still not be resounding success, if other companies with better strategies and effective implementation target the same opportunity. There is another, far less satisfactory, outcome that can occur from a combination of poor strategy and strong implementation. If the ineffective strategy is aggressively implemented without modification (that is, with no mid-course corrections), the result will only be bad results faster.

This discussion suggests that it is very limiting to think of strategy and implementation as static. In reality, they should be in continual change, especially in a rapidly developing technology-intensive environment. Effective implementation involves continuing to ask the key questions which were outlined at each stage of our process, on customers, competitors, capabilities and resources, profitability, etc.—as the strategy is introduced to the market. No strategy is perfect from its very inception, so effective implementation means *learning* about what improvements are necessary, then modifying the strategy, implementing the changes, learning from how the strategy is received, and so on. As Figure 11-2 portrays, central to the whole process are the key questions for managers that have been outlined through this book.

FIGURE 11-2: Strategy, Implementation, and Learning

This process produces a strategy that is continually fine-tuned by the learning that occurs as key questions are addressed during the implementation process. In a changing environment, particularly a rapidly changing one like an advanced technology setting, this approach is much more effective than simply developing a strategy, laying out an implementation plan, and blindly following it. Figure 11-3 portrays this process.

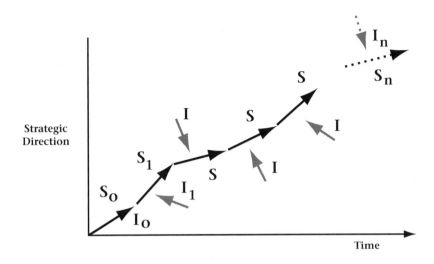

FIGURE 11-3: Implementation's Effect on Strategy

In the diagram, S_0 denotes the original strategy, and I_0 the plan for implementing it. The learning that occurs during this implementation process is fed back into a continuing round of strategy development, resulting in a modified strategy, S_1, and I_1 for implementing it. This round of strategy, implementation, learning, strategy modification, etc., as shown in Figure 11-3 continues forever. The emergent strategy is produced in a step-by-step process, rather than by management fiat, based on an initial analysis at one particular point.

There are two fundamental errors you can make with implementation. The first is to pay insufficient attention to it by assuming that an announcement of the new strategy, and (perhaps) the logic underlying it, will be sufficient to persuade the necessary people to change their behavior. While this mistake results from little or no attention being paid to the issue of how to make the new strategy happen, the second kind of error often happens when a great deal of effort is invested in determining who should do what to whom and when. And then, come hell or high water, that's what is done! The problem here is not lack of attention to implementation, but lack of flexibility. In the changing environment where you are doing business, no strategy or the action plan for executing it can be frozen in place. There must be capacity built into the plan for learning and modification.

A Process for Managing Implementation

If we lowered a microscope on the "Implement the Strategy" box in the overall Winning Market Leadership Process, what we would see is Figure 11-4. This diagram introduces a model for managing implementation of a strategy. It begins at the point of departure of this chapter, that is, after a business opportunity has been identified, a strategy for capitalizing on it has been developed, and its profitability has been analyzed.

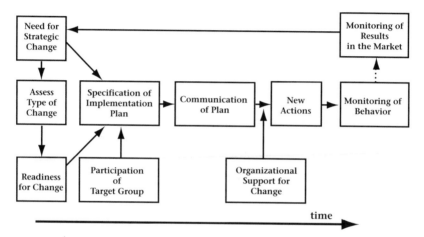

FIGURE 11-4: A Process for Managing Implementation

We will discuss this process in depth, so it will be only briefly introduced now. Implementation of the new strategy clearly requires people in the firm to change their behavior. (See Chapters 4 and 8 for analysis of necessary changes in behavior of customers and other members of the market web.) As previous discussion has indicated, the change required may be uncontroversial and purely evolutionary, or it may involve major modifications of your company's existing policies, procedures, and resources.

The people affected may or may not be ready to make the necessary change. One important factor in their willingness to change is the switching barriers (like the existing performance evaluation and compensation plan) that exist. In large part, their readiness to alter their behavior depends on how well they understand the urgency of the need to change. Is it a situation where the firm is in crisis and the status quo is clearly not acceptable, or is it a situation where those who are supposed to change don't see the need and will resist efforts to implement the new strategy? Depending on the perceived urgency of the need for change, and the readiness to change, there will be more or less consultation in the process of deciding how the strategy will be implemented. This plan must be effectively communicated to the people affected, both inside and outside the firm, and organizational support for the change must be gauged. If these steps have been carried out effectively, new behavior results. This behavior should be monitored and reinforced, as should the results of the altered behavior. The model is iterative, because the whole execution of a strategy is iterative. It proceeds a step at a time; then, based on the feedback obtained at any stage, a new need for change emerges and engenders a response.

An Example

Using an extended example, we will develop and illustrate the major areas of the implementation process. This example deals with the European operations of a global chemical company that produced a specialty product which had a number of potential applications. The company penetrated the European market over a 10-year period by concentrating on large firms in the application areas where the chemical made up a high percentage of the total cost of their product. Not surprisingly, these were the price-sensitive customers. They had little need for technical support in using the chemical, especially after their initial adoption. Sales representatives for the product reported to the country sales organization, which in turn reported through a country sales manager to a country managing director. Objectives for the country organizations were based largely on volume and market share.

Although the strategy had been successful in gaining 18% of a large market over 10 years, and volume targets were met in most countries, corporate profitability targets were not being met by a significant degree. A major reason was the continued focus on the most price-sensitive segments. A new marketing manager was appointed for the business. Based on an audit of the external situation, he decided that a very different strategy was required, focusing on smaller, less price-sensitive applications where in the selling process more emphasis could be placed on his organization's excellent technical service capability. He needed to realize higher prices (by about 4% on average) across the mix of accounts, and he wanted prices to be administered centrally rather than regionally. These changes had profound implications for the sales force—new applications and industries to learn, new customers to call on, and a new basis of selling (the "whole product," including technical service, rather than primarily price). This manager's approach to the situation, and the organization's response, will be used to illustrate various stages of the implementation model in the sections which follow.

The Case for Change

A new strategy requires that new actions must be taken to make it occur. Unless someone's behavior changes, the new strategy will never leave the ground, and the firm will be left with the status quo.

The Need for Strategic Change

Key factors in the implementation process are the amount of change that is required, and the urgency with which it must be implemented. The kinds of strategic changes we are dealing with in this book tend to be major changes with some element of urgency. Small changes where there is no hurry to implement are not likely to make significant differences in operating results. Relative to other industries, advanced technology businesses are inherently fast-paced with major resource commitments required to back up key strategic decisions. Change occurs at a high rate, and successful companies in this type of business must be very good at assessing risk so that enough of their big bets pay off that they can pay for the losers and still maintain a healthy return. Therefore, the situations we are analyzing in this book tend to be primarily in Quadrant 4, and secondarily, in Quadrant 3 of Figure 11-5.

		Magnitude of Strategic Change	
		Small	Large
Urgency	Low	1	2
	High	3	4

FIGURE 11-5: Describing Strategic Change

There are other important aspects of the need for change. One important element of the situation is how visible the need is. In some situations, the imperative for change is apparent to all concerned; failure to react to a situation is seen by everyone as having dire consequences. This was the situation that Barco, the leading manufacturer of projection systems for portraying data and graphics, faced in 1989 when Sony surprised them at a major industry trade show with a projector that had a faster scan rate and a better picture. Clearly, unless Barco reacted very quickly, their technical leadership in the industry would be lost.

Another key factor in assessing need for change is the *readiness* of key managers and other employees for implementing the strategy. For example:

- Do they *know* that they have to change?
- Are they aware of what they have to do to implement the strategy?
- Are they well-equipped for making the necessary changes?
- Are they capable of executing the necessary tasks?
- Are they committed to performing them?
- Do they see the linkage between changing and the organizational reward system?

In the case of our European chemical company, the answer to most of these questions was no. The sales force did not know they had to change until they received a memorandum from the new marketing manager in Geneva. The manager thought rapid change was necessary, but the sales force felt that everything was fine. At most, they believed, some fine-tuning would take care of the problem. Furthermore, the sales force had only a modest understanding of the external market conditions compelling a change (namely, the likelihood of a price war) and they lacked knowledge of the new target customers in the smaller, less price-sensitive applications. To make the situation even more difficult, they had sold on the basis of price for so long that selling on value required a major adjustment. Suffice it to say, that in this situation there was not great readiness to change among the main actors who would have to implement the strategy.

Types of Change

Different implementation processes are required for different types of change. A very useful model for considering types of change was described by Fry and Killing.[2] They proposed that change situations can be classified into one of three categories: anticipatory, reactive, and crisis. The differences among the types of change are seen in Figure 11-6, which Fry and Killing call "The Crisis Curve." The vertical axis in the chart, labeled Strategic Performance, describes how well the current strategy is working in the marketplace. Usually, financial performance lags strategic performance, because there is a certain amount of inertia in most markets. For example, even when a strategy has become "tired," there are enough switching barriers for customers and other members of the market chain such that not all business is lost to competitors in the short run.

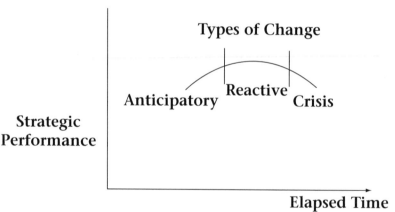

FIGURE 11-6: The Crisis Curve

Crisis Change

In crisis situations, almost anyone who looks at the situation recognizes that the existence of the business is at risk. If a new strategy is not developed and implemented rapidly, the whole company or business unit could fail. In these circumstances, people are ready to

---

[2] See Joseph N. Fry and J. Peter Killing, *Strategic Analysis and Action*, 2nd Edition, (Scarborough, Ontario: Prentice-Hall Canada Inc., 1989). Their work was subsequently extended in a paper by Sandra Vandermerwe, *Long Range Planning* (April 1995), pp. 79–91.

change because they are aware and committed, but the business could be in such a weakened condition that its capability to support change is questionable. Cash (and available credit) are likely to be scarce. Some of the most capable people, who saw the crisis coming earlier, have likely left the organization or are on their way out. Furthermore, senior managers might lack credibility with people inside the organization and outside it. After all, these leaders were steering the ship when it went into crisis. Are they the people to steer it out?

Anticipatory Change

At the other end of the curve is anticipatory change. This situation describes IBM during the 1980s very well. Here the situation was the exact reverse of the crisis situation. Capability of the firm to implement a new strategy was high. The business had been profitable, and it had good relationships with market chain members and customers. Management's credibility was high, and recruiting was easy. The problem was that most people didn't initially recognize that there was a problem. The strategy was working well, and the income statement showed it, so why change? The major issues in anticipatory change are developing awareness of the need to change, and commitment to implementing the new strategy. Only a few people see that change is required, let alone what has to be done to win in a new environment that most people don't even see emerging.

Reactive Change

These circumstances are between those observed in anticipatory and crisis situations. The signals are clearer than in the anticipatory situation, so more than a few individuals agree on the need for a new approach. However, there is not yet a well-grounded feeling of strategic discomfort in the business. With regard to capabilities, the business is still in good shape; although it does not have the strength it had a few months earlier, it certainly isn't in the situation of diminished capacity that a crisis brings.

Figure 11-7 summarizes our discussion of types of change situations encountered in implementing a new strategy.

Type of Change	Strategic Performance	Visibility of Requirement For Change	Readiness For Change	Available Resources
Anticipatory	Improving	Not visible	Low	High
Reactive	Plateauing	Somewhat visible	Medium	Medium
Crisis	Declining	Highly visible	High	Low

FIGURE 11-7: Summary of Characteristics of Change Situations

> Viewed in the light of the crisis curve, our European chemical business faced a serious situation. The new marketing manager was sure that the business was in crisis, and he acted accordingly. He felt that the business was doomed unless the profitability problems were solved, and solved quickly. Since he estimated that there was greater than 30% excess capacity in the industry at that time in Europe, he felt that his business (with the largest, most price-sensitive customers) was highly vulnerable. Consequently, believing that he had very little time to act, he worked out a new strategy in his first weeks on the job and announced it with a memorandum to the sales force which was dispersed through Europe. What compounded the problem, however, was that the sales force was back at the anticipatory level on the curve. Most of them thought all was well with the business. They certainly were not enthusiastic about taking the personal effort and risk necessary to implement the new strategy, by learning new applications in new industries and making cold calls on firms in these industries and, perhaps, jeopardizing their annual salary raises. With the wisdom of hindsight, it seems clear that the leader of the change should have spent time developing common perceptions of the situation so that he could get buy-in for an ambitious program of rapid change.

As this example illustrates, when there are major differences in perceptions of urgency of the change between the managers who design the strategy and those who must change their behavior, problems can result (see Figure 11-8). The only situation in which rapid implementation and low resistance are likely to occur is when both groups, strategists and key implementers, believe that it is a crisis situation. When both parties see the conditions as anticipatory, there is likely to be low resistance, but it can take a long time to realize a significant change.

		Viewpoint of Strategy Developers	
		Anticipatory	Crisis
Viewpoint of Those Who Must Change	**Anticipatory**	High consultation Low direct conflict Slow, or no change	Confrontation Very high resistance to change
	Crisis	Impatience Frustration with leadership	Rapid implementation Low resistance

FIGURE 11-8: Resistance to Change

Specification of the Implementation Plan

It is time to plan out the specifics of how the strategy will be implemented. Specification of the implementation plan can be looked at from two perspectives. First, you can ask a series of questions that must be addressed in an implementation plan. Second, you can outline especially important implementation considerations that come up in technology-intensive businesses.

Implementing a new strategy or significantly modifying the existing strategy may require profound changes in many parts of your organization. For example, the jobs of the sales teams or the customer service teams may need to change in a major way if they are to play the role you want them to play in your new strategy. As Figure 11-9 describes, recruiting, selection, training and other aspects of the management system might need modification to insure that the new roles can be effectively carried out.

FIGURE 11-9: Aligning Organization, Policies, and Procedures to Encourage and Enable People to Carry Out Their New Roles

The Questions

What questions need to be addressed in detailing your implementation plan? We address these questions with reference to the European chemical company as an illustrative example.

Who must change?   In the chemical company, the major changes to implement the new strategy had to be made by the sales representatives, the technical support team, and the country sales managers.

What must they change?   The sales representatives had previously called on only a few large accounts in application areas that used high volumes of the company's product. To implement the new strategy, they now had to learn new industry applications, call on potential customers, and sell on the basis of a whole product of which technical service was a major part, rather than on price alone.

Who is affected by the change?   Your new strategy can have significant effects on other employees in the company, and also on people and businesses outside the company, including existing customers. In this situation, the sales representatives reported to sales managers in various countries in Europe. These sales managers each supervised a territorial sales force which consisted of one or two sales representatives for this particular product and 10 to 15 representatives for other chemical products that the company manufactured. Supervisory practices and the reward structure for the overall sales force were geared toward volume and market share. Now the marketing manager for the product in question wanted the sales managers to focus their sales representatives on achieving dollars of gross margin, and to reward the sales representatives accordingly.

Besides the sales representatives and their managers, another group who would certainly feel the effects of the new strategy was the technical support team. Demand for their services in reaching the new segments would increase, and technical service costs would rise. External to the company, the group who could be most strongly affected was the existing customers. There was some confusion among the sales representatives when the new plan was announced about whether the proposed price increase (approximately 4% in average price realized) necessarily meant higher prices for the existing accounts, who had been sold largely on a price basis.

When must the key steps occur?   If the situation is at the crisis point, action must be taken virtually immediately. If the situation is anticipatory, there likely needs to be a considerable education and persuasion phase before significant behavioral changes occur. Because the manager in our example believed he was in a crisis situation, he specified immediate action from the sales force, without an educational program. Not surprisingly, the sales force, which did not report directly to him, initially rejected his proposals.

What are criteria for success? Two kinds of measurement could apply here: measurement of behavioral change (the inputs that you make to the change process), and measurement of results in the marketplace (the outputs). In our example, criteria of the former sort included a number of calls on competitive accounts, and a number of calls in new industries. The final result expected was equivalent or greater volume at much greater contribution margins.

What resources are required to support the new behavior? These resources can be financial (e.g., dollars for incentives, for new personnel, or for technical development) or non-financial (e.g., senior management support, or allocation of training resources). In our example, support from senior management would have been very helpful—if the managers of the countries had overtly supported the changes, it would have undoubtedly been much easier to get the country-based sales managers and sales representatives to change. Also, there was a real need for resource allocation to training for the sales force—to augment their ability to sell on a non-price basis, and to teach them about potential new industries.

What resistance to the new strategy is anticipated? Will the people affected by the change embrace it, or, more likely, will they oppose it? What form will this opposition take? Will it be active confrontation, or passive resistance that might be disguised as acceptance? Sometimes in situations of Anticipatory Change, it can be difficult to engage people in dialogue, because they perceive no need for action. A good implementation plan must analyze where the resistance might be expected to occur, how it will express itself, and how it might be overcome. In a situation where those affected agree there is a crisis, there will likely be less resistance than in a situation that is at the anticipatory level of the crisis curve. Of course, as we saw in our example, the perceptions of the builders of the new strategy and those most strongly affected might not be the same.

In our example, the marketing manager who was the champion of the new strategy perceived that he had a crisis on his hands, but those most affected by the new strategy (the sales force and the country sales managers) were back at the anticipatory level. Not surprisingly, strong resistance to the new program resulted once the sales force realized that the new market manager was serious about wanting significant change, and wanting it soon. This resistance was manifested in complaints to the country sales managers and the overall country managers, and through them, to the new marketing manager's director.

What reinforcement should be offered to support behavioral change? This raises the issue of reward and punishment, and, of course, financial and non-financial reinforcement. At times, designers of the change pay little attention to this important consideration, perhaps feeling that the logic of the case for the new strategy will be sufficiently persuasive in itself. However, they are perhaps forgetting that change has a cost to those who must alter their behavior. In the case of our European chemical company, the initial strategic plan made no provision for reinforcing the desired behavior. Since the sales representatives were part of a large organization with an overall policy of paying the sales force on a straight salary, large shifts in compensation practice were not possible. However, after the initial resistance was experienced, a change was made to ensure that, for sales representatives of this product line, annual bonuses were paid based on success generating total contribution margin, rather than simply sales revenue. The other form of reinforcement that proved very effective was recognition. A series of meetings was initiated between the marketing manager and the sales representatives from around Europe. Difficulties and successes with implementing the new strategy were discussed. Recognition of early successes was important reinforcement for the new strategy.

What organizational support is needed? This question deals with ways in which the organization can remove barriers and provide assistance to implementing the change. Can changes in organizational policies be made to smooth the path for the new strategy? Perhaps the organizational unit implementing the change could be exempted from following organizational policies in hiring or capital authorizations, for example. Flexibility might be permitted in interpreting salary policies, by permitting special incentives. In our example, company policy called for all sales representatives to be compensated 100% on salary. However, the system was flexible enough to permit bonus payments and salary increases for the sales representatives to be awarded on the basis of performance with new accounts and on contribution margin, rather than sales revenue.

Answering these questions results in an implementation plan. However, in developing your plan, you will probably encounter an internal, cross-functional challenge that is particularly important in technology-intensive businesses.

The Challenge

In our experience, an important aspect of implementing strategy in technology-intensive businesses is developing the internal teams to deliver customer interface strategies, and to deliver on the service promises in your strategy. Decisions were made on these critical interface strategies and service promises when you completed the winning strategy (Chapter 9). To deliver these, in most instances, you will be faced with the challenge of cutting across functional, hierarchical, and organizational boundaries to assemble teams at the interfaces between you, your customers, and other critical members of the market web associated with the opportunity. Doing so raises a number of organizational and management issues that must be considered.

Organizational Issues

You must decide whether your new cross-functional teams should be aligned against sets of customers on a formal, permanent basis. If your environment is changing quickly, it might make sense to have the membership on the teams somewhat fluid, under the guidance of an account manager. You will also need to consider how to integrate your teams into the mainstream organizational structure, and how to provide them with the support they will require—for instance, communication systems, shared information access, and decision support systems.

Leadership

Detailed analysis of the job to be done by the teams will lead to conclusions about the aptitude, attitude, skills, and knowledge required to lead these teams. Based on the requirements for leadership, you will have to decide how much formal and informal authority the team leaders should have.

Rewards and Recognition

Likely, your organization previously had some means of rewarding sales representatives based on the results they achieved. Now you need to think about designing systems to evaluate and recognize contributions of the whole team to the success it achieves.

Transitional Issues

If moving to some sort of team-based customer interface strategy means a big change for your organization, you need to give some thought to managing the transition. For instance, how do you get those successful "Lone Rangers" in the sales organization to become team players? Perhaps training is the answer for some, but perhaps you also need to recruit some new people who have different skills and interests.

Once the implementation plan has been laid out, you need to consider how it should be communicated.

Communicating Implementation

The communication of the plan is critical to winning acceptance of the new strategy and motivating the behavioral changes required. Basic communication issues must be addressed before any announcements or pronouncements are made.

Target of the Communications Effort. Who should be informed about the new strategy? Clearly, all those who are affected by it, either directly or indirectly.

Message. What should the message be? To a great extent, this will depend on the segment you are trying to reach. Those most strongly affected, that is, those who will have to undergo the greatest changes in behavior, should get detailed, tailored communication about the new strategy, why it is necessary, what the implications are for them, what changes in behavior are expected from them, what support for the new behavior will be provided, and how their performance measurement and compensation will be affected. This is a stage where the 10 steps of the Winning Market Leadership Process can be useful. Taking these change-affected individuals through the opportunities considered before this one was chosen, and then the development of a strategy that can provide competitive differentiation and positive cash flow, should convince them that the changes being asked of them are important. Others, depending on the impact of the new strategy on them, receive only a subset of this information.

Besides the content, the style of your communication is also important. The appropriate communications style to employ is a function of four factors:

1.   The visibility of the need for the new strategy
2.   The clarity of the strategic direction
3.   The sense of urgency in the situation
4.   The degree of trust required between sender and receiver

In a crisis situation, for example, the message should be unequivocal in making the case that indeed a crisis exists, and that rapid action must, and will, be undertaken. The communication is a call to action heading in a clear direction. In contrast, back in an anticipatory situation when much more time must be taken to get to the point of major behavioral changes, your first stages of communication should reflect the slower pace of change. Precise strategic direction is probably not altogether clear, and a sense of trust between communicator and receiver on the need for change must be established. Your communication in this latter situation might announce a task force (with heavy representation from those groups who can contribute to the development of an effective strategy, and those groups who will be strongly affected by the change) to study the situation in the marketplace. The style in this situation is much less abrupt, definitely not a call to action. You should be aware, however, that if you put a task force to work on the issue, you will be expected to listen carefully to their findings.

Media and Source.   If at all possible, it is preferable to have the implementation plan communicated in person by one of the leaders of the new strategy. Certainly, this personal communication should be done for all those who are most affected by the new strategy. This process lends credibility to the message, shows confidence in the strategy, and permits dialogue with the people who developed the new strategic direction. Therefore, chances of miscommunication are minimized, and the builders of the new strategy have the maximum opportunity for feedback. This is especially important when they believe that the business unit is in a crisis situation.

Figure 11-10 outlines approaches to communication in relation to the crisis curve. In a crisis situation, a more prescriptive approach is required because time does not permit the luxury of extensive consultation about defining the problem. At the reactive level of change, there is greater need for, and more time available for, consulting those who will be implementing the new strategy. In a reactive change situation, communication style should reflect the fact that most people are not yet aware of the need for a significant change, and there is a requirement for bringing them on board by including them in the process of understanding the need. In a sense, the task of communications is to "co-opt" them into the process by inviting them to participate in understanding the situation in the market.

Place on the Crisis Curve	Tell them	Sell them	Consult them	Co-opt them
Crisis	X	X		
Reactive		X	X	
Anticipatory			X	X

FIGURE 11-10: Approaches to Communications

Timing. The timing of the announcement of the new strategy should be part of the plan. One danger of premature communication is that competitors obtain information in time to prepare an effective reaction to the new course of action. Also, a pitfall of very early communication is alerting potential internal opposition to the new strategy before the details are all worked out. However, this can be an opportunity to improve the strategy by listening to the objections and using the process to help in selling these people on the need for a new strategy. Indeed, equal or greater problems exist with delaying the announcements. Then you run the risk of adding steps and time to the critical path of implementation, because objections and constructive ideas will surface only very late in the process when the announcements take place. As well, delays increase the likelihood that some of the key actors hear about the new strategy from the office or industry grapevine, without the planned explanation of reasons for change and steps in implementation. The information obtained this way can be very inaccurate, and it is highly likely to be incomplete.

In our example of the European chemical company, communication was not explicitly considered to be a significant issue at all. The new marketing manager communicated the new strategy without the underlying rationale in a memorandum that was sent to the sales representatives and their managers around Europe. Since the change was major, and it was seen as very threatening to the key players, what resulted was a firestorm of unproductive criticism that "poisoned the well" against the new strategy and its sole architect. It forced a series of intense meetings with the European sales force and managers in which a consultant was used in a mediating role during the heated discussions. These meetings did serve the useful purpose of clearing the air between the two sides, and they proved to be an effective, if belated, communications tool to help each understand the position of the other. They also proved to be a very useful forum for sharing the results of early successes, once a few territories started to show results with accounts in the new applications areas.

Monitoring Implementation

The implementation plan should include a design for monitoring performance; behavior and resources in actually carrying out the strategy (inputs to the process), and results in the market (outputs).

The measures chosen should be related to the objectives of the new strategy, the key behavioral changes necessary to implement it, and the criteria for its success. Measurement of outputs lets you answer the question "Was the strategy a success?"; measures of inputs help you to understand why by enabling you to diagnose problems that arise. For instance, have the planned resource allocations actually occurred? Objectives considered should be both financial (e.g., profit and cash flow) and non-financial (e.g., speed of response to customer inquiries, or customer satisfaction). Measures in the market should be taken at the level of a product/market/technology opportunity, that is, on a segment-by-segment basis rather than on the entire market.

Once decisions are made about the measures to be taken, the next steps are to budget for and carry out the necessary data collection, to review the results of the process, and to feed the information back to modify the strategy and its implementation appropriately. It is far better to focus on a few key measures that can be directly tied to the delivery of the strategy and its results, rather than to measure everything possible, "in case it's needed later."

> To return one final time to our European chemical company example, several measures were monitored in implementing the strategic change. On the input side, the key measure was number of sales calls on the new, less price-sensitive segments. With regard to outputs, key measures were numbers of accounts converted, sales volume, and price realized.

While the monitoring stage of the implementation process is quite straightforward, it is important that it not be ignored. The saying that "if you don't measure it, you can't manage it" fits very well here.

Conclusion

Implementation is an important part of the Winning Market Leadership Process. How well the strategy is implemented is every bit as important to future success as the competitive power of the strategy itself. An effective implementation process insures that the intended strategy is delivered. Then, if the results are less than predicted, diagnostic efforts can be centered on the elements of the strategy, rather than on unproductive discussion of whether the problem lies with the strategy or its implementation. Furthermore, as conditions in the market change, they are observed during implementation and fed into the process so that appropriate changes can be made.

This chapter completes our review of the stages of the process of Winning Market Leadership. Our concluding chapter deals with running the management system that drives this whole process.

Key Questions for Executives and Managers

- How great is the need for change in implementing this strategy? How visible is this need for change? How fast does the implementation have to be done? What are criteria for the success of the strategy? What resistance to the new strategy is anticipated? Who will oppose it? Why?

- Specifically what changes in behavior have to be made in order to execute the strategy? Specifically when must the key steps occur? Who are the key people who will be responsible for implementing the strategy? How ready are the key implementers for the changes they will have to make in order to carry out the strategy?

- What resources are required to implement the strategy successfully? What budget is required? What personnel resources? What training for key people who will be undertaking new behavior? Is senior management support required? If so, in what form? What policies and procedures will need to be modified in order to execute the strategy? What reinforcement is needed to support the new strategy, i.e., what rewards can be offered for positive results, what consequences for negative results?

- How will the new strategy be communicated? Who are the targets of that communication? What will the message be for each specific audience? Who will deliver the message? How will it be delivered? When?

- Is a process for feedback and review in place? What are the key measures that will be monitored—both internally (are the necessary behaviors being carried out) and externally (how are customers and key market chain members reacting to the new strategy)?

CHAPTER TWELVE
&

The System That Makes the Process Happen

Introduction

So far we have developed the Winning Market Leadership Process, an iterative planning process to generate profitable strategies for opportunities within your strategic business unit (SBU). The process, with its 10 major strategic question areas, is one that a team of managers and individual contributors work through to refine strategy for existing market opportunities, and to evaluate and develop strategies for potential opportunities. This process allows your team, over time, to take a market opportunity, ask strategic questions that force you to make difficult strategic choices, and develop and refine a winning strategy for the opportunity. The process is shown in Figure 12-1.

However, developing winning strategies needs not only a powerful process, but also a planning system that encourages, reinforces, and enables the use of the planning. Organizations have planning systems to ensure that planning does occur and that planning in the different strategic business units, functions within business units (such as operations), and shared corporate resources (such as central R&D) occurs in a coordinated manner. This process allows top management and business unit management to make crucial resource allocation decisions with a complete knowledge of the major initiatives planned or under way in the corporation. In this chapter, the focus is on the organization's planning system.

We begin with a discussion of why most organizations have some form of organized planning system. We look at a typical planning system in a large, sophisticated organization and how the Winning Market Leadership Process can be integrated into such a planning system. We then argue that within great planning systems, effective strategic market planning processes have certain distinguishing characteristics. Finally, we discuss some of the fundamental aspects of companies and planning systems that create an environment that encourages great planning and the development of winning strategies.

Planning Systems

The purpose of planning is to encourage effective strategic thinking that leads to making informed choices about which opportunities to target with which strategies. A planning process, such as our Winning Market Leadership Process, refers to the series of strategic questions that a team of managers and individuals address over time to make the tough choices about their business opportunities.

The planning system, on the other hand, refers to the structure that is built around the process to encourage it to occur in a manner aligned with overall organizational objectives and timetables. Planning systems are based on rules (such as deadlines for certain planning activities), guidelines (such as assumptions about economic conditions), and norms (such as the "openness" of the planning process). Identifying who will be involved in the process at what times, and in what decision-making roles, is a critical issue since it determines whether the critical questions will be asked by the right people at the appropriate time.

Figure 12-2 shows a typical alignment of planning process activities with a planning system. Here the system indicates in very broad terms which levels of an organization are most involved in planning activities from the beginning of the development of the plan to implementation of the plan. As will be discussed later in this chapter, most planning systems include more than one cycle of involvement of the different levels in an organization. The shaded boxes in the diagram indicate the areas of the planning process that receive

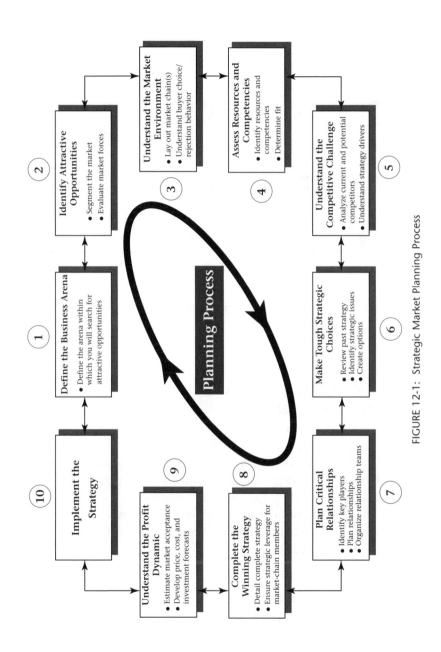

FIGURE 12-1:   Strategic Market Planning Process

the most attention in a particular cycle of this planning system. But the reality of effective planning in a fast-moving technology-intensive business is that most areas are likely to be visited during each planning cycle.

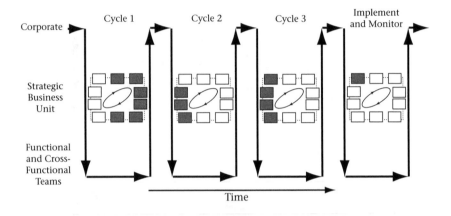

FIGURE 12-2: Areas of the Planning Process that Receive Most Attention at Different Cycles in the Planning System

Need for Planning Systems

In small, entrepreneurial organizations, there may be very little need for an organized planning system. The strategic market planning process may be done very informally and intuitively on a continual basis, perhaps even within the head of one individual. However, even here, one can make strong arguments that periodically this individual, or a small team, should sit down and systematically review the opportunity or opportunities the organization is pursuing. There is even a benefit from recording some of this in order to create a corporate memory.

Improved Coordination

In mid-sized and larger organizations, an organized system often develops to help make the planning process happen in a more systematic and thoughtful way. There is a need for alignment, coordination, and communication both within a strategic business unit (SBU) and certainly among the SBUs in a larger corporation.

One area that requires a good deal of coordination is the achievement of overall corporate goals. Organizations often have ambitious financial goals. These goals may involve not only high profit or earnings per share growth, but also low volatility in these financial measures. Many companies, particularly publicly traded companies, want to show a strong upward trend, often on a quarterly basis, in their earnings per share. This requires a good deal of coordination between the different SBUs. If one SBU is investing heavily to develop an attractive new opportunity which initially will generate large losses, others within the organization must be able to compensate for these short-term losses if corporate profits are to grow.

In addition, many corporations want to actively manage the business risk across their portfolio of market opportunities. This may result in corporate management being unwilling to pursue very attractive, but highly risky opportunities within a particular SBU. On the other hand, it could allow SBUs to pursue risky opportunities depending on the status of the overall company portfolio. Coordinated portfolio management is a key outcome of a good planning system.

And finally, corporate management might see the need to enter attractive new opportunities in order to secure the long-term growth of the organization. This could mean pursuing new market segments, new functionality, new technologies, and/or new value-adding roles. In some cases, pursuing new opportunities might require the coordinated activities of units in different SBUs. These opportunities may not be the most attractive ones for the individual SBUs, but they may be crucial to the corporation's success in the overall market.

In the mid-1990s, when Hewlett-Packard made a corporate decision to pursue the digital photography market, a number of Hewlett-Packard divisions around the world were required to be involved and to act. Contributing to the digital photography initiative was not always in the best short-run interests of the individual Hewlett-Packard divisions. Many of them had more attractive opportunities closer to their core businesses. But for the corporate good, these divisions were encouraged to pursue digital photography opportunities in a coordinated fashion.

Allocation of Scarce Resources

A second major reason for the use of formal planning systems is to manage and focus the allocation of scarce resources to those opportunities that promise the greatest likelihood of contributing to the overall objective. Again, if each of the individual SBUs selects its own opportunities without considering the cumulative impact of these moves across the whole corporation, significant resource scarcities might occur that would prevent any of the business units from achieving their objectives. For example, too many demands might be placed on a central research and development (R&D) organization, and the R&D organization would be unable to respond effectively. Similarly, the demands for capital to invest in the various businesses might exceed the ability of the organization to raise the necessary funds.

Design of a Planning System

Factors Influencing the Design of a Planning System

Planning systems vary significantly from one organization to another. There is no one right planning system—the planning system should be designed to fit the organization's strategy and its internal and external environments. A company that has a corporate strategy of identifying small niche markets and developing highly tailored product and service "packages" to meet the needs of these niches is likely to need a very different type of planning system than a company that uses a cost leadership approach in all its businesses. In the former case, the planning system should be designed to encourage managers who are very close to the primary customers to develop innovative solutions to customer needs. In the second case, the system is likely to be more top down and internally oriented with a heavy focus on cost reduction and cost control.

Internal factors, such as the sophistication of an organization's people, influence the design of the planning system. When employees are highly educated professionals, many of them will want to, and will have the skills to, participate in developing their company's strategies. They will also be able to participate in more sophisticated planning tasks. The situation will be quite different in an organization where the workers have low educational levels and planning skills, and the planning system should reflect this.

External factors, such as the turbulence of the company's markets, can also influence the design of the planning system. A company operating in a highly turbulent market must have a highly flexible planning system that facilitates quick reviews and fast decision making. Plans may have to be revisited three or four times a year. Here, an "annual plan" can lock in decisions that are wrong-headed, or it can motivate implementing decisions that no longer fit market realities. A company or SBU operating in a more stable, mature market may need to schedule a major planning review only every two or three years. The cautionary note here is that even this organization needs to be on the lookout for emerging opportunities, and the planning system needs to be designed to encourage this.

> It is unlikely that the planning system that has been designed to meet the needs of another organization will perfectly fit the needs of your organization. You should always be suspicious of any individual who claims there is one "right" planning system that can be used in any technology-intensive company. On the other hand, the Winning Market Leadership Process is more robust. Asking good strategic market questions about the right things travels well across opportunities, planning systems, and companies.

Planning systems have to be organized, but they do not have to be bureaucratic. However, planning systems frequently do become that way. Whole departments are established to manage the planning system and planning process, or even worse, to do the planning. Guidelines and templates are developed to "help" managers do their planning in the right way. The result of this type of system is that the plan can become the end, not the means for making more effective strategic choices for the organization. "Success" becomes finishing the plan, throwing it on a bookshelf, sending the final copy to the corporate planning department, and the managers sitting back in their chairs and thinking, "Thank God, it's over for this year." If managers exhibit these attitudes, the planning system is a failure.

While some central support can be useful and necessary to manage the planning system, the objectives of the support system should be to help your operating managers make the hard choices and then develop great strategies for the opportunities in their businesses in a way that contributes to the achievement of the corporation's overall objectives. The operating manager should know her business better than any planner. Larry Bossidy, CEO of Allied Signal, captured this well when he stated, "I want the people running the business to be the strategic planners. I think it is my responsibility to be the strategic planner, and I don't want a host of bureaucrats running around almost in opposition to the people running the business. Part of the responsibility of a business leader is to be the strategist." [1]

Major Planning System Design Decisions

In designing the planning system, top management must deal with a number of key questions. These can loosely be organized into four sets of issues: participation, scope, timing, and monitoring and control.

Participation

Participation deals with the question of who gets involved in your planning process, when, and in what roles. Most executives in technology-intensive businesses recognize that planning cannot be the exclusive responsibility of top management teams at the corporate and SBU levels. Customers, competitors, and technologies are all changing far too rapidly in technology-intensive environments for the members of top management teams to have a good understanding of what is really happening in the organization's various markets. So, in most technology-intensive businesses, it is important to involve a cross-section of individuals from the whole organization in different aspects of planning.

It is important to include not just the decision makers in the process, but also the people who will be responsible for implementing strategy. In essence, what you want is input from the people with the best and most up-to-date knowledge that is relevant for making choices and implementing those choices. Well-educated and knowledgeable individuals populate most technology-intensive businesses, and these individuals often would like to have a role in establishing the direction and making the important decisions that have an impact on their livelihood. People with critical knowledge include managers and individuals, such as salespeople who are in contact

---

[1] "Larry Bossidy Won't Stop Pushing," *Fortune*, January 13, 1997, p. 136.

with customers, particularly lead users, key suppliers, and key complementors.

Let's go even further. Your company can directly involve key partners in parts of the planning process so that their views and input are heard directly by a broad cross-section of managers. Why not bring in customers, important suppliers, and other members of the market web to help refine and vet plans? If a customer reacts negatively to a plan, it is typically because there is not enough value-add in the plan from their perspective. It is better to know this sooner rather than later.

Hamel has argued that if revolutionary strategies are to emerge in a business, senior managers must supplement the hierarchy of experience with a hierarchy of imagination.[2] He argues this can be done by ensuring that a broad cross-section of the organization, down to low-level individual contributors, should be involved in the strategy development process. He looks for "new voices" to be added to the process. Clearly, senior management in your organization must also be heavily involved in the planning process.

At Emerson Electric, a company well known for its rigorous planning since the 1950s, the CEO and several members of his top management team spend over 50% of their time in planning activities. Chuck Knight, the CEO, has said, "We devote so much time to planning because that is when we identify business investment opportunities in detail—and because good planning takes time."[3] This rigorous and time-consuming planning at Emerson Electric has contributed to an enviable record of financial performance matched by few, if any, companies in the world that operate in similar types of markets.

Scope

One issue you must deal with in designing a planning system is the scope of the system. An important element of this is time horizons. Some companies in technology-intensive markets argue that planning beyond two or three years makes little sense given the volatility of the markets in which they compete. Ed McCracken,

---

[2] Gary Hamel, "Strategy as Revolution," *Harvard Business Review* (July-August 1996), pp. 69–82.

[3] Charles F. Knight, "Emerson Electric: Consistent Profits, Consistently," *Harvard Business Review* (January-February 1992), pp. 57–70.

the former CEO of Silicon Graphics, once said, "Long-term planning weds companies to approaches and technologies too early, which is deadly in our marketplace and many others. No one can plan the future. Three years is long term. Even two years may be. Five years is laughable."[4] In other industries, including natural resources and some high-technology industries like aircraft and large jet engines, planning horizons of 10 years or more are not uncommon.

A second dimension of scope refers to the level of detail in plans. Here again, there is great variation depending on the firm's strategy and its internal and external environments. A dominant company in a fairly stable market might do an annual operating plan in great detail down to such things as developing the plan for each promotion for the next year. Other companies, in faster moving environments, or where the market is being driven by a competitor, may have to do some of their detailed planning on much shorter notice.

Timing

An important issue related to timing is the frequency of planning. Formal planning systems in most organizations are built around an annual cycle. For a business operating in a very stable environment, this may be too frequent. Some companies deal with this by allowing a business unit in such an environment to go through only a partial planning process on an annual basis. A full-scale planning review is scheduled every few years, or when there is a significant change in the situation facing the business. In most technology-intensive businesses, the plan may need to be revisited more than once a year, due to unexpected developments externally in the market or internally within the organization. This exercise may be simply an updating of the existing plan developed during an annual planning cycle.

A second issue to do with timing is the schedule for planning during the year. Some organizations, such as Emerson Electric, believe that rigorous planning is essential for corporate success and spread the planning process out over the entire year. In these

---

[4] Stephen E. Prokesch, "Mastering Chaos at the High-Tech Frontier: An Interview with Silicon Graphics's Ed McCracken," *Harvard Business Review* (November-December 1993), pp. 135–144.

organizations, some aspect of planning is under way somewhere in the organization at all times. At the other extreme, some technology-intensive organizations try to compress the planning process into one or two off-site meetings per year.

While off-site meetings can be useful for getting people together to focus on important issues, it is dangerous to compress the planning process so highly. Too intense a process means that only a limited amount of the knowledge in the organization is tapped in the planning process. It also discourages individuals from going out in the market to consult with customers and other market chain and web members in order to determine whether key assumptions underlying strategy are in fact valid.

The challenge is to find a schedule that helps your managers recognize the importance and value of planning, that provides sufficient time to do a thorough job, and that builds the commitment of the organization to the plans. It is not uncommon in a number of technology-intensive businesses for the formal planning process to occur over a six-month period with a series of formal checkpoints throughout the year. Formal and informal updates can, and should, occur throughout the year as conditions warrant—planning is continuous and iterative.

Monitoring and Control

An important element in any planning system is the control system and the key variables that are monitored in the business. In order to determine how well your plan is doing, it is essential to monitor both key inputs and outputs. Understanding the inputs tells you whether the plan is being followed; monitoring the outputs tells you whether the plan is working. Planning is about making strategic choices, allocating resources, and changing behaviors to support those choices. Therefore, it is important to track the key resources to determine if they are, in fact, allocated where they are supposed to be. For example, did research and development funds get allocated to the high-priority projects? Did the sales force call on the accounts that were deemed to be strategic? Did the "No" decisions stick?

Additionally, you must monitor the results being achieved. The only way that managers learn what works and what doesn't work is by comparing actual results to predicted results. Here, you are not just looking for situations where the target results are not achieved, but also for situations where the target results are overachieved. If a particular strategy or tactic works better than management anticipated, it is important to understand why. It is only by gaining this understanding that you learn to do a better job of making strategic choices in the future, and learn to anticipate the impact of certain choices on performance in the marketplace.

In setting up any sort of process to monitor key inputs and outputs, you must be selective. The system should be designed to encourage managers to focus on those few key variables that have the biggest impact on business success. Unfortunately, in too many companies, the focus is almost exclusively on financial performance. While this is obviously important, it can lead to top management in an SBU focusing on meeting their next quarterly target, rather than ensuring that a major new product program comes to market on time and on budget. A number of high-technology companies, including Advanced Micro Devices (AMD) and Analog Devices, are using the balanced scorecard approach to monitor a variety of key performance measures for their businesses. A balanced scorecard provides managers with a coherent set of performance metrics based on a company's strategic objectives. These measures go well beyond normal financial metrics. Advanced Micro Devices carefully monitors customer-based measures, such as on-time delivery; and measures of internal business processes, such as new product development; as well as more traditional measures of financial performance and quality.[5] Xerox not only measures customer satisfaction, but also ties the results into the compensation of managers and salespeople.

No One Right Planning System

As the above discussion suggests, there is no one right planning system. A good planning system fits the organization and its environment and it focuses managers on the critical factors in their business.

Internal factors, such as the size of the organization, the educational level of the employees, the history of planning in the organization, the length of new product development cycles, and the style

---

[5] Robert S. Kaplan and David P. Norton, "Putting the Balanced Scorecard to Work," *Harvard Business Review* (September-October 1993), pp. 134–142.

of top management all have a significant impact on the design of the planning system.

External factors, such as the rate of change in the market, the intensity of competition, and the degree to which your company is a leader or follower in its industry can also influence the design of the planning system. One important element that can substantially affect a planning system is the urgency for action that the external environment imposes on the organization. As discussed in our chapter on implementation (Chapter 11), how an organization plans is likely to be quite different if it is responding in an anticipatory way to looming changes in its market compared to if it is responding to a crisis brought on by environmental change that is already negatively affecting its performance.[6]

Where significant change is anticipated but has not yet occurred, a planning system that encourages a lot of participation is ideal. This allows the whole organization to recognize the need for change and to participate in developing the response. The process is likely to be slow but can build high commitment to a carefully considered response to the anticipated change. Where the corporation is already in crisis, many of the people in the organization are more willing to tolerate a planning system that relies on a few trusted individuals or a team to understand the problems and develop a "solution." The danger is that not all the relevant information may be considered, and deep commitment to the change will not be present in the organization, which increases the implementation challenge.

Finally, a company's objectives and strategy can have a major impact on the design of the planning system. A company wishing to encourage revolutionary change needs to develop a different planning system than one that is generally happy with its performance and feels that only minor, evolutionary change is needed. A related example is companies that have been successful in building powerful customer value and profit creation models that they want to leverage across all their business units. That is, no matter what market opportunity they are looking at, they tend to "play the game" in much the same way. Clearly here the planning system would be quite centralized and structured and would allow management within the SBUs to fine-tune strategies within the broad strategy set by the company.

---

[6] Joseph N. Fry and J. Peter Killing, *Strategic Analysis and Planning*, Third Edition (Scarborough, Ontario: Prentice Hall Canada Inc., 1995), Chapters 11 and 12.

Balanced Interaction

In technology-intensive markets, good planning requires balanced interaction between top management, and managers and individual contributors who are very close to the market. Senior managers, with an overview of the business and the market environment, are often in the best position to supply the broad strategic perspective essential to providing strategic direction. On the other hand, middle managers and individual contributors have the narrow focus that contributes to a deep knowledge of customers, competitors, and markets that is essential to develop winning strategies and execute them effectively. A good planning system encourages productive dialogue among all levels in the organization.[7]

Unfortunately, in many organizations this does not happen. In some cases top management makes decisions that lead people lower down in the organization to shake their heads, when they recognize how out of touch with the market their leaders are. A large number of CEOs of Fortune 500 companies have come up through non-marketing functions and may not take the time to stay in tune with the market at the opportunity level. Scott Adams with his Dilbert cartoons has highlighted some of these situations in a humorous way.

At the other extreme are companies that empower people at the SBU or lower levels in the company to make important choices, but give them no strategic direction or vision. In this case, the empowered people do their analysis, make choices, and develop plans based on limited knowledge of the overall market environment and corporate strategic direction. When their decisions are communicated to top management, one of two things happens. Top management sees the plan, recognizes that it is out of touch with the strategic direction of the corporation and says no. After months of intensive work, the team is demotivated and unlikely to make a similar effort in the future. On the other hand, if top management says yes, over time the corporation will go off in dozens of different, often conflicting, directions. At some point, this lack of focus can very well lead to disaster.

Balanced interaction between the top management teams, SBU leadership, and those lower down in the organization leads to better, more executable plans in the marketplace that are aligned with overall corporate direction.

---

[7] These are important elements of what Day calls adaptive planning. See George S. Day, *Market Driven Strategy* (New York: The Free Press, 1990), Chapter 3.

Planning System in a Large, Sophisticated Company

The Winning Market Leadership Process can be readily integrated into the strategic planning system of a large organization. A typical planning system is shown in Figure 12-3. The 10 areas of our process fit into this broad corporate planning system.

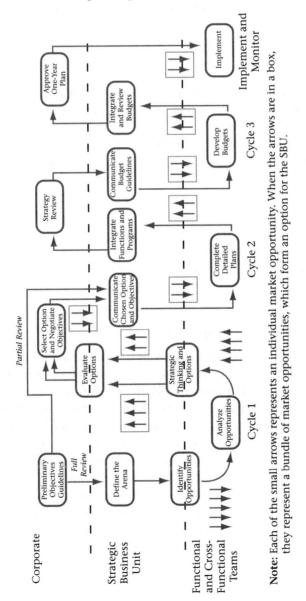

FIGURE 12-3: Planning System in a Large, Sophisticated Organization

Note: Each of the small arrows represents an individual market opportunity. When the arrows are in a box, they represent a bundle of market opportunities, which form an option for the SBU.

Overview of the Planning System

The generic planning system shown in Figure 12-3 involves three levels in the organization: corporate, SBU, and functional and cross-functional teams. The system provides for two basic possibilities. The first is a full review, where an SBU engages the complete planning system during each planning period. The second possibility is a partial review, where SBU management and corporate management decide that little has changed and that no useful purpose is served by doing a full review in this particular planning period. The full review involves three cycles in the SBU's development of the plan and budgets. In the case of a full review, there are three formal points of dialogue between corporate management and the management within the SBU, and hopefully, numerous opportunities for productive discussion between the two.

We now discuss each of the three cycles in the planning system and discuss the linkages between them and the Winning Market Leadership Process.

Cycle One: Develop Options for SBU

In most organizations, strategic planning begins with corporate management providing some preliminary objectives and guidelines—the prologue.

Objectives and Assumptions

The preliminary objectives and assumptions cover a number of areas. The objectives usually include financial objectives, such as cash flow or profits or operating margins. They might include non-financial objectives, such as market share goals. For example, in 1991 General Electric set stretch corporate objectives for 1995 of 10 inventory turns and 15% operating margins. At the time these objectives were set, GE corporately was achieving 5 inventory turns and had a 10% operating margin. Similarly in 1996, General Electric widely communicated its intention to double revenues coming from the services side of its business by the year 2000. Obviously, the objectives for particular SBUs within General Electric are more or less stringent than the overall corporate objectives, depending on the nature of the business and the circumstances of the business unit.

A second area covered in the prologue is environmental assumptions, including assumed growth rates for the economies in which the company is operating and anticipated inflation levels. Finally, companies use these preliminary objectives to get SBUs to focus on new emerging issues that top management feels could be important for the overall success of the organization. For example, some companies in the late 1990s asked each SBU to consider the impact of several European countries adopting a common monetary unit (the EMU).

Opportunities

With these preliminary objectives and assumptions, the management of the SBU begins the Winning Market Leadership Process by defining the business arena. Once the arena for the SBU has been established, top management of the SBU, probably in conjunction with key managers and individuals in the different functions, identify the opportunities to be examined in this particular planning cycle (see Chapter 2). Usually, these are a combination of existing opportunities that the SBU is already pursuing and new, potentially attractive opportunities. In Figure 12-3, let's assume that five opportunities are going to be examined by the SBU.

At this stage, cross-functional teams are assigned to look at each of the five opportunities. Each team works through the Winning Market Leadership Process and puts a particularly heavy emphasis on Areas Two to Five in Figure 12-1: Identify Attractive Opportunities (Chapter 3), Understand the Market Environment (Chapter 4), Assess Resources and Competencies (Chapter 5), and Understand the Competitive Challenge (Chapter 6). However, they do not just confine themselves to analysis at this stage. They also make tentative decisions about whether the opportunity looks viable; if it does, they do some preliminary thinking about the appropriate strategy, the key relationships, the winning strategy, and the likely financial implications of pursuing that opportunity. These are shown as Areas Six to Nine in Figure 12-1: Making Tough Strategic Choices (Chapter 7), Manage Critical Relationships (Chapter 8), Complete the Winning Strategy (Chapter 9), and Understand the Profit Dynamic (Chapter 10).

In Figure 12-3, we assumed that only four of the five opportunities emerge from that process. The cross-functional team working on one of the opportunities decides that it is not attractive and has decided to eliminate that opportunity from further consideration. At this point, the dialogue with the SBU management becomes more intense (the SBU management team continues to work with the cross-functional teams as the opportunities are analyzed), but now, working together, they have to decide which options to present to top corporate management. In this example, one of the four remaining opportunities was dropped after some hard strategic examination by SBU management and the teams about which opportunities to move ahead with. At the end of this discussion they see two broad options: Option A is to focus on the two existing opportunities, but to make some significant changes in strategy for both of these. Option B also involves the two existing opportunities and the same set of changes, but it also envisions going after one other major new opportunity over the planning horizon. Members of the SBU team and the cross-functional teams debate the pros and cons of these two broad options, Options A and B. SBU management finally decides to present top management with the two options. The two options have different implications corporately since they have different resource requirements and significantly different cash flow and profit implications.

In a meeting with top management, the SBU management team lays out the two options and their implications. After discussing and reviewing the options that have emerged from deliberations with the other SBUs, top management eventually decides the SBU should pursue Option A.

Cycle Two: Detailed Planning for Selected Option

Once top management has committed to an option and provided the SBU with revised objectives, the SBU management team now communicates the chosen option and the objectives for the SBU to key people within the unit. The cross-functional teams, often significantly increased in size, working with the functions now begin developing detailed plans for the two selected market opportunities. Again, as part of this process, a review of Areas Two to Five is undertaken to determine if there have been any significant changes that need to be considered in developing detailed plans.

Usually, most of the focus during this cycle is on Areas Seven, Eight, and Nine. This attention ends up involving all the functions in the business unit. New product plans are developed and refined. R&D and engineering put together their functional new product development activities and cost reduction programs. Manufacturing develops its strategy to support each of the two opportunities, as does marketing and sales, and human resources. As the detailed plans are pulled together for the two opportunities, SBU management get involved in setting priorities as conflicts emerge between the needs of the two different opportunities. If there is a resource scarcity in one of the functional areas, certain activities might have to be outsourced. In other cases, the conflicts may force you to revisit the set of opportunities being carried forward.

When detailed planning is complete for each of the opportunities, as shown in Area Eight, the SBU makes a strategy review presentation to top management. Undoubtedly, the detailed planning will have led to some changes in strategy, resources needed, and probable results.

Cycle Three: Develop Budgets and Detailed One-Year Operating Plan

Once corporate management gives its blessing at the review, the SBU management communicates budget guidelines to the various functional and cross-functional teams as these teams begin developing the one-year operating plan and the associated budgets. After these budgets have been integrated and reviewed by SBU management, they may or may not go back to top management for final approval. In some cases, the final presentation of the plans and budgets occurs at a planning conference, so that top management in all of the SBUs gain a better understanding of the activities of their peers and potentially see the opportunity for productive cooperation among SBUs.

Implementation and Monitoring

The plan now moves back into the SBU for implementation (Area Ten, Chapter 11). The control system in the organization starts to monitor key inputs and key outputs. Sophisticated organizations go beyond simply monitoring what happened compared to what was supposed to happen. General Electric, for example, monitors performance against the world as it turned out to be, not the world on which the plan was based. Here, top management is most concerned with how well the SBU anticipates change and deals with it.

In some organizations, after every iteration of the annual planning system, management conducts a "postlogue." In the postlogue, an attempt is made to critique the planning system and to try to gather constructive suggestions from the people involved about how it could be made more effective.

An Effective Strategic Market Planning Process

Within the context of the planning system, an effective strategic market planning process has a number of distinguishing characteristics. It:

- Is both integrated and iterative
- Is question driven
- Combines hard data with soft intuitive judgment
- Focuses on implementation
- Recognizes that the process is as important as the plan
- Encourages managers to say no
- Challenges industry and company norms.

Our Winning Market Leadership Process displays all these characteristics.

Is Both Integrated and Iterative

The process is integrated and iterative. By integrated we mean a process that is complete and helps managers ask the important strategic questions in an integrated way. Changes in any one of the areas in Figure 12-1 necessitate a re-thinking of some of the other areas. Integration also comes from having a shared framework such as the Winning Market Leadership Process, a shared vocabulary, and shared information which is encouraged by this process.

It is iterative in the sense that managers don't just work through the process once in a sequential manner—this is not a serial process. Inevitably, as managers work around the process, they will gain new insights, or ask new questions that cause them to revisit an area they have already dealt with. In the earlier discussion about the integration of the Winning Market Leadership Process with a typical corporate strategic planning system, it was pointed out that managers would work through most areas of the planning process at least two or three times.

Is Question Driven

Strategy and planning are not about having good answers—they are about asking great questions. Our Winning Market Leadership Process encourages this, since it is a set of integrative questions leading to tough strategic choices. As Hamel suggests, "We should spend less time working on strategy as a 'thing' and more time working to understand the preconditions that give rise to the 'thing'."[8] We contend that one of the preconditions is the ability of the people in your company to ask great questions.

Combines Hard Data with Soft Intuitive Judgment

In technology-intensive markets, managers seldom have enough hard data to make the important strategic choices. If they wait until the data are available, somebody else will probably have seized the opportunity. Thus, there is an important role for informed judgment. These conclusions are not guesses, but judgments based on informed interaction with customers, competitors, and people within your own organization.

Focuses on Implementation

An effective strategic market planning process pays as much attention to implementation as it does to strategy development. You must always keep an eye on how you are going to make a strategy or tactic work. Too often, managers develop strategies and tactics that look wonderful on paper, but are impossible to implement effectively in the marketplace. This is why it is so essential to have some of the people responsible for implementation on each of the cross-functional planning teams that drive a planning process. These people bring the cold reality of the marketplace and internal challenges into the conference room.

---

[8] Gary Hamel, "Killer Strategies That Make Shareholders Rich," *Fortune*, June 23, 1997, p. 84.

Recognizes That the Process Is as Important as the Plan

Great managers recognize that the process is more important than the plan produced at the end of it. They worry a great deal about involving a representative cross-section of the organization in the planning process, so that these individuals feel they have contributed to the development of the plan and understand the rationale for the decisions that are made—they add "new voices" to the process. A good manager does not expect consensus to occur in a large organization. However, resistance to change is greatly reduced if individuals feel they have a voice in the process by which the important decisions are made. Involving many people takes additional time, and time is always at a premium in a technology-intensive business. But if the time is not taken at the planning stage, much more time is wasted as a result of poor or unenthusiastic implementation of the plan.

Engagement in the process also results in people carrying around shared visions; shared frameworks, concepts, tools and language; and a shared understanding of the critical market segment/functionality/technology/value-adding role maps associated with opportunities being pursued. It is better to have these as shared mental models rather than as plans on shelves. Process encourages this and the result is that planning becomes a deeply embedded capability in an organization as opposed to an exercise to be carried out at a particular time.

Encourages Managers to Say No

One of the most difficult tasks facing managers at all levels in an organization is saying no. It is easier to continue to say yes. An effective strategic market planning process provides managers with the process, information, and analysis that encourages them to say yes or no and not maybe. Top management should create the culture, perhaps by example, where it is expected that managers at all levels have the courage to make clear strategic choices and minimize the number of maybes. Managers must know what not to pursue as well as what to pursue.

Why do so many otherwise effective managers have so much trouble saying no? Saying no makes people unhappy, and these are loyal, hard-working employees, who have months of their lives invested in a particular project. Managers don't want to demotivate these employees and perhaps even lose them to a competitor. Other managers are simply reluctant to put all their eggs in one or two baskets. They would rather spread the risk. The obvious danger is that limited resources are spread over too many projects with insufficient resources devoted to any of the projects to ensure success.

An effective strategic market planning process helps with both these issues. A good process can help all the people involved in the process see more clearly why no is the most appropriate response to certain opportunities. In these cases, if the analysis is thorough and discussed openly, most reasonable people, albeit reluctantly, understand why their pet project should not proceed. A good process can also dramatically reduce the number of maybes, since better information will be available to point to either yes or no. Projects are not allowed to take on lives of their own, but are subject to thorough analysis early, before significant resources are committed. Early no decisions are much more palatable than late no decisions, since people have less of their lives invested in the project at that point. An early discussion of the business arena (Area One in Figure 12-1) can immediately eliminate many potential opportunities that simply don't fit in the part of the arena in which the SBU has chosen to compete.

However, every SBU will have at least a couple of maybe opportunities in its portfolio at any time. One way to get control over these opportunities is to lay out the ground rules for continuing to keep these opportunities alive. Management might collectively decide to continue to pursue the opportunity only if certain conditions are met. If the conditions are not met, the opportunity is killed. If this is clearly communicated to the team, the ground rules are clear and a subsequent termination is likely to be much more palatable.

Challenges Industry and Company Norms

A strategic market planning process should not be so rigid that it pre-cludes you from breaking the rules in your industry—changing the rules of the game. For instance, slavish devotion to a current busi-ness definition could prevent you from seriously considering radical opportunities. Hamel claims that it is the rule breakers that develop killer strategies. Companies such as Microsoft, Nike, Harley-David-son, and Virgin Atlantic changed the basis of competition in their industries. According to an MCI/Gallup survey of opinions of CEOs, in times of rapid marketplace changes, 62% of the newcomers in these markets succeeded by profoundly changing the rules of the game.[9] A good planning process encourages market-driving risk tak-ing where appropriate.

Key Success Factors in an Effective Planning System

The discussion above highlights the characteristics of a powerful planning process. What we look at now are some of the underlying fundamentals of the company and the planning system that lead to planning with these characteristics. These fundamentals include: effective teams, a supportive corporate culture, integration of the planning process with other key processes, and effective support sys-tems (see Figure 12-4). Not having these foundations in place creates significant barriers to effective and powerful market planning.

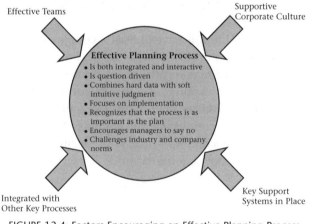

Effective Teams

Supportive Corporate Culture

Effective Planning Process
- Is both integrated and interactive
- Is question driven
- Combines hard data with soft intuitive judgment
- Focuses on implementation
- Recognizes that the process is as important as the plan
- Encourages managers to say no
- Challenges industry and company norms

Integrated with Other Key Processes

Key Support Systems in Place

FIGURE 12-4: Factors Encouraging an Effective Planning Process

[9] Hamel, p. 72

Effective Teams

A fundamental requirement for generating powerful strategic market plans is having teams of people asking the questions and addressing the issues. Having effective teams is easier said than done. What makes the challenge difficult is that teams that do effective planning typically cross functions, hierarchical levels, geographic locations, and organizational boundaries. In addition, in some cases planning teams are informal teams so that cohesion and leadership often emerge as opposed to being structured up front.

Membership and Structure

The nature and membership of the team can vary depending on the planning situation. This could involve a core team plus supplementary members as required. For example, one study suggests that when a radically new strategy based on radically new products is developed, technical activities require greater integration. When working on strategies related to existing opportunities and low-innovation products, a higher level of integration among the team members is required when conducting launch activities such as designing and detailing the marketing program and implementing the product launch.[10]

In our planning process the teams should be addressing all the questions in the process and they should be structured to achieve this goal. Specific functional teams should not be assigned to specific questions because of their perceived strengths. For example, don't put the financial folks in charge of looking at the profit dynamic. Everyone needs to understand the financial implications of the decisions and choices being made within the planning process. Team membership can include participants from outside the organization at various stages of the planning process. Customers, end users, suppliers, and other members of market chains and market webs can all play significant roles in developing appropriate strategies. Integrating these people into the team structure can create challenges which go beyond those faced when dealing with internal barriers to team effectiveness.

---

[10] Michael Song and Jinhong Xie, "The Effect of R&D-Manufacturing-Marketing Integration on New Product Performance in Japanese and U.S. Firms: A Contingency Perspective," *Marketing Science Institute Report*, 96–117.

Effective market planning teams are typically not functional teams, do not live at one level in the hierarchy, and do not live at one location. Effective teams get over the barriers and boundaries often established within organizations to ensure that a rich mixture of people, perspectives, and ideas gets into the planning process. This suggests the need for a "boundaryless" environment in your organization to allow these barriers to be crossed.

Finally, the team that has been assigned to the planning process, although its membership might change over time, needs to be at least explicitly identified and recognizable. There should be no question in anyone's mind as to whether he or she is on the team or off the team. Teams must also know their boundaries. How far can a team go? When do other people have to be brought into the picture?

Shared Perspectives

We believe that teams function well when they have common objectives, a shared vision, and a set of concepts and frameworks shared broadly across the team. Clear objectives give the team direction, but the other thing that happens with clear objectives is that the team develops a sense of potency or power—it develops a sense that it in fact can generate great strategies.

Part of the shared perspective can come from networking, interaction, and common educational experiences where cross-functional teams work on projects related to planning or perhaps not even related to the planning mission. American Management Systems (AMS) and IBM use organizational and team-level simulations to give participants hands-on experience in developing group solutions to problems. Other organizations invite sales, field service, and R&D professionals to join marketing managers as full participants during marketing leadership development programs. A spin-off of these interactions is the building of respect and trust which enhances the planning.

Rewards and Recognition

One of the key drivers of team effectiveness is the compensation and reward system. If members of the team are continuously referring back to their functional areas for rewards, recognition, and compensation, a sense of being on a team—"teamness"—will not develop. This does not mean that the entire compensation and reward system should be based on what people do as team members, but at least part of it should be. Clear objectives backed up by associated rewards and recognition go far in assisting team effectiveness.

Team Process

Another dimension of effectiveness is focusing on the team process itself. Team members must be on guard to recognize process problems and to reassess process effectiveness continuously. There must be openness and candor—a tough environment—to ensure that the process stays on track.

Finally, there must be continuous and visible top management support for the planning teams. If top management doesn't encourage an effective process and does not continuously highlight the importance of teamwork in planning, it will not happen.

Supportive Corporate Culture

Your organization must have a culture that supports planning. The dimensions of such a culture include:

- Developing a strong "market orientation." The planning process starts externally and continuously refers to customers and competitors in the process. It does not start internally looking at costs and capabilities. A market-oriented organization is vigilant to changes in the environment, processes those changes, and widely shares the resulting information across functions and locations.

- Focusing on reduced time to market. Those organizations which are successful in reducing this time have the greatest number of opportunities available to them, and the most options to pursue. Reduced time to market often creates opportunities to become market leaders as opposed to market followers.

- Creating a "boundaryless" organization

- Encouraging questions as opposed to imposing answers

- Insisting on clear yes/no choices being made and a culture that respects and values "no" decisions

- Developing a shared vision of where it is going and how, and which opportunities to pursue

- Recognizing that planning takes time and that planning is as important as, if not more important than, putting out day-to-day fires

You can see organizations that have a culture supportive of planning and developing great strategies. You see organizations where employees spend time walking in the customers' shoes. Intuit demonstrates a market-oriented culture by staffing its customer service lines with a variety of employees so that they get a strong understanding of customer needs and issues. It even has employees visit customers in their homes to observe them using Intuit's software. Other firms insist on creative job assignments where technical people take on other roles in the organization, which can again enhance planning effectiveness.

Nokia demonstrates the kind of culture that leads to great strategies. This Finnish company sitting at the edge of the Arctic may theoretically not have a good view of what is going on. They work hard to send engineers and others into different cultural environments and to change their experience base. This has resulted in such things as the Nokia engineers coming up with the colorful bright red, yellow, and blue cellular telephones that opened up a whole new market for the company. You need a culture that allows these "Eureka" experiences to happen.

Integration with Other Key Processes

An effective strategic market planning system forces clear and close links to other key processes, such as the new product development process. In our experience, the new product development process is often disconnected from the planning process and managed by different people. The people driving the new product development process have a tendency to consider the market and financial issues early on, and then push ahead with the technical and production related issues. Instead of continuously revisiting changes in the marketplace and revisiting assumptions, the team permits these technical issues to dominate. Tight integration into the market planning process may avoid this.

By tightly integrating the marketing planning process and the new product development process, there are fewer opportunities for the important questions that are asked in our Winning Market Leadership Process to be overlooked. You want all people involved in new product development, not just the marketing people, to be frequently asking the critical questions we have been discussing. What you don't want is the new product development process strictly becoming technologically and functionally oriented. An effective planning system ensures that these processes are integrated.

Key Support Systems in Place

Support systems are the grease that help the planning system work effectively. This grease has three major components. The first is information based on data and technology. A key underpinning of a great market planning system is the capability for managers to access information to help them answer the planning questions. An additional aspect of this is that all those involved in the planning process should have access to similar information bases to allow integrated and iterative questions to be asked and answered. Finally there needs to be a balance between the internal and external information available in the data base—most companies err on the side of too much internal cost data and not enough information on customers and competitors.

The second component that enables great planning is the communication systems. To enhance team effectiveness and to ensure shared objectives and frameworks, you must have the ability to communicate among the members of the team that are asking the planning questions. This becomes difficult when your organization expands geographically so that team members are not at the same location. An example of a communications systems which really does support planning, new ideas, and new opportunities exists at one of the world's leading pharmaceutical manufacturers. In this situation, great ideas are shared. When managers first sign on to their system in the morning, a list of great ideas comes up on the screen. These ideas capture the experiences of managers around the world. In this company there is a culture that encourages the sharing of experiences, and a communication system to make it happen.

The third ingredient is a monitoring and control system that focuses on the key metrics. A top manager who had worked for two leading technology-intensive companies in his career noted how the monitoring and control process was an important enabler. Both companies he had worked for stated publicly that the key to their future success was developing a stream of successful new products. The manager noted that one of these companies, Hewlett-Packard, put its words into practice. He recalled that at each strategy review meeting, senior management at Hewlett-Packard focused on the new product programs in the division. How were they doing? What could they do to make sure that these new product programs were on time in getting to the market? Corporate management at Hewlett-Packard believed that if the plans were well formulated and the new product programs were successful, the financials would take care of themselves. At the second company, the manager noted that most of the time at each strategy review meeting was spent on the financial performance of the division. Was it going to meet its quarterly profit numbers? The focus on the financials in the second company resulted in a very different culture and a very different allocation of where the managers spent their energy and time. This company became internally as opposed to externally focused.

In summary, when looking at the foundation of a great market planning system, we see organizations where teams are effective, where the corporate culture allows planning to happen, where the market planning process is intimately integrated with other key processes, and where the key support systems are effective.

Conclusion

A very effective strategic planning system and process can provide significant benefits to an organization beyond the development of better plans.

The planning system can be a powerful tool to improve communication and reinforce the culture within an organization. The Hewlett-Packard example above illustrates this point well.

Finally, a truly effective strategic market planning system helps create an organization of "informed opportunists."[11] In almost all

---

[11] Robert H. Waterman, *The Renewal Factor* (New York: Bantam Books, Inc., 1987).

technology-intensive businesses, plans are wrong in at least some detail the moment they are developed. An effective strategic market planning system develops an organization of informed opportunists, each of whom knows the general direction in which the business unit is trying to go. Thus, when an unexpected opportunity emerges in the market, a salesperson will know whether this is an opportunity that could help the organization achieve its objectives. Or is this an opportunity that, if pursued, could dilute the focus of the organization and reduce its chances of achieving its objectives? Technology-intensive businesses are complex with important decisions being made by dozens, if not hundreds or thousands of people on a weekly basis. It is critical that they all understand the general direction the organization is trying to go. The strategic market planning system and process, if effectively implemented, can help achieve this important objective.

Key Questions for Executives and Managers

- Do you have an appropriate planning system for your organization?

    - Are you involving the right people in the organization in the planning? Are you involving those with access to key planning information and those who will play major roles in the successful implementation of any plan?
    - Is the scope of the system right in regard to such things as the planning horizon and the level of detail in the plans?
    - Is the timing right? Is the frequency of planning and strategy reviews appropriate for the company's various SBUs? Is planning scheduled at the right time during the year? Is there enough time in the planning process for the required data to be gathered and analyzed?
    - Is there an adequate monitoring and control system in place that focuses on key inputs and outputs? Are you using a balanced scorecard or are you relying too heavily on financial measures?
    - Is there an appropriate amount of interaction between top management and lower levels in the organization to

---

ensure that both broad strategic issues and detailed market knowledge are incorporated into planning?
- Is the planning process effectively integrated with the strategic planning system of the organization? Does it focus on achieving overall corporate objectives?

- Does the planning system encourage an effective strategic market planning process that:

  - is both integrated and iterative?
  - is question-driven?
  - combines hard data with soft intuitive judgment?
  - focuses on implementation?
  - recognizes that the process is as important as the plan?
  - encourages managers to say no, when appropriate; that is, forces difficult and clear strategic choices and allocation of resources?
  - allows you to break the rules?

- Are the fundamentals that drive powerful planning in place, such as:

  - effective teams to ask the important questions?
  - a corporate culture which encourages planning and an external focus?
  - strong ties between the market planning system and other key processes, such as the new product development process?
  - effective support systems, such as appropriate information, communication, and monitoring systems?

INDEX
∞